ISRAEL
AND
LATIN AMERICA:

THE
MILITARY
CONNECTION

ISRAEL
AND
LATIN AMERICA:
THE
MILITARY
CONNECTION

BISHARA BAHBAH
with
LINDA BUTLER

Foreword by
Stanley Hoffmann

ST. MARTIN'S PRESS • New York
in association with the
INSTITUTE FOR PALESTINE STUDIES • Washington

All rights reserved. For information, write:
Scholarly & Reference Division,
St. Martin's Press, Inc., 175 Fifth Avenue, New York, NY 10010

Printed in the U.S.A.

ISBN 0—312—43770—6
ISBN 0—312—43771—4 (pbk.)

Library of Congress Cataloging-in-Publication Data

Bahbah, Bishara.
    Israel and Latin America: The Military Connection.

    Includes index.
    1. Munitions—Israel. 2. Military assistance,
Israeli—Latin America. 3. Israel—Military relations—
Latin America. 4. Latin America—Military relations—
Israel. I. Butler, Linda, 1946-   . II. Title.
UF535.I7B35 1986   382'.45623'0095694   86-1904
ISBN 0—312—43770—6
ISBN 0—312—43771—4 (pbk.)

The Institute for Palestine Studies
would like to thank *Linda Butler*
for her extensive editing of the
original manuscript.

To the memory of my father

Assad Rizek Bahbah

*for the sacrifices he made
to educate his children*

Contents

List of
Tables and Figures

Tables

Figure

Foreword

This excellent study by Bishara A. Bahbah throws light on one of the most important developments of contemporary world affairs: the international arms trade. It is also an objective and searching contribution to the understanding of Israel's role in the world. The study documents the rise of Israel's arms industry, analyzes the reasons for it (the imperative of greater self-sufficiency above all) as well as its importance for the Israeli economy, and shows the decisive role played in the expansion of the arms industry both by the Israeli government and the U.S. government (particularly in the form of co-production and licensing agreements).

Above all, this work is a case study. It describes the ties created by arms sales between Israel and several Latin American countries. These have turned to Israel as a major supplier not only because of the needs created by local disputes or the political importance of their military forces, but also because of Israel's willingness to tailor exports to such needs (e.g., counterinsurgency weapons) and to impose no restrictions for reasons of moral and political distaste (e.g., human rights). The paradox of Israel supplying the anti-Semitic military junta of Argentina in the 1970s and early 1980s is one of the more unsavory aspects of this relationship.

Furthermore, Bahbah's work is not merely descriptive. He provides a sober analysis of the motives of the actors and a critical but unimpeachable evaluation of the results achieved by Israel. He shows Israel's continuing dependence on the United States, both negatively—although Israel's arms exports to Central America soared when the United States under President Carter suspended shipments to repressive regimes, they fell when the

Reagan administration reversed this course—and positively—the use of Israel by the United States as a proxy and a supplement to its own efforts. He also shows that the arms trade, although beneficial for the economy, has brought Israel few political benefits: almost none in South America and very limited gains in Central America. Indeed, the close ties between Israel and various dictatorships have had disadvantages—as in the case of Nicaragua which froze and subsequently severed its diplomatic ties with Israel following the overthrow of the Somoza dictatorship and Argentina where the new democratic regime of President Alfonsín has tempered its military ties with Israel.

It can only be hoped that future studies will examine other cases of arms exports, for instance those of France and of the United States, with the same dispassionate rigor and empirical thoroughness as this scholarly and thought-provoking book by a promising young writer on political affairs.

Stanley Hoffmann
Chairman, Center for
European Studies
Harvard University
Cambridge, Massachusetts

Acknowledgments

This study could not have been completed without the assistance and the contributions of many people. Much appreciation is due to Professors Stanley Hoffmann and Lisa Anderson of Harvard University. They both graciously agreed to supervise my doctoral dissertation from which this book has been developed. They spent much time reading and evaluating the manuscript. Much more significant to me, however, was their faith in my ability to research and write a manuscript of several hundred pages on a subject rarely written about.

Professors Walid Khalidi and the late A.J. Meyer played an important role in helping me secure the financial resources needed to free me from other obligations and to allow me to concentrate on research and writing. Their recommendations to various foundations are greatly appreciated.

Many thanks are due to the American Palestine Educational Foundation (subsequently known as the Jerusalem Fund), the Earhart Foundation, and the Department of Government and the Center for International Affairs at Harvard University for the financial aid they provided to cover my travel, research, and living expenses.

During my travels in Latin America, I was helped by many people. Their indispensable assistance made it much easier for me to locate sources of information and to make my way around a region that I had never been to before.

I would also like to thank my friends Walid and Nabil Shihadeh who had to listen to me, more than often, reading parts of my work to them. My wife, Heather, was very understanding whenever work on this book confined me and prevented me from being with her.

Finally, I would like to thank Mary Neznek of the Institute for Palestine Studies for coordinating and incorporating all the changes, one draft after another.

Grateful acknowledgment is also made to the following for permission to reprint previously published material: *Middle East Economic Digest* for the tables from "Latin America and the Middle East," *Middle East Economic Digest: Special Report*, September 1981, and to the Middle East Research and Information Project for use of the table, "Foreign Investment in Israel's Military Industries," which appeared in "Israel: the Sorcerer's Apprentice," by Esther Howard, *MERIP Middle East Report* 13 (February 1983).

CHAPTER ONE

Arms Exports and Israeli Government Policy

Tucked away in an article on Israeli-Latin American relations written by a former Israeli ambassador to Bolivia and Peru is the passing remark that "a considerable percentage of Israeli defense industry exports go to Latin America" and that "for obvious reasons very little has been published about this subject."[1] It is true that, aside from fragmentary coverage in press reports, the military dimensions of these relations and, in particular, weapons transfers have not received the attention they deserve. Indeed, the only book devoted to Israeli-Latin American relations treats the military aspect of these relationships more or less on a par with diplomatic, economic, and even cultural ties.[2] Therefore, this study seeks to remedy the gap with a more sustained treatment of the subject, not only for its intrinsic interest—Israeli-Latin American relations now being dominated by the military component—but also because Latin America provides a good starting point for shedding light on the Israeli arms industry and export policies, and their implications and consequences both for Israel and the areas in which it operates.

But why study the Israeli arms industry and arms export policy in the first place? Despite the spectacular growth and geometric increase of its exports over the past decade,* Israel's present sales, which are somewhere between $1 and $2 billion (see Table 1),† are dwarfed by those of the big suppliers. The United States, Soviet Union, France, and Great Britain together

---

* According to *MERIP Reports* (February 1983, p. 18), Israel's arms exports increased more than tenfold from 1970–80, from $100 million to $1.25 billion. Stockholm International Peace Research Institute (SIPRI) reports that they doubled from 1979 to 1980 to reach $1.2 billion. (*World Armament and Disarmament Yearbook 1982* [London: Taylor and Francis, 1982], p. 188). The U.S. General Accounting Office's *U.S. Assistance to the State of Israel* (uncensored draft, Washington, D.C., April 1983, p. 42) has Israel's military exports tripling from 1977-81, from $400 million to $1.2 billion.

† Given the highly classified nature of information concerning Israel's arms sales (they do not appear as such in national trade statistics, but rather are scattered in various categories—metal, machinery, and electronics), estimates concerning Israel's importance as an arms supplier differ widely.

control no less than 77 percent of the market,[3] compared to Israel's share of 0.6 percent to 4 percent.[4] And while its rank as

Table 1.   Israeli Arms Sales (millions of US dollars)

Year	Reported Low	Reported High	Only Available Figure
1960s (late)	$ 60[a]	—	—
1970	—	—	$100[b]
1971	N.A.	N.A.	—
1972	—	—	90[c]
1973	53[d]	$ 100[e]	—
1974	—	—	100[f]
1975	200[g]	500[h]	—
1976	250[i]	1,000[j]	—
1977	250[k]	400[l]	—
1978	400[m]	1,000[n]	—
1979	750[o]	928[p]	—
1980	1,250[q]	1,600[r]	—
1981	1,200[s]	2,100[t]	—

N.A. = Not available.

[a] Stockholm International Peace Research Institute (SIPRI), *World Armament and Disarmament Yearbook 1979* (London: Taylor and Francis, 1979), p. 181.

[b] Esther Howard, "Israel: The Sorcerer's Apprentice," *MERIP Reports* 112 (February 1983): 19.

[c] SIPRI, *Yearbook, 1973*, p. 356.

[d] *New York Times*, 15 June 1977, p. 3.

[e] Andrew Pierre, *The Global Politics of Arms Sales* (Princeton, New Jersey: Princeton University Press, 1982), pp. 235-36.

[f] These were the exports of only one company, Tadiran, in the first 8 months of 1974. The data for the whole year is not available (*Ha'aretz*, 5 September 1974).

[g] *The Israel Export and Trade Journal* 28 (March/April, 1976): 10.

[h] *New York Times*, 15 January 1977, p. 1.

[i] *The Israel Export and Trade Journal* 29 (June/July 1977): 19.

[j] *New York Times*, 15 January 1977, p. 1.

[k] *Los Angeles Times*, 18 August 1981.

[l] *New York Times*, 15 January 1977, p. 3.

[m] *New York Times*, 19 November 1978, p. 1; SIPRI, *Yearbook, 1979*, p. 181.

[n] *El Nacional* (Mexico City), 14 November 1978.

[o] *Los Angeles Times*, 18 August 1981.

[p] *Time Magazine*, 18 May 1981, p. 39; *Boston Globe*, 23 August 1981.

[q] *Los Angeles Times*, 18 August 1981; SIPRI, *Yearbook, 1982*, p. 188; *Boston Globe*, 23 August 1981.

[r] *8 Days*, 11 July 1981.

[s] Jane Friedman, "Israel's Uzi Submachine Gun," *New York Times*, 7 February 1982; *Jerusalem Post*, 5 February 1982 ($1,300 million).

[t] *Al-Fajr Palestinian Weekly*, 19–25 February 1982. Quoting Ya'acov Meridor, Israel's minister for economic coordination.

the eleventh largest arms supplier on the world market* is no mean achievement for a country of Israel's size, why not study, say, the Italian arms industry which is consistently ranked higher?

The Significance of Israeli Arms Exports

The significance of the Israeli arms industry does not lie in these figures; nor even in Israel's achievement, unmatched elsewhere, of producing within scarcely a decade combat-tested high performance military equipment ranging from sophisticated defense electronics to state-of-the-art main weapons systems. Rather, the significance lies in what has become Israel's absolute imperative to export arms. Dependence on arms sales is such that: a defense minister pledges upon assuming office to step up arms production and exports in order to improve the country's sagging balance of payments;[5] the governor of the Bank of Israel publicly states that arms exports kept the country from going under economically;[6] and a prime minister, introducing a strategic dimension, comments that as long as Israel's security situation remains the same, there is no alternative but to push arms.[7] From this dependence on arms exports, all else is derivative: Israel's close cooperation with what have been delicately termed "regimes with serious image problems";[8] the increasing salience of Israel's "advisory" and other "services" to such regimes as an adjunct to sales; and finally, Israel's growing involvement in the global strategies of the United States. It is with these consequences that this study of Latin America is concerned.

---

* SIPRI, *Yearbook 1981*, p. 188. It should be noted that since SIPRI includes in its calculations only major items, such as aircraft, tanks, and naval ships, and totally excludes small arms, ammunition, and defense electronics which constitute, according to SIPRI itself (*Yearbook 1982*, p. 188), the bulk of Israel's military exports, this ranking may be considered conservative. Other sources rank Israel as seventh (*New York Times*, 15 March 1981) and even fifth (a 1981 CIA report, cited in Ignacio Klich's "Guatemala's Back Door Arms Deals," *8 Days*, 11 July 1981). Aaron Klieman estimates its rank at fifteenth (*Israel's Global Reach: Arms Sales as Diplomacy* [McLean, Va.: Pergamon-Brassey's, 1985], p. 207).

The story of Israel's arms industry since it was seriously launched in 1967, besides being a record of successive achievements and technological advances, is the story of its growing centrality to the Israeli economy. Over the years industrial development has been channeled into the arms sector. As former Defense Minister Moshe Arens pointed out: "every country should be dealing in those products in which it has a comparative advantage. . . . Israel's largest comparative advantage is in military products, because these demand advanced technology on one hand and military experience on the other."[9] Today, it can be said that no country in the world is as dependent on arms sales as Israel. The Jaffa orange is fast being edged out of the public consciousness by the Uzi submachine gun as Israel's major export. Israel is the largest per capita arms exporter in the world. Arms exports constitute about 16 percent of its total exports[10] compared with 4.5 percent for the United States,[11] 4 to 5 percent for France,[12] and 2.5 percent for Great Britain,[13] which gives Israel the world's highest ratio of military to total exports as well.[14] Conventional wisdom has it that dependence on arms exports reaches a danger point when these exports exceed 25 percent of industrial exports,[15] and Israel has exceeded this limit, with one-fourth to one-third of its industrial exports being arms.[16]

Arms exports play a crucial role in shoring up an ailing economy. Israel's foreign debt in 1984 stood at $24 billion, the largest in the world on a per capita basis.[17] Its trade deficit soared from $834 million in 1972 to $2,329 million in 1981.[18] With declines registered in agricultural exports, and with tourism, traditionally a large foreign currency earner, falling off in recent years, the contribution of military sales is needed to help offset the worsening balance of trade and steadily declining balance of payments.

No less important in a society where people traditionally look to the government for job opportunities and the maintenance of a certain standard of living, is the position of the military as the largest employer in the country. This is particularly relevant in light of job losses in other industries. As many as 120,000

Israelis are employed in defense industries,[19] including 64,000 in the twelve largest military companies alone. This means that up to 40 percent of the industrial labor force and close to 10 percent of the total labor force are employed in the arms industries.* Since over half of Israel's military production is exported, it can be assumed that about 5 percent of the total labor force is employed on exports, compared to 0.3 percent for the United States[20] and 0.45 percent for France.[21] Underscoring the vital link between arms sales and employment, Defense Minister Yitzhak Rabin in March 1985 told 4,000 employees slated for layoff by the Israel Military Industries (TA'AS) that the only way to save their jobs would be to increase exports.[22]

Nor is the issue simply an economic one. Weapons exports are essential for the well being of the Israeli defense industries as a whole, which in turn are seen as the cornerstone of the country's security. Arms production outgrew the domestic base in the mid-1970s.[23] By the beginning of the 1980s, the Israeli Defense Forces (IDF) were purchasing only about 38 percent of the country's arms production.[24] The rest was sold abroad. This export orientation is not the result of some ephemeral policy, and this proportion of exports is required by the very structure of the industry. Regardless of how many wars Israel may fight, its domestic market, unlike those of the United States and the USSR, is not large enough to provide the economies of scale required for the development of main weapons systems such as tanks, missiles, boats, and aircraft. It is not merely a question of lowering unit costs; development costs of major weapons are such that the projected export volume determines whether or not a project can be undertaken in the first place. The Lavi aircraft, for example, which is scheduled for production in the 1990s and whose development is expected to cost $2 billion,[25] could never have been undertaken without the expectation (now proven to be overly

---

* According to the Bank of Israel, Israel's labor force in 1982 was 1.3 million, of which 309,000 were in the industrial sector (cited in Aaron Klieman, *Israel's Global Reach*, p. 57.)

optimistic) that 70 percent of the projected production would be exported.[26] Without exports, some industries would collapse and certain projects would have to be abandoned.[27]

Thus, with as much as 60 percent of its output exported (compared with about 25 percent for the United States* and the United Kingdom[28] and up to 41 percent for France[29]),† the arms industry is able to run at or close to full capacity. Consequently, in an emergency, Israel can commandeer production earmarked for export, as was the case during the prolonged fighting following the invasion of Lebanon in the summer of 1982. Furthermore, with the high rate of turnover between generations of sophisticated weaponry, foreign orders allow Israel to sell models that are being replaced by new generations and thus move ahead to new levels of sophistication. Finally, arms export earnings help to support the research and development that enables Israel to maintain a leading edge in weapons technology. Reflecting the sense of urgency attached to the arms export policy, Israeli scholar Aaron Klieman states that arms transfers "are no less critical today for the survival of the state than is its parallel program of weapons procurement."[30]

Problems of Arms Export Dependence

While arms exports may be beneficial in the short run and are clearly indispensable in present conditions, there is a price to be paid. Recent studies on the country's arms industry by Israeli scholars reflect a growing concern about the long-term economic

---

* According to the American Enterprise Institute, only one corporation of the top ten contractors with the U.S. Defense Department in 1977 was heavily dependent on foreign sales. The reliance of the others on exports averaged 12 percent (*Defense Review* 2 [1978], p. 10).

† This explains why France has been more liberal than the United States in its arms sales policy. Nonetheless, only 4 to 5 percent of France's exports consist of arms, and only 300,000 employees of a labor force of 22 million are engaged in the arms industry (Andrew Pierre, *The Global Politics of Arms Sales* [Princeton, N.J.: Princeton University Press, 1982], p. 85). It is clear that the contribution of arms exports to the French economy is not comparable to that of Israel.

and political effects of dependence on weapons transfers.[31] Economically, this high concentration in one area makes Israel vulnerable not only to events beyond its control in client states but also to sudden fluctuations in a traditionally highly volatile market—fluctuations which, if large enough, could send shock waves through Israeli society. Politically, the arms exporting imperative to which this dependence gives rise could involve Israel in foreign adventures or relationships that ultimately may be detrimental. Likewise, the growing levels of strategic cooperation with the United States have serious implications for the independence of action that Israel claims to cherish.

Israel frequently maintains that its arms deals are concluded within the framework of larger political or security considerations. As former Defense Minister Ariel Sharon commented, Israeli security interests are to be met "by an active effort to increase our exports to countries who share our strategic concerns."[32] While one seriously doubts whether contemporary Ethiopia or Khomeini's Iran shares many of Israel's strategic concerns, there is no question that supplying arms to these regimes has furthered Israel's political interests, given Ethiopia's checkered relationship with the Sudan and Iran's war against Iraq. Similarly, Israel's budding military relationship with the Mobutu regime in Zaire, whose security concerns could scarcely be guessed at, advances Israel's interests by reinforcing its foothold in sub-Saharan Africa.

Nevertheless, there are many instances in which maximization of sales rather than diplomatic concerns appears to be the overriding factor in Israel's course of action. It is difficult to find the strategic benefit of supplying Argentina against Great Britain during the Falklands/Malvinas War or Sri Lanka in its war against the Tamil separatists. Furthermore, efforts to fit Central America into the framework of the Arab-Israeli conflict on the basis of a Palestine Liberation Organization (PLO) presence in Nicaragua (which has yet to be substantiated as more than moral support) remain unconvincing. In a pattern that may be typical in situations where there are no compelling political factors against arms sales, the initiative appears to lie with the purveyors of arms, frequently with far-reaching consequences. Thus, according to Aaron Klieman of Tel Aviv University, Israel's domestic arms sales diplomacy is "the product of an internal process, the foundations of which rest upon an exceptionally broad consensus among Israelis supportive of Israel in the role of arms supplier."[33]

Although Israeli arms reportedly have found their way to sixty-two countries in Asia, Africa, Europe, and the Americas (Table 2), serious obstacles impede export capabilities. The Soviet bloc is off-limits as are, *a fortiori*, the Arab states (the largest purchasers of arms) and most Muslim countries. Most of the industrialized countries either produce their own weapons or purchase them from NATO allies. Many potential third world buyers, Israel's natural clientele, prefer to avoid the political risks of visible arms purchases from Israel, especially if other sources are available. Thus, Israel is forced to pursue a particularly aggressive arms sales drive in the markets that remain, using every competitive advantage it can summon. For Israel the chief competitive advantage, aside from the weapons themselves, is expertise in counterinsurgency techniques and the control of popular resistance.

What sets Israel apart from most other suppliers, then, is not necessarily the concentration of clients with regimes at war with their own people. In the intense competition for markets, few suppliers disdain sales to such governments, although France, traditionally chided for its lack of fastidiousness in selecting clients, discontinued sales to South Africa and Chile under its socialist government.[34] Rather, Israel is notable for the close advisory relationships it forges with these client regimes as a sales inducement. The salience of these relationships, themselves an outgrowth of the need to export, leaves Israel vulnerable to international criticism and political isolation. On a more pragmatic level, the fact that these client regimes are unpopular and hence unstable makes the risk of a sudden loss of a market, such as with the overthrow of the Somoza government and of the Shah of Iran, more than hypothetical.

Finally, the arms export imperative has important implications for Israel's relations with the United States. Relatively minor, but nonetheless worthy of mention, is the friction that

Table 2.   Israeli Arms Customers by Region

Country	Reference Source
Africa	
Central African Republic	Interview with Naomi Chazan, coordinator, Africa Research Unit, the Truman Institute, Hebrew University, Cambridge, Mass., April 1983.
Ciskei (South African homeland)	Aaron Klieman, *Israel's Global Reach*, 1985, pp. 135–142; and *Hadashot*, 15 October 1984, p. 1.
Ethiopia	*New York Times*, 19 November 1978.
Gabon	Ignacio Klich, "Israeli Arms," *South*, April 1982; interview with Naomi Chazan.
Ghana	Stockholm International Peace Research Institute (SIPRI), *Arms Trade Register, 1975* (London: Taylor and Francis, 1975), p. 36.
Kenya	*New York Times*, 19 November 1978.
Liberia	Aaron Klieman, *Israel's Global Reach*, 1985, pp. 135–142; and *Hadashot*, 15 October 1984, p. 1.
Malawi	Gregory Orfalea, "Arms Buildup in the Middle East," *The Link* 14 (September-October 1981): 7.
Morocco	Aaron Klieman, *Israel's Global Reach*, 1985, pp. 135–142; and *Hadashot*, 15 October 1984, p. 1.
Nigeria	Benny Morris, "Arms at Any Price," *Jerusalem Post*, 4 June 1982.
South Africa	*Uno Mas Uno*, 14 November 1978.
Swaziland	Aaron Klieman, *Israel's Global Reach*, 1985, pp. 135–142; and *Hadashot*, 15 October 1984, p. 1.
Tanzania	*Ibid*.
Uganda	SIPRI, *Arms Trade Register, 1975*, p. 89.
Zaire	*Salt Lake Tribune*, 15 December 1982; and *Los Angeles Times*, 13 January 1983.
Zimbabwe	*Uno Mas Uno*, 14 November 1978.

(continues)

Table 2.   (continued)

Country	Reference Source
Asia	
Burma	SIPRI, *Arms Trade Register, 1975,* p. 3.
China	*Barricada* (Managua), 22 January 1981; *Nuevo Diario* (Managua), 31 August 1982; "China Has Secret Military Pact with Israel," *Salt Lake Tribune,* 21 November 1984; and *Jerusalem Post,* 15 October 1984, p. 1.
India	Carl Alpert, "Making and Selling Arms Helps Keep Israel Free—But It Bothers Her," *Jewish Week,* 13 August 1982.
Indonesia	SIPRI, *World Armament and Disarmament Yearbook 1981,* p. 224.
Malaysia	*Uno Mas Uno,* 14 November 1978.
Nepal	SIPRI, *Arms Trade Register, 1975,* p. 37.
New Guinea	Aaron Klieman, *Israel's Global Reach,* 1985, pp. 135–142; and *Hadashot,* 15 October 1984, p. 1.
Philippines	U.S. Congress, House Committee on Foreign Affairs, *Economic and Military Aid Programs in Europe and the Middle East,* 96th Cong., 1st sess., 1979, p. 84.
Singapore	*Monthly Review,* January 1973, p. 58.
South Korea	*Uno Mas Uno,* 14 November 1978.
Sri Lanka	SIPRI, *Arms Trade Register, 1975,* p. 41.
Taiwan	*Uno Mas Uno,* 14 November 1978.
Thailand	*Agencia Latino Americana De Informacion,* 17 November 1977; *Christian Science Monitor,* 27 December 1982.
Europe	
Austria	SIPRI, *World Armament and Disarmament Yearbook 1977,* p. 276.
Belgium	*Israel Export and Trade Journal,* May 1977.
France	Jane Friedman, "Israel's Uzi Submachine Guns," *New York Times,* 7 February 1982.
Great Britain	*Ibid.*

Table 2.   (continued)

Country	Reference Source
Greece	*New York Times*, 19 November 1978.
Romania	*Jerusalem Post*, 4 June 1982.
Switzerland	*Jewish Telegraphic Agency*, 23 December 1981.
West Germany	*Los Angeles Times*, 29 July 1981.
Latin America	
Argentina	*New York Times*, 9 May 1982, p. 6; and *Washington Post*, 16 December 1982.
Bolivia	SIPRI, *World Armament and Disarmament Yearbook 1977*, p. 311.
Brazil	*Latin America Weekly Report*, 24 December 1982, p. 11.
Chile	*Yediot Ahronot*, 25 January 1979; and SIPRI, *World Armament and Disarmament Yearbook 1982*, p. 410.
Colombia	SIPRI, *World Armament and Disarmament Yearbook 1982*, p. 210; *Latin America Regional Reports—Andean Group*, 22 January 1982, p. 1.
Costa Rica	*Financial Times*, 22 October 1982.
Dominican Republic	Ronald Slaughter, "Israel Arms Trade Cozying to Latin Armies," *NACLA Report* 16 (January–February 1982): 52–53.
Ecuador	*New York Times*, 19 November 1978.
El Salvador	*New York Times*, 19 November 1978; and SIPRI, *World Armament and Disarmament Yearbook 1982*, p. 213.
Guatemala	*Christian Science Monitor*, 28 October 1981; and *Latin America Weekly Report*, 5 September 1980, p. 8.
Haiti	Ronald Slaughter, "Israel Arms Trade Cozying to Latin Armies," pp. 52–53.
Honduras	*Latin America Weekly Report*, 17 December 1982; and *Guardian*, 26 January 1983.

(continues)

Table 2.   (continued)

Country	Reference Source
Mexico	*Excelsior,* 14 March 1982; and *Jerusalem Post,* 12 January 1981.
Nicaragua	*Newsweek,* 20 November 1978, p. 68; and *Latin America Weekly Report,* 16 May 1980.
Panama	SIPRI, *World Armament and Disarmament Yearbook 1976,* p. 275; and *Excelsior,* 25 February 1977.
Paraguay	SIPRI, *World Armament and Disarmament Yearbook 1977,* p. 332.
Peru	*Latin America Weekly Report,* January 1982, p. 3.
Venezuela	SIPRI, *World Armament and Disarmament Yearbook 1982,* p. 237.
Middle East	
Iran	*New York Times,* 19 November 1978 and 24 August 1981.
Lebanon	*New York Times,* 19 November 1978.
Turkey	*Christian Science Monitor,* 6 January 1977, p. 1.
North America	
United States	*Washington Post,* 21 July 1982; and *Israel Business and Investors' Report,* August 1981.
Canada	*Jewish Telegraphic Agency,* 7 January 1982; and *Excelsior,* 11 April 1977.
South Pacific	
Australia	*Israel Export and Trade Journal,* September 1973, p. 26.
New Zealand	Aaron Klieman, *Israel's Global Reach,* 1985, pp. 135–142; and *Hadashot,* 15 October 1984, p. 1.

arises as a result of Israel's emergence as a supplier on the world market. That Israel is viewed as a potential competitor in the field was made clear in the congressional debates over U.S. funding for the development of the Lavi jet fighter. In view of rising U.S. protectionism and the many facilities accorded the Israeli arms industry (discussed in detail in Chapter 2), this tension is likely to increase. Another point of friction is the U.S. control of sales of Israeli products containing U.S. components, which includes virtually all of Israel's main weapons systems. Washington's willingness to exercise that prerogative, as when the proposed sale of Kfir jets to Ecuador was initially vetoed, has led to considerable ill-feeling.

In other ways, too, the growing sophistication of the arms industry, far from enhancing the country's independence as was the original intent, has actually made Israel more dependent on the United States than ever before. Thus, in addition to Israel's perennial dependence on economic assistance and for military hardware that it cannot produce itself, dependence on the United States now encompasses funding for major defense projects such as the Lavi fighter aircraft and the Merkava tank, technology transfers, licensing agreements, and data packages, as well as the approval of many sales to third parties. In turn, this situation encourages *quid pro quo* arrangements in which Israel, in order to obtain better markets for its weapons and with the expectation of rewards at the bilateral level,[35] helps the United States when it is unable to act overtly itself due to congressional opposition or other constraints. The extent of this dependence will make it increasingly difficult for Israel to turn down requests from Washington due to a constant need to prove itself and its usefulness. As Klieman points out, "each instance of close military cooperation strengthens Israel's claim that it has the right to be regarded as an ally and strategic asset, while at the same time justifying American support for Israel as payment for services rendered."[36] While these services are at present most visible in Central America, this pattern could be easily repeated wherever political considerations prevent the United States from acting directly on its own behalf.

The Latin American Experience

This study looks at all these issues with reference to Latin America, and particularly at several selected states in the region. There are a number of reasons why Latin America provides a good starting point for examining Israel's arms export policy. No other region of the third world has had as continuous a relationship with Israel, both diplomatically and militarily. Apart from Nicaragua, Guyana, and Cuba, all the Latin American countries have diplomatic ties with Israel. This provides a regional context lacking for other major Israeli arms buyers (such as South Africa) which are scattered geographically. Furthermore, arms sales are most concentrated in this region. Not only has Latin America been Israel's primary market, but at least eighteen of the Latin American states have purchased Israeli arms. By focusing on Israel's military relations in Latin America, using concrete examples rather than theoretical formulations, this study seeks to present a clearer understanding of Israel's arms export policy and marketing strategies, the appeal of its weaponry, the local and international factors behind its success, and the vulnerability of arms sales to international and domestic changes. Through the study of Latin America, a profile of Israel's arms clients emerges as well. Finally, this book hopes to bring out the achievements and shortcomings of Israel's export policy as a whole, including the gap between expectations and results.

NOTES

1. Nathaniel Lorch, "Latin America and Israel," *Jerusalem Quarterly*, no. 22 (Winter 1982), pp. 70–84.
2. Edy Kaufman, Yoram Shapiro, and Joel Barromi, *Israel and Latin American Relations* (New Brunswick, N.J.: Transaction Books, 1979).
3. Aaron S. Klieman, *Israel's Global Reach: Arms Sales as Diplomacy* (McLean, Va.: Pergamon-Brassey's, 1985), p. 207.
4. *Ibid.*, p. 208.
5. The *New York Times*, 24 August 1981.
6. Dr. Moshe Mandelbaum, talking about 1982, quoted in *Ma'ariv*, 18 October 1982, cited in Klieman, *Global Reach*, p. 69. Also quoted in Moshe Lichtman, "Israel's Weapons Exports," *Monitin*, July 1983.
7. Shimon Peres, quoted in Lichtman, "Weapons Exports."
8. Klieman, *Global Reach*, p. 47.
9. *Jerusalem Post*, 7 September 1983, cited in Klieman, *Global Reach*, pp. 100–101.

10. Yoram Peri and Amnon Neubach, *The Military Industrial Complex in Israel: A Pilot Study* (Tel Aviv: International Center for Peace in the Middle East, 1985), p. 69.
11. Daniel Southerland, "Israeli Economy Said to Depend Heavily on Export of Weapons," *Washington Post,* 22 March 1985.
12. *Financial Times,* 5 March 1981.
13. *Ibid.*
14. Alex Mintz, "The Military-Industrial Complex: The Israeli Case," *Journal of Strategic Studies* 6 (September 1983): 112; Victor Perera, "Uzi Diplomacy," *Mother Jones,* July 1985, p. 43.
15. Klieman, *Global Reach,* p. 204.
16. *Ibid.,* p. 65.
17. *Ibid.,* p. 62.
18. *Foreign Trade Statistics,* vol. 24, no. 12 (Tel Aviv: Central Bureau of Statistics, 1973), pp. 35–37; Central Bureau of Statistics, *Statistical Abstract of Israel, 1982* (Jerusalem: Hed Press Ltd., 1982), pp. 213–214.
19. Klieman, *Global Reach,* p. 57.
20. Andrew Pierre, *The Global Politics of Arms Sales* (Princeton, N.J.: Princeton University Press, 1982), p. 79.
21. Stockholm International Peace Research Institute (SIPRI), *World Armament and Disarmament Yearbook 1982* (London: Taylor and Francis, 1982), p. 183.
22. *Jerusalem Post,* 12 March 1985, cited in Jane Hunter, "Israel and the Contras: A Bigger Role," *Israeli Foreign Affairs* 1 (May 1985): 7.
23. Aaron Klieman, *Israeli Arms Sales: Perspectives and Prospects* (Tel Aviv: Jaffee Center for Strategic Studies, 1984), paper no. 24, p. 26.
24. Tom Segev, "Israel's Arms Exports," *Koterit Rashit* 4 (April 1984).
25. Peri and Neubach, *Pilot Study,* p. 60.
26. Hirsh Goodman, "Fighter in a Fog," *Jerusalem Post,* 19 February 1982.
27. Klieman, *Israeli Arms Sales,* p. 36.
28. Klieman, *Global Reach,* p. 59.
29. Pierre, *Arms Sales,* pp. 84–85.
30. Klieman, *Global Reach,* p. 193.
31. Peri and Neubach, *Pilot Study,* p. 60; Klieman, *Global Reach,* p. 193; Mintz, "Military-Industrial Complex," p. 112.
32. Efraim Inbar, *Israeli Strategic Thought in the Post-1973 Period* (Jerusalem: Israel Research Institute of Contemporary Society, 1982), pp. 24–29, cited in Klieman, *Global Reach,* p. 193.
33. Klieman, *Global Reach,* p. 92.
34. "French Arms Exporters: Making a Killing," *Economist,* 20 October 1984, p. 73.
35. Edy Kaufman, "View from Jerusalem," *Washington Quarterly* 7 (Fall 1984):46.
36. Klieman, *Global Reach,* p. 45.

CHAPTER TWO

Israel's Arms Industry

I srael launched its military industry on a large scale in the wake of the June 1967 war under the impetus of the arms embargo declared by France, its major supplier. Within a few years, the nation had developed an advanced arms industry unmatched in the third world in terms of technological sophistication.

By 1972 Israel was producing a domestically designed combat jet with a speed of Mach 1.5, as well as its own armored fighting vehicle. Three years later, it introduced what is now commonly known as the Kfir C–2 fighter jet, the most sophisticated fighter ever manufactured in a developing country.[1] Moreover, as marketing began for its own air-to-air missiles and sea-skimming infrared missiles, work was being done on a new generation of supersonic cruise missiles. Then in 1981 the new Barak antimissile missile defense system was unveiled. Israel has also designed and developed its own battle tank, the Merkava, which has an armor so advanced that shells fired by a World War II tank would simply bounce off it. Highly computerized and carrying twice the amount of ammunition as other tanks, the Merkava also has an explosion suppression system, developed by the Israeli firm Spectronnix. The Merkava uses an inert agent to stop an explosion within sixty milliseconds before burns are caused.[2] In addition to light arms, ammunition, and communications devices, other Israeli-manufactured weaponry includes remotely piloted vehicles, electronic and antielectronic warfare systems, and naval equipment ranging from command and control systems, missiles and antimissile guns to a variety of patrol boats. The Dvora, for instance, is a 71-foot boat with an operational range of 700 nautical miles powered by two MTU marine diesel engines. Carrying two Israeli-made Gabriel sea-to-sea missiles and two 20-mm cannon or 50-inch machine guns, the Dvora has about twice the firing power of similar class boats. Thus, by December 1981 Israel's chief of staff, Rafael Eitan, was able to boast that his country had "unlimited potential in the military, industrial and security fields and is able to produce everything it needs to protect itself."[3]

Reasons for the Development of the Arms Industry

Unreliability of Suppliers

Survival, the Israelis say, is the principal reason for their decision to build a domestic military industry.[4] As a state established by force of arms in an alien and hostile environment, Israel was by necessity a society built on military readiness and a preoccupation with security matters. A series of wars has required continual rearmament, making it only natural for Israel to develop a defense industry of its own. This tendency has been reinforced by repeated demonstrations of the country's vulnerability to the pressures of suppliers, which have never hesitated to withhold or delay arms shipments either as punishment for Israel's actions or to influence its policy.

Never was this vulnerability more forcefully revealed than in 1967, when France imposed an arms embargo on the eve of the Six-Day War. Because Israel relied almost exclusively on France both for fighter jets and heavy arms, the embargo had a tremendous psychological impact. This situation was compounded by another embargo imposed by the United States.[5] By demonstrating Israel's dependence on imported weapons in a moment of crisis, the French embargo served as a catalyst for Israel's resolve to develop a full-scale military industry at least to minimize the impact of future interruptions in arms supplies.

Arms procurement problems had plagued the Zionists in Palestine from the 1930s, and clandestine weapons plants, which formed the basis of the pre-1967 arms industry, had been created in response to those problems. Nor did expanded production capacity bring an end to this vulnerability. Embargoes or threats of embargoes have continued constantly to reinforce Israel's determination to pursue an arms production policy. A brief survey of the more important embargoes will illustrate this point.

At the time of the first Arab-Israeli war in 1948, the United States, Great Britain, and several other countries imposed an arms embargo on both combatants,[6] forcing the Haganah, the group in charge of Zionist arms procurement, to scramble for arms supplies on the world's black market. Although Britain and the United States lifted their arms embargoes in 1953, Canada cancelled an earlier Israeli order for twenty-four Canadian-built CL–13B Sabre 6 fighters on the grounds that renewed hostilities seemed imminent.[7] Two years after France's 1967 embargo, President de Gaulle imposed another in retaliation for Israel's destruction of thirteen Lebanese commercial airliners stationed at the Beirut airport—which was a reprisal for a *fedayeen* attack on an El Al aircraft in Athens in which one person died. The second embargo resulted in a "redoubling of efforts to enlarge local production and to do away with dependence on overseas arms."[8]

The United States, in the meantime, became Israel's principal source of the sophisticated and heavy equipment it was unable to produce. By May 1970 Israel had received most of the seventy A–4 Skyhawk fighters and three trainers ordered from the United States in 1966 and 1968, as well as forty of the fifty F–4 Phantom fighters and six reconnaissance aircraft ordered in December 1968. An additional 100 Skyhawks and 25 Phantoms were also expected.

However, the replacement of France by the United States as Israel's major supplier merely transferred the seat of pressure from Paris to Washington. At the height of the "war of attrition" with Egypt in 1970, the United States "held in abeyance" an urgent Israeli request for arms. In so doing, the United States hoped not only to induce the Soviets to show similar restraint vis-à-vis its Arab clients, but also to establish some distance from Israel to ease the pressure on friendly Arab regimes.[9]

In July 1971 following the breakdown of negotiations conducted under the supervision of United Nations Emissary Gunnar Jarring, the United States imposed another embargo on a shipment of Phantom and Skyhawk planes that had been ordered by Israel and approved by Congress earlier that year.[10] Since the Phantoms constituted the Israeli air force's principal strike force, Israel took the embargo very much to heart and exerted its own pressure by adamantly refusing to proceed with the Suez Canal discussions until the planes were delivered. Meanwhile, a letter, dated October 15, 1971, signed by seventy-eight U.S. senators, was sent to President Nixon calling for the resumption "without further delay" of the F–4 Phantom deliveries. Israel's case was also aided by the Soviet Union's pledge to increase military assistance to Egypt. The United States finally gave in and Skyhawk deliveries proceeded in November 1971 and Phantom deliveries in March 1972.[11]

These deliveries became particularly important because within less than a year Syria and Egypt launched a surprise attack on Israel which began the fourth Arab-Israeli war. With the eruption of hostilities, Great Britain imposed an arms embargo on the region and refused to ship tanks and tank engines to Israel under previously signed contracts.[12] It was this embargo that led to the development of the Merkava tank.[13]

The United States has frequently resorted to the threat of embargo to influence Israeli policy. In March 1975, when U.S. Secretary of State Henry Kissinger was unable to persuade Israel to pull back from the Sinai passes and oil fields in exchange for Egyptian political concessions, the Ford administration declared its intention to "reassess" Middle East policy and restricted the flow of arms and economic aid to Israel.[14] Moreover, following Israel's first major invasion of Lebanon in 1978, President Carter wrote a note to Prime Minister Begin warning that Israeli failure to withdraw from Lebanese territory would compel the United States to halt arms shipments.[15]

In 1976 and 1978, the United States imposed special restrictions on the use and shipment of cluster bombs to Israel. A few years later, during the 1982 invasion of Lebanon, the Reagan administration suspended shipments of cluster bombs altogether to induce Israel to negotiate the exodus of Palestine Liberation Organization (PLO) guerrillas from Beirut and to end the siege of the city. But this embargo was more symbolic than substantive, since Israel was already manufacturing its own cluster-type bombs.[16]

On a number of occasions, the United States also imposed temporary embargoes on the shipment of F–15 and F–16 warplanes to Israel. In June 1981 this was done in response to Israel's bombing of downtown Beirut and destruction of Iraq's nuclear reactor.[17] Deliveries were suspended in December 1981 following Israel's annexation of the Golan Heights and again in April 1983 to pressure Israel to withdraw from Lebanon.[18]

These actions by its closest ally and most important arms supplier strengthened Israel's determination, in the words of Defense Minister Moshe Arens, "to reduce our dependence on arms supplies from outside."[19] While Israeli policy makers are aware that total self-sufficiency can never be achieved, they are confident that domestic production can limit the effectiveness of outside political pressures, which will give Israel more leeway to pursue its own policies rather than having to accommodate the concerns of its suppliers.

Economic Factors

The development of an indigenous Israeli arms industry was principally a response to security needs in order to be free from the political pressures of suppliers. But economic factors played a role as well. With war or the threat of war virtually a way of life, Israel's defense requirements placed a tremendous burden on an economy beset by chronic deficits and a permanent need for foreign aid in order to function.* From 1966 to 1972 Israel's military imports grew from $116 million to $800 million per year.[20] Furthermore, the arms buildup following the 1967 Arab-Israeli War accounted for half the country's trade deficit in 1968, according to Moshe Kashti, director-general of Israel's Defense

---

* Between 1966 and 1972 Israel's military spending increased fivefold in absolute terms and two and a half times as a percentage of the gross national product (GNP). Defense spending reached a peak in 1975, consuming some 35 percent of the GNP. Although it declined in the late 1970s, reaching a low of 22 percent of the GNP (*Financial Times*, 25 May 1981), defense spending rose again in 1980 to register $5.4 billion, or 31 percent of the $17.7 billion budget. This figure does not include the $1.4 billion in military aid allocated by the United States to compensate for losses from the peace treaty with Egypt. (*Time*, 18 May 1981, p. 38). By 1981 Israel's defense spending reached the equivalent of 27 percent of the GNP (*Financial Times*, 25 May 1982). According to the Stockholm International Peace Research Institute (SIPRI), Israeli military spending is among the highest in the world relative to the size of the GNP, total public spending, and population (*World Armament and Disarmament Yearbook 1984* [London: Taylor and Francis, 1984]).

Ministry. Kashti felt that the resulting shortage of foreign reserves constituted the "most dangerous problem Israel faces in this regard."[21] Following the Six-Day War, the use of foreign assets to purchase military equipment tripled in one year. At that rate it was feared that Israel's foreign monetary reserves would reach a point beyond the "permissible line" within two or three years.[22]

Expanded domestic arms production promised to alleviate many of these problems. Of the arguments advanced at the time, which are still used to justify Israel's arms policy, four stand out. First, domestic production would reduce the quantity of military imports and thus narrow, or lessen the increase of, the expanding trade gap. Not only would import substitution save foreign currency, it would also save domestic funds since local products would be less costly than foreign ones. Second, employment opportunities, not only for the labor force but also for highly skilled professionals, would be created, helping to stem the brain drain and attract skilled immigrants. Third, research and development activities would have a spillover or spinoff effect in the nonmilitary sector, spurring the technological advancement of sophisticated industry. Fourth, the profits from foreign sales would earn foreign currency above and beyond the saving through import substitution. In apparent demonstration of the wisdom of embarking upon local arms production, the burden of military imports on Israel's trade deficit declined from an average of 42.8 percent in 1968–72 to a low of 13.4 percent in 1976–80,[23] encouraging the country to expand the arms industry further.

There may be another, less tangible, reason for the development of a domestic arms industry. As stated by the head of planning of the Israeli Defense Forces (IDF), reliance on foreign suppliers has grave consequences "for our political independence, but also for the national pride and values of Israeli society as a whole."[24]

History of the Industry

Although Israel did not seriously set about developing its sources of supplies until the late 1960s, the arms industry is older than the state itself, tracing its origins back to the days of the Haganah. Zionist pioneers worked in small, underground workshops manufacturing and repairing various types of small arms, ammunition, armored vehicles, and other types of military hardware.[25] These military workshops (collectively known as Israel Military Industries [IMI or TA'AS], Israel's pioneer defense firm) were founded around 1933. Subsequently, the defense firm proved to be "not only a major agent of [Israel's] survival in the War of Independence, but the mold and nucleus of [the] Military Industry to come."[26] In May 1948 when the British left Palestine, the Haganah came out from underground and began to set up other military factories and workshops.

In the early 1950s, these independent and often overlapping workshops were brought under a single management and incorporated into the military concerns that were founded alongside TA'AS. Among these new entities were the Israel Aircraft Industries (IAI), originally known as Bedek or the Institute for the Reconditioning of Planes, and the National Armaments Development Authority (RAFAEL).[27] The main emphasis in the first two decades of the new state of Israel was on the procurement of weapons from outside sources,[28] although modern military production lines were established during that same period.

Initially, the arms industry was geared to repairing and overhauling tanks, aircraft, and electronics systems that could not be replaced easily or cheaply.[29] When reconditioning of some old planes that had been withdrawn from service was started, it was discovered that there was a lucrative market for them in the Far East and Latin America.[30] This prompted Israel, largely under the influence of David Ben-Gurion, to purchase equipment from armament factories closed at the end of World War II. The equipment, which was bought virtually at scrap metal prices, was overhauled and transformed into usable and relatively inexpensive military hardware for export.[31] Indeed, the IAI made its first big profits after purchasing discarded military equipment from other countries, reconditioning it, and turning it into "first-class flying craft."[32]

During this time, the manufacture of arms, mainly ammunition, mortars, and small arms, was being pursued. Furthermore, Israel was also assembling French planes and other weapons systems, on a limited basis, and was itself producing certain parts for these systems. By 1966–67 the groundwork for the armaments industry had been solidly laid, and production of some 400 different small arms items[33] was valued at about $80 million.[34]

Even before the June 1967 war and the French arms embargo, there were proponents of a large-scale arms industry within the government. In 1966, when the country was in economic recession, detailed plans were discussed for the expansion and diversification of the military industry to meet domestic and export needs.[35] Over the years, a debate had crystallized around this issue. One side, headed by Defense Ministry Director-General Shimon Peres,* included many Defense Ministry officials, and advocated total self-sufficiency in arms production: Israel should develop and produce all the combat material required. The other faction, headed by Army Chief of Staff Yitzhak Rabin, included many senior officers of the Israeli Defense Forces (IDF), and believed that domestic weapons production should involve only such items as could be competitively and economically manufactured locally, with the larger, heavier systems purchased from abroad. This faction advocated the production of less sophisticated systems and the development of the capacity to adapt large, imported items, such as aircraft, tanks, and armored personnel carriers, to suit national needs.[36]

The debate was ended in 1967,[37] with the shock of the French embargo spurring Israel to the radical reorientation of its arms industry "towards fulfillment of its all-encompassing ideal— the total supply of all requirements in arms and munitions of every kind, their components, auxiliary equipment, spare parts,

---

* Shimon Peres held this post from 1953 to 1967, during which time he took direct responsibility for programs involving applied military research and development. Under his influence the ministry took over the arms industries, expanded into aviation, established an electronics division, and pushed ahead on nuclear research and development (Aaron Klieman, *Israeli Arms Sales: Perspectives and Prospects* [Tel Aviv: Jaffee Center for Strategic Studies, 1984], paper no. 24, p. 11).

explosives, propellent fuels, chemicals and all else needed for the defense of the state."[38] Thus, the military industry underwent a swift and far-reaching expansion. The sense of urgency to achieve independence from foreign suppliers led the country into an unprecedented industrial revolution. The groundwork, however, had been laid in the rapid industrialization of the 1950s when factories had been set up all over the country to feed, clothe, and employ a population that had doubled within three years due to immigration. In the early stages, the government imposed restrictions to protect the fledgling industry. However, once it was firmly established, the country was opened to international competition, and the less efficient firms were weeded out or improved their standards.[39]

The thrust of this "industrial revolution" was directed toward the manufacture of military equipment. Consequently, 1967 can be said to mark the beginning of the militarization of the Israeli economy. According to Aaron Klieman, after the June 1967 war under the impetus of defense industrialization, Israeli society was transformed from a rural economy based on citrus exports to a highly industrialized one, producing electronics and high-technology items.[40] Production at existing defense industries, such as IAI and TA'AS, was stepped up, and many civilian production lines were converted to military ones. With the shift from France to the United States as the principal supplier of heavy military equipment, factories were transformed to develop and manufacture complementary weapons and ammunition for American arms.* This provided a further boost to expansion by requiring new production lines and organizational changes.[41]

The government instituted a policy of co-opting civilian firms for defense projects.[42] Military production lines were installed in a number of industrial plants, such as Amcor, Tadiran, Soltam, and Volcan, which later served as subcontractors to the military industries supplying intermediate products, parts, and

---

* The shift to U.S. weapons also released large stocks of French weapons systems, such as Mirages and Super-mysteres, which were upgraded and sold abroad, mainly in Latin America.

accessories for finished systems.[43] This policy is still maintained and large numbers of civilian workers in nondefense industries continue to work on military projects. As a result, about 800 companies, many of them civilian, are currently involved in defense projects. About 160 civilian plants were used as subcontractors for the Kfir jet fighter.[44] According to information revealed to the Knesset's Economic Committee, 180 of the 200 plants working on the Merkava tank and about 40 percent of the parts needed for its production were supplied by the private sector.[45] The Israel Military Industries (TA'AS) subcontracts to about 500 civilian manufacturers,[46] and it is the official policy of the government-owned RAFAEL to subcontract as much as possible to civilian firms.[47] Although as military needs are met many companies have branched out to produce sophisticated equipment for medical, scientific, and other industrial purposes in addition to that for military use, the main emphasis continues to be on arms development. For example, between 1977 and 1982 70 percent of the electronics industry's production was of a military nature, as opposed to only 10 to 15 percent in communications.[48]

Israeli employment statistics are a good indication of the militarization that followed the Six Day War. Prior to 1967 less than 10 percent of the Israeli work force was involved in the military sector. By 1980 approximately one-fourth of the total labor force, or 300,000 people,* and one-half the industrial labor force worked in the military sector, including the armed forces. The growth of Israel's two largest military industries during this period reflects the same trend. The work force of the Israel Aircraft Industries (IAI)—which produces the Kfir fighter jet, the Arava STOL (short take-off landing) plane, Gabriel sea-to-sea missiles, Dabur and Dvora missile boats, and pilotless reconnaissance planes—grew from 4,461[49] in 1966 to 22,500 in 1980.[50]

---

*Of these, 120,000 were employed directly in the defense industry (see Aaron Klieman, *Israel's Global Reach: Arms Sales as Diplomacy* [McLean, Va.: Pergamon–Brassey's, 1985], p. 57).

During this period, Israel Military Industries (IMI or TA'AS)—which produces Uzi submachine guns, Galil assault rifles, rocket launchers, "path-clearing" and other bombs, and a variety of ammunition, including HEAT (high explosive antitank) ammunition—grew from 4,521[51] to 14,500 employees.[52]

Militarization soon paid off. By the time France declared its second arms embargo in January 1969, Israel was domestically producing most of the items that were withheld.[53] Domestic arms production had risen by 50 percent that year, while manpower had increased by 20 percent over 1968 levels. Investment had almost doubled over the same period.[54] By 1972 Israel claimed that it was producing one-fourth of its total weapons requirements,[55] a percentage that reached one-third by 1976.[56] Meanwhile, the value of its arms production was estimated at $500 million in 1973, representing a fivefold increase over 1966.[57]

It was especially after 1973 that the industry acquired a high degree of sophistication, enabling it to produce advanced military equipment ranging from tanks and jet aircraft to precision-guided "smart weapons," microelectronics, and rocket-propelled engines for sea-to-sea and air-to-air missiles. This success, particularly in view of the size of the country, its lack of natural resources, and the short time in which the industry was developed, has been a source of considerable national pride. The arms industry has given Israelis not only a sense of security, but provided foreign currency and, in many cases, a vehicle for reaching and influencing the third world.

The Elements of Success

The success of the Israeli arms industry can be attributed to a combination of domestic and foreign factors. On the domestic side, there is a large pool of highly skilled workers, scientists, and engineers, a government policy that actively encourages arms production and military research, and a broad public consensus favoring arms production and arms exports. On the foreign side, there are extensive investments and technology transfers from abroad which have been crucial to the development and expansion of the industry.

Domestic Factors

Israel's best resource is its human resource. It has the highest per capita concentration of scientists and engineers in the world: an average of 3 out of every thousand Israelis is engaged in full-time research and development, as compared to 2.5 per thousand in the United States and 2.4 per thousand in Japan.[58] About 500 Israeli companies are active in research and development, and this number increases by about 100 every year. Moreover, the number of scientists and engineers (currently 10,000 and 20,000, respectively) in a country of over three and one-half million is increasing at an annual rate of 16 percent.[59]

Because of Israeli government policy, the nation's research and development efforts are concentrated in the military sector. By the early 1960s, Israel was spending $5 to $10 million on military research and development at a time when total military expenditures amounted to only $200 million. This figure increased from $20 to $30 million in 1966–67 and almost doubled in 1969–70 to reach $50 million.[60] Of all government expenditures for research and development, 46 percent goes to the military sector, as compared to 2 percent in Japan, 3 percent in Holland, and 8 percent in Canada.[61]

Israel has also mobilized a highly skilled labor force whose salary levels, low relative to Western standards, make possible less costly products. Government subsidies of research also lower costs to between one-third and one-quarter of those in the United States or Europe. Less tangible but equally important is the motivation of workers, nearly all of whom are members of Israel's military reserves. In the words of an IAI official, "everyone who works here is emotionally involved." Workers are urged in the name of patriotism to manufacture equipment "good enough for your sons" to use.[62]

But the most important domestic factor in the development and success of the Israeli arms industry has been the preponderant role played by the government. The government took over and consolidated the various enterprises of the prestate period, centralized and nurtured weapons research in the RAFAEL Armament Development Authority and was in the forefront of the country's industrialization efforts. In addition, after the June 1967 war, the Procurement and Production Administration was established to encourage local and civilian defense manufacturing.[63] For a long time, the military industry's factories were departments of the Defense Ministry or affiliated with it, and only later achieved administrative autonomy.[64]

Most of these industries are still state-owned, including the two largest companies, IAI and TA'AS, which together employ over 10 percent of the country's industrial work force. RAFAEL, Israel's largest research and development institution, which is responsible for developing advanced and sophisticated items such as guided weaponry and electronic warfare equipment, electro-optics, thermal imaging, and missile detection systems, is a division of the Defense Ministry. MASA, which produces the Merkava tank, grew out of the IDF's renovation and maintenance centers and is directly responsible to the chief of staff. Israel Shipyards, manufacturer of naval craft including the Reshef missile and gunboats, is also government-owned. Other companies, such as Tadiran, a major manufacturer of military communications equipment, got their start through funding from the Defense Ministry—which had joint ownership before selling its half to GTE, which subsequently sold it to Koor Industries (Koor is owned by Histadrut, the Israeli labor federation) which already owned the other half. Likewise, Elbit, a leading defense computing firm, began as a joint venture between the Defense Ministry and Elron. Many of the nongovernment firms subcontract to the defense establishment. (See Table 3 for an overview of the major Israeli arms manufacturers.)

All military research and development and manufacturing is subject to the direct or indirect control of the Defense Ministry.[65] The government pays for the means of production, covers the

Table 3. Major Israeli Arms Firms

Firm	Year	No. of Employees	Sales ($U.S. in millions)	Exports ($U.S. in millions)	Comments
Israel Aircraft Industries (IAI)	1983	20,000	$1,000	$500–600	The largest industrial enterprise as well as the largest single employer and industrial exporter in Israel. Five major divisions are engaged in aircraft production from designing to building. Produces the Kfir and the Westwind and formerly manufactured the Arava plane. Currently engaged in the production of the Lavi.
Israel Military Industries (IMI)	1982	14,500	535	350	Government-owned firm, with 31 factories. Principal manufacturer and supplier of small arms and ammunition sold abroad. Of 500 exportable products, the Uzi submachine gun and the Galil assault rifle are the best known.
Tadiran	1984	12,000	600	245	One of the largest exporting firms. Best known for air-conditioners and radios. Produces intelligence-gathering and electronic warfare equipment, the Mastiff drone, nightsensing devices, and tank range-finders. Current production includes all types of military communications gear.

RAFAEL	1983	6,000	300	9	Responsible for research, design, and development of new defense systems "to preserve the qualitative superiority of the IDF," and to solve pressing battlefield problems as they arise. Developing new generations of air-to-air missiles, firing computers, electronic and physical means of deception, "smart" bombs, and electronic means of disruption and blockage.
Elbit	1983–84	1,800	119	42–50	Makes specialized radio and communications equipment for Israel's armed forces and specialized computers and coding systems.
Elta	1983	1,800	N.A.	25	Makes electronic warning and radar systems.
Soltam	1982	1,750	80	60	Specializes in mortars and mortar shells and also makes heavier mortars, diverse types of ammunition for mortars, and cannons for long-range artillery.
Urdan	1983	1,300	N.A.	17	Formed to support the Merkava tank program to make parts such as the hull, turret, and suspension. Produces armored steel parts and kits for tank construction and upgrading.
Bet Shemesh Engines	1983	1,300	30	N.A.	Main company that develops, plans, manufactures, overhauls and repairs turbojet engines.

(continues)

Table 3. (continued)

Firm	Year	No. of Employees	Sales ($U.S. in millions)	Exports ($U.S. in millions)	Comments
Electro-Optics (El-Op)	1982	1,200	80	15	Makes advanced technologies such as passive night-vision systems, direction-finding instruments, range-finders, long-range observation systems, and compasses. Most are military in nature.
Elisra Electronic Systems	1983	1,170	50	12	Major supplier of early warning equipment and components.
Israel Shipyards	N.A.	1,100	N.A.	N.A.	Constructs naval craft, including hydrofoil patrol boats and the Saar. The Reshef missile and gunboat is the most successful item.

Sources: Aaron Klieman, *Israel's Global Reach: Arms Sales as Diplomacy* (McLean, Va.: Pergamon, Brassey's, 1985); Yoram Peri and Amnon Neubach, *The Military Industrial Complex in Israel: A Pilot Study* (Tel Aviv: International Center for Peace in the Middle East, 1985); and Aaron Klieman, *Israeli Arms Sales: Perspectives and Prospects* (Tel Aviv: Jaffee Center for Strategic Studies, 1984).

Note: A majority of these firms are either wholly or partially owned by the Israeli government.

N.A. = Not available

development costs of all new weapons systems, whether developed by state-owned or private firms,[66] and coordinates efforts when more than one firm is involved. Finally, the government is responsible at the highest level for the sale of all weapons manufactured in Israel. Decisions concerning arms sales are made by the Ministerial Committee on Weapons Transfers, composed of the prime minister, foreign minister, defense minister, and the minister of industry and commerce.[67] In authorizing exports, information is received from the IDF concerning what defense items cannot be sold and from the foreign minister concerning what countries cannot be recipients of arms.[68] The day-to-day business of coordinating and implementing authorized arms transfers is handled by the Defense Ministry, and more particularly by a special department called the Defense Sales Office (SIBAT), headed by the deputy general director for arms exports. In addition to reviewing all prospective arms deals and sales applications and seeing each sale through from export licensing to post-sales servicing, SIBAT is involved in marketing, advertising, initiating and developing contacts with potential clients, and acting as an intermediary between the client and the appropriate organization. Thus, SIBAT represents the government, the IDF, and private defense industries in all sales.[69] Industry sales offices, agents, and private arms merchants all go through this office; whatever their status, they, in effect, work as an extension of the Defense Ministry.

The government predisposition toward expanding military production and increasing arms exports is strengthened by the high representation of the professional military in Israel's political elite. Mossad, the Border Police, the Civil Guard, the Civilian Administration, and the Airports Administration are all headed by senior IDF officers.[70] Generals often become heads of the various defense industries, government-owned and civilian alike,[71] thereby predisposing the civilian industries in the direction of military production.[72] According to Mintz, one-third of all retired generals from 1948 to 1977 embarked upon full-time political careers,[73] and there has been a marked increase in the number of senior reserve officers in the cabinet and the Knesset since 1967. Moreover, although before the 1967 war the defense minister had always been a civilian, since then four senior IDF officers—Moshe Dayan, Ezer Weizman, Ariel Sharon, and Yitzhak Rabin—have occupied the post.

There are similar ties between the government bureaucracy and the defense industries. The most obvious example is former Defense Minister Moshe Arens, who was a senior executive with the Israel Aircraft Industries (IAI) before entering politics. A number of Knesset members also act as representatives of military industries.[74] Furthermore, government figures have also been directly involved in arms sales or have had close ties with firms or individuals acting as arms merchants. Ezer Weizman, for example, was a partner in Elul Technologies, a major middleman for the export and import of arms, and Moshe Arens was associated with an arms dealing company called Kibernetikes.[75] The unparalleled symbiosis among the government, the military, and the arms manufacturing firms is a powerful influence toward arms sales.

This predisposition is not only supported by the military industries but also by the labor unions, the scientific community, and the IDF. Furthermore, an overwhelming share of public opinion sees large-scale arms production and export not only as essential to the national security and economy but also as a source of prestige, a testimony to the ability and technological prowess of a small developing state. These elements form what Klieman calls the "pro-arms coalition."[76]

Foreign Factors

But however impressive the research and development, whatever the quality of the labor force, and whatever the commitment on the part of the government, the arms industry would not have progressed far beyond the stage of producing ammunition and light arms or reconditioning surplus stocks without the tremendous contributions from abroad, both in terms of capital and technology transfers. The extent of foreign investment in Israeli arms firms is shown in Table 4.

Table 4. Foreign Investment in Israel's Military Industries

Corporation	Israeli Subsidiary (date founded)	% Owned	Products
Aarhus Chefabrik	Hayes (Ashdod) Ltd.	N.A.	N.A.
American Electronic Laboratories (AEL)	AEL Israel Ltd. (1967)	37	avionics, military electronics
Astronautics Corp. of America Ltd.	Astronautics C.A. Ltd. (1970)	100	avionics, generators, etc.
Control Data Corporation	Eljim Ltd.	100	military computers
	Eltek Ltd.	67	N.A.
	Elbit Computers Ltd. (1966)	37	electronic warfare equipment
	Contahal Israel	50	N.A.
	World Technologies Israel Ltd.	1	N.A.
	Control Data Israel	100	N.A.
	Elron	N.A.	N.A.
Austin Instruments Inc. (NY)	Precision Mechanism Ltd.	2	electronics, mechanical goods
Chromalloy America Corporation	Turbochrome	2	engine turbines
Designatronics Inc.	Automatic Coil of Israel Ltd.	N.A.	electronics, mechanical components
Digital Equipment Corp.	DECSYS Computers Ltd.	100	military computer parts
General Telephone & Electronics	Tadiran Israel Electronics Industries	45[3]	military electronics, computers, communications equipment
	Advanced Technologies Ltd.	N.A.	N.A.
Gerber Scientific Inc.	Beta Engineering & Development Ltd.	54[4]	anti-guerrilla detection systems, mine detection devices

(continues)

Table 4.   (continued)

Corporation	Israeli Subsidiary (date founded)	% Owned	Products
Intel Corporation	Intel Israel	100	electronic computers, computer circuits
Information Magnetic Corp.	SDSI Scientific Data Systems Israel	N.A.	N.A.
Itek Corporation	Sci-Tex Corporation	N.A.	optical systems
KMS Industries Inc.	KMS	N.A.	military avionics, computers
Kulicke & Soffa Industries Inc.	Kulso Ltd. Monsel Electronics Industries Ltd.	N.A. N.A.	N.A. N.A.
Landseas Corporation (NYC)	Landseas Israel (1962)	N.A.	electronics, computers
Locke Technology Inc.	Laser Industries	N.A.	N.A.
Mennen Greatbach Electronics	Mennen Electronics	N.A.	N.A.
Metal Working Laser International	Metal Working Laser, Ltd.	N.A.	computer welding machinery
Microwave Associates	Science-Based Industries (Technion)	N.A.	N.A.
Motorola Inc.	Motorola Israel	100	military communications systems
Neuchatel Suisse Holding Financiere Industriele	Israelectra, Ltd.	N.A.	computers, military electronics
Pioneer Systems Inc.	Pioneer Enterprises Aerodyne, Ltd.	N.A.	N.A.
Rand Information Systems	Arand Iltam		computers computers
Teledyne, Inc.	Teledyne Intercontinental, Ltd.	N.A.	electronic control systems
Turbomecha	Ormat Turbines, Ltd.	N.A.	N.A.
TRW	Iscan Blades	N.A.	spare parts for Mirage, Phantom, Kfir engine

Table 4.   (continued)

Corporation	Israeli Subsidiary (date founded)	% Owned	Products
VALTEC	Fibronics Communications Equipment	N.A.	
Veeco Instruments	Islambda Electronics	100	N.A.
Vishay Intertechnology	Vishay Israel (1969)	100	N.A.
Whittaker Corporation	Orhte Engineering	2	trucks and aircraft

Note: Table reprinted with permission of *MERIP Reports*. Even at the time of its publication, this table was incomplete. Since 1983 the amount of foreign investment has increased while there has been no appreciable disinvestment (Jim Paul, editor, *MERIP Reports*, statement of 28 October 1985).

N.A. = not available
[1]Joint venture with World Technologies and Elron.
[2]Joint venture with IAI
[3]With Koor Industries, Ltd.
[4]Jointly owned with Clal Industries (established in 1963 with the backing of Rockefeller Brothers and Associates).
[5]Joint venture with Elbit.

Aside from the enormous amount of financial aid* without which ambitious industrial military projects could not have been undertaken, Israel has relied on foreign friends, governmental and otherwise, to provide technology. Most of the technology or expertise in arms manufacture prior to 1967 was obtained from France or West Germany, and the bombs and unguided surface-to-air rockets manufactured by Israel during that period were patterned on European models. Not only were machines, tools, and production lines imported from Europe but so were entire industrial military plants.[77] In the late 1950s, an agreement was negotiated with the French firm Fouga for the assembly of twelve

---

* The United States funded one-third of Israel's defense budget from 1977–78 to 1981–82. By 1982–83 this had risen to 37 percent. The United States also provides Israel with large amounts of aid to keep the economy afloat: Israel is the largest recipient of U.S. Economic Support Fund (ESF) aid in the world, receiving 30 percent of the total in 1982–83 (SIPRI, *Yearbook 1984*, pp. 105–106).

Magister trainer jets in Israel. Many parts for the plane were subsequently produced domestically, and when the production of the French-made wings lagged, Israel purchased entire wing assemblies from Heinkel, the West German firm that manufactured the Magister under license from Luftas.[78] Moreover, by replacing many of the metal components with fiberglass ones, Israel improved upon the original product—a pattern that has become typical.

After the decision to develop a full-scale weapons industry at the close of the 1967 war, Israel, in its quest for technology, approached a number of foreign companies to develop certain products jointly. In 1969 Bet Shemesh Engines Ltd. was established as a subsidiary of France's Turbomecha, and Israeli technicians were trained in France so that Shemesh could produce engines on its own.[79]

Most Israeli weapons contain a large number of foreign components. According to the U.S. Comptroller General's 1983 report, *U.S. Assistance to the State of Israel*, most of Israel's exports in 1981–82 contained an import component of about 36 percent. Even in the electronics field, about 35 percent of the technical expertise was acquired from the United States.[80]

In many instances, however, foreign borrowing goes beyond the mere use, in Israeli products, of foreign components obtained under licensing agreements or technology transfer. Indeed, many of Israel's products are basically improved and adapted versions of existing foreign weapons systems. A U.S. official cited in *Aviation Week and Space Technology* went so far as to complain that "in many cases the Israelis use a U.S. system, make minor modifications, and then claim it is not a U.S. weapons system and sell it for export."[81] Most domestically produced aircraft are actually adaptations of France's Mirages. Furthermore, when assistance was not spontaneously offered, other means of procurement were used. In 1969 Israeli agents stole the blueprints of the French Atar 9–C engines used in the Mirage-3 and Mirage-5 aircraft. Armed with detailed plans for both engine and air frame, Israel secretly began building the Mirage and fitting it with an Atar engine. The aircraft, code-named the Nesher, or Eagle,[82] first flew in 1971 and was later used during the October 1973 war.

The Barak, or Lightning, fighter aircraft is an improved version of the Nesher, based on the Mirage-3 air frame but powered by a U.S.-designed J–79 engine.[83] It was also fitted with Shafrir air-to-air missiles, themselves virtual copies of the American-made Raytheon AIM–9D/G missile.[84] By the fall of 1973, Israel had built five Baraks which were used extensively during the October war. Beginning in 1970, modifications were also introduced on the American-made A–4H and A–4E Skyhawks so that they would be similar to the A–4N Skyhawk. Naval and offensive weapons were added to the old planes, and the outer body was modified to make it resemble the new model more closely.

Israel's famous Kfir C–2 fighter bomber, which is now in its second generation, was built using the stolen blueprints of France's Mirage-5, to which the powerful American-made General Electric J–79 engine was added. Although the plane is essentially a hybrid of the French aircraft and a U.S. engine, the extent of redesign work made it "for all practical purposes . . . Israel's first indigenous warplane."[85] The Kfir was also equipped with air-to-air and air-to-surface missiles and sophisticated, domestically designed radar and communications equipment.[86]

Israel also made use of foreign military equipment that had become obsolete compared to highly advanced state-of-the-art weaponry, building several new hybrid weapons from the parts of outdated equipment. Thus, the Isherman and Supersherman tanks were built from old French M4 and U.S. M50 Shermans, and the T1–67 was built from about 300 Soviet-made T–54/55 tanks captured in the June 1967 war.[87] The Galil assault rifle, one of Israel's best-sellers on the international market, is simply a lighter version of the Soviet-made Kalashnikov rifle.[88]

Israel continues to have access to European technology because it is eligible for technological assistance as a member of the Common Market's free-trade area, but European input into the Israeli arms industry has diminished considerably, particularly since the late 1960s.[89] Instead, the United States has emerged not only as the principal source of Israel's highly sophisticated weaponry, but also as an indispensable partner in its arms industry.

The contribution of the United States to the Israeli arms industry has been diverse and extensive.

1. The United States has promoted, and at times even funded, military research and development at Israeli academic institutions. Annex A of the March 19, 1979, U.S.-Israeli Memorandum of Agreement covers joint research and development.[90] The two countries renewed a research and development agreement in March 1984 stipulating an exchange of information on "procurement and logistics."[91] Part of the U.S. funding of Israeli research and development comes from the recycling of a portion of Israel's loan repayments. In addition, since 1977 the Binational Research and Development Foundation has been a major conduit of financing for Israeli companies interested in developing and manufacturing products specified by U.S. concerns. Moreover, Israel has benefited from the mobility of engineers and scientists engaged in U.S. defense projects or weapons laboratories. Between 1967 and 1972 about 3,000 American technicians and scientists emigrated to Israel.[92]

2. U.S. technology has also been instrumental in the development of Israel's domestic arms industry. According to Klieman:

> The Americans have made virtually all their most advanced weaponry and technology—meaning the best fighter aircraft, missiles, radar, armor, and artillery—available to Israel. Israel, in turn, has utilized this knowledge, adapting American equipment to increase its own technological sophistication, reflected tangibly in Israeli defense offerings.[93]

The basis for the technology transfer is set out in the Master Defense Development Data Exchange Agreement, which was signed by the United States and Israel on December 22, 1970, and "permits and facilitates the exchange of information important to the development of a full range of military systems including tanks, surveillance equipment, electronic warfare, air-to-air and air-to-surface weapons, and engineering."[94] According to the United States Comptroller General's 1983 report on U.S. aid to Israel, 25 separate data exchange annexes covering individual projects had been concluded up to August 1982.[95] Between 1975 and 1977 alone 100, complete technical data packages were made available by the United States at no charge or at nominal prices, thus saving Israel considerable expenditures on research and development.[96]

3. Joint ventures and subsidiary relationships between U.S. and Israeli firms have provided access to U.S. technology. IAI and the U.S. company Chromalloy jointly own Turbochrome Ltd., a hard metal coating facility in Israel that utilizes the expertise of the parent firm.[97] In October 1984 the Israeli defense computer company Elbit purchased 70 percent of the stock of the Boston-based Inframetrics Inc., which designs and manufactures advanced infrared and night-vision systems for imaging radiometers, in order to "broaden its technological base in the field of advanced sensors," since the scanning system developed by Inframetrics has "a wide range of applications in both civilian and military spheres."[98] Because 48 percent of the company had been owned by the U.S. firm Control Data Corporation (CDC),[99] Elbit had access to the expertise of the U.S. parent company. Although Control Data sold its share of Elbit, it continues to hold substantial interests in a number of other Israeli firms that manufacture electronics equipment. Tadiran, Israel's third largest exporter of military goods, was until recently a subsidiary of the transnational General Telephone and Electronics Company (GTE). Iscan Blades, a manufacturer of Mirage, Phantom, and Kfir spare parts, is a subsidiary of the U.S. company TRW. Beta Engineering and Development, which produces antiguerrilla detection systems and mine detection devices, is more than 50 percent owned by Gerber Scientific. AEL Israel, which produces avionics and military electronics, is 37 percent owned by American Electronic Laboratories. Israel's success in attracting foreign investors is due mainly to the important benefits and subsidies it offers on foreign capital investments, as well as concessions on research and development costs, training, and rental of plant and premises.[100]

4. Israel often uses its purchases of U.S. military equipment as a lever to obtain concessions from the vendor "particularly where technology is involved."[101] In most cases, commercial agreements between a U.S. firm and Israel specify the rent-free use of the vendor's equipment for production in Israel, waiver of

research and development costs, the delivery of simulation packages, and lists of parts and suppliers. For example, Israel purchased Litton's LW–33 weapons delivery system for the F–4E and RF–4E contingent upon a phased program of technology assistance and know-how to qualify IAI as a prime subcontractor with work equal to 25 percent of the total contract. Similarly, in purchasing the Samson rocket-powered gliding decoy from Celesco Industries (since renamed Brunswick), Israel insisted on the transfer of the technology data and threatened to halt other contracts unless the U.S. State Department approved the manufacture of components in Israel.[102] Although permission was originally refused, the United States subsequently lost interest in the decoy and Israel was allowed to take over the technology involved. It went on to produce the Samson drones whose performance in the June 1982 war was such that in February 1984 the United States purchased the weapon itself.[103]

Co-production or licensed production agreements are particularly prized, not only to acquire technology but also for commercial reasons. Israel reportedly made $100 million over three years from manufacturing aircraft parts under a 1972 agreement.[104] In addition to demanding co-production of certain components as a condition for purchasing weapons systems from U.S. firms, Israel has used political leverage to obtain authorization for such agreements from the U.S. government. In a secret addendum to the 1975 Sinai Agreement, U.S. Secretary of State Henry Kissinger promised cooperation in future military co-production projects.[105] Two years later, as part of the price for concessions in the Geneva negotiations scheduled for 1978, Israel requested rights for the co-production of armored XM–1 tanks, torpedoes, Maverick and Hellfire ground-to-ground missiles, and sophisticated radar and electronics equipment.[106]

A number of Israeli requests for co-production agreements have been turned down, and the United States has, on occasion, expressed concern about the use of U.S. funds and technology to create an export-oriented industry in competition with U.S. industry.[107] In February of 1976 former President Gerald Ford vetoed a request for co-production of 40 percent of the F–16 warplanes sold to Israel.[108] Co-production concessions for the McDonnell-Douglas F–15 were also refused.[109] Nevertheless, according to the U.S. Comptroller General's 1983 report on U.S. assistance to Israel, "the U.S. has permitted Israel to co-produce U.S. defense equipment through licensed production 'at a higher level of technology' than it has any other FMS credit recipient."[110] Presently, leading U.S. arms producing firms such as McDonnell-Douglas, General Dynamics, General Electric, Pratt and Whitney, and Garrett AiResearch all have licensing agreements with Israel for engines and other aviation components.[111]

5. Under the March 19, 1979 Memorandum of Agreement, Israeli firms are allowed to bid on certain U.S. defense contracts that do not have Buy American Act restrictions. Although the Defense Department has not formally kept track of subcontractor awards, the U.S. Comptroller General's report quotes a Defense Department official as estimating that Israeli firms subcontracted for $50 to $100 million worth of goods under the Memorandum of Agreement in 1981 alone.[112] One deal under the memorandum was a $39 million contract awarded to Tadiran to supply AN/VRC–12 radio equipment for U.S. Army tanks and ground vehicles, even though a number of U.S. firms could have handled the job. One Dallas-based firm, E-Systems, formally protested the Pentagon's decision in June 1982, but the protest was denied.[113]

Moreover, Israel has been the sole producer of some pieces of equipment for American weapons. Cyclone Aviation Products, Israel's largest private manufacturer of airplane parts, is the sole producer of a gun access door for F–15 planes. Again, the U.S. government subcontracted the work to an Israeli plant even though production capability is available in the United States. Saudi Arabia reportedly has refused to accept delivery of the F–15s it ordered until the parts manufactured in Israel are removed.[114]

Similarly, McDonnell-Douglas has subcontracted an Israeli firm to produce conformal fuel tanks and equipment pods to be fitted to the outside of the F–15 aircraft (which increases the combat range by 550 miles). This example gives some idea of the complexity of these arrangements. When McDonnell-Douglas, the plane's manufacturer, came up with the concept for the tanks, the U.S. Air Force did not have the research and development funds available. Wanting these additions on the F–15s it had ordered, Israel stepped in with funds provided under U.S. military assistance and paid McDonnell-Douglas to develop the tanks. The United States subsequently gave permission to produce the fuel tanks in Israel, and the U.S. Air Force ended up ordering the tanks for its own planes from Israel, as well as those slated for sale in Saudi Arabia.[115]

Following the 1979 Memorandum of Agreement, the United States enhanced the facilities accorded to Israel under a Memorandum of Understanding on Strategic Cooperation signed November 30, 1981.* This memorandum included the "Defense Trade Initiative," a joint U.S. State Department and Defense Department effort to increase the competitiveness of Israel's military industries and to facilitate the Defense Department's procurement of up to $200 million a year in Israeli-made military equipment. But an Interagency Defense Trade Task Force, established in April 1981 to implement the commitment,[116] determined that the United States could not procure enough Israeli equipment on a competitive basis to achieve the goal.[117] In any event, the 1981 Memorandum and Defense Trade Initiative were suspended by the United States following Israel's formal annexation of the Golan Heights in December 1981. The 1979 Memorandum of Agreement remains in effect, however, and the list of Israeli military items exempt from Buy American Act restrictions under Annex B has been expanded from the original 610.[118]

6. The United States has also allowed Israel to buy the exclusive rights to produce U.S.-designed military equipment, introduce modifications, and sell it abroad. In 1967, for example, Israel bought the rights to an American jet which it subsequently called the Westwind executive jet. The Israeli version, however,

---

* Indeed, the United States has emerged as a significant customer for Israeli military hardware. In 1978 military products accounted for 26.5 percent of Israel's total exports to the United States. By 1980 the figure had grown to 37 percent (*Israel Business and Investor's Report*, August 1981).

is powered with a different engine, albeit one of U.S. production. The Westwind has been marketed both as an executive jet and as a military reconnaissance plane,[119] and some 300 had been sold by September 1984.[120] In 1981 IAI began working on an advanced generation of the jet, the Westwind Astra. With a speed of Mach 0.8 and a range of 3,000 nautical miles,[121] the Astra has been marketed since late 1984.[122]

7. According to *Aviation Week and Space Technology*, sales contracts for U.S. equipment to Israel often contain a requirement for maintenance in Israel "even when it is not considered economical."[123] Bedek Aviation, IAI's division for overhauling and repairing planes, acquired its expertise in servicing thirty types of civilian and military aircraft at least partly from its U.S. partner Chromalloy Inc.[124] In 1972 the United States permitted Israel to establish facilities for repairing the Phantom's J–79 engine and subsequently helped it to build those facilities. It also helped Israel build the facilities to assemble, under license, 67 percent of the J–79 engines used to power the Israeli-built Kfir aircraft.[125] Toward the end of 1984, Israel agreed to "loan" without charge twelve Kfirs to the United States to simulate Soviet MIG–21s in dogfighting exercises in return for a three-year, $70 million maintenance contract for the Kfirs.[126]

8. Finally, the Israeli arms industry and military exports have benefited enormously from the flexibility the United States allows in "creative or liberal uses" of U.S. Foreign Military Sales (FMS) funds.[127] Israel received $13.5 billion in FMS credits from 1974 to 1981, a figure representing over half the total of all the FMS-financed exports ($24.85 billion).[128] According to U.S. law, FMS loans and grants must be spent on the purchase of military equipment from U.S. manufacturers. Of the $3.4 billion of exemptions granted by the Pentagon, no less than 98.5 percent were to Israel,[129] thus allowing it to use U.S. military aid to buy its own products. In 1982 the United States allowed Israel to use $100 million of its FMS funds to purchase Israeli-made military equipment.[130] In its 1984 aid request, Israel asked that $20 million of its FMS credits be used for procurements from its own arms industry. Israel has also proposed that other recipients of

U.S. military aid be allowed to use FMS credits to buy Israeli goods.[131]

The United States has also allowed Israel to make trade offset arrangements for purchases using FMS credits. Consequently, even when buying U.S.-made equipment with U.S.-provided funds, Israel can insist that the supplier buy back a specified percentage of the contract value in Israeli goods or services (Israel generally asks for 25 percent on purchases of $1 million or more).[132] Offsets are common under regular commercial arms sales, but in a survey conducted by the Aerospace Industries Association of America and the Electronics Industries Association covering contracts signed between 1975 and 1981, only four countries (Israel, Spain, Korea, and Greece) were found to have made them with FMS credits. Israel accounted for 87 percent of the dollar value of these offsets.[133] However, offsets do not always translate into cash; U.S. firms are not as likely to follow through with their commitments.

Unique among FMS recipients, Israel has been allowed to use credits not only to buy its own products but also for the actual development of weapons systems. In what was to have been a one-time-only exception, Israel was permitted to transfer $107 million in foreign aid originally earmarked for the purchase of U.S. M–60 tanks to the development of a third production line for the Merkava tank. This exception was followed by another, in 1979, when the Carter administration allowed the use of $181 million in aid to develop a modified version of the Pratt and Whitney F–100 jet engine which powers the U.S. F–15 and F–16 aircraft.[134]

But the most ambitious use of FMS credits was for the development of the Lavi fighter bomber, which is expected to enter full-scale production in the 1990s.[135] The development costs of the project, originally estimated at $750 million, jumped by 1982 to $1.5 billion,[136] while the unit "fly-away" cost was estimated at between $9 and $11 million, depending on the number of aircraft sold.[137] The project, estimated to generate 20,000 jobs,[138] was undertaken at a time when the Kfir project was coming to an end, raising the specter of widespread layoffs of scientists, engineers, and technicians.[139]

The Lavi was to be Israel's restriction-free jet fighter, a further step in the direction of military self-sufficiency (the 1976 veto by the United States of Israel's proposed sale of twenty-four Kfirs to Ecuador was an impetus to the project).[140] Yet seldom has Israeli dependence on the United States stood in sharper relief than with the Lavi. Israel lacked not only the funds but also the technology to produce the aircraft on its own. Moreover, the presence of a large number of U.S. components in the plane, including Pratt and Whitney engines built under a licensing agreement, gives the United States the power to veto sales to third countries. The Lavi was in fact the subject of a selective embargo in 1982, when Washington refused to grant permission to use American technology in the Lavi as a punitive measure following the invasion of Lebanon. Permission to proceed was granted only in April 1983, when the Israeli withdrawal from Lebanon was thought likely.[141]

In terms of technology, in May 1983 Israel was granted licenses for the import of twenty-five items, including fabrication technologies for the Lavi's wing and tail structures, a computerized flight-control system, and other high-technology equipment.[142] The Pratt and Whitney F-100 jet engine is being modified and developed for the Lavi project. Other systems expected to be modified for the Lavi include jet fuel starters developed by Sundstrand/Garrett AiResearch, emergency power systems developed by Garrett AiResearch, and other systems such as the fuel and hydraulic systems, the oxygen system, and the environmental control system.[143]

In terms of financing, in November 1983 Congress approved an amendment to the foreign assistance bill authorizing $550 million of FMS credits to fund the Lavi's development, including $250 million to be spent in Israel on electronics and avionics and $300 million to be spent in the United States.[144] But controversy surrounding the project continued. In testimony to the House Foreign Affairs Committee in the spring of 1984, Defense Secretary Caspar Weinberger argued that it was folly for Israel to develop a fighter that could be purchased at lesser cost from the United States, and that since the American administration had not invested "a cent" in the development of the Lavi's American counterpart—the F-20 manufactured by Northrop—he could see no reason why the United States should help fund an Israeli fighter that would compete with the F-20.[145] Other opponents focused on the possible loss of jobs in the United States resulting from the loss of F-16 and F-15 sales to Israel,[146] as well as on the principle of paying for the research and development of competing defense products.[147] But proponents of the project prevailed, and the House Foreign Affairs Committee earmarked another $400 million for the Lavi.[148] By December 1984 the U.S. involvement in the aircraft was worth about $710 million in 99 contracts let to some seventy U.S. firms.[149]

Israel's calculations on the Lavi are all based on the assumption that the aircraft will be easily marketable. Israel itself will buy 300, the United States is considered a potential market for at least 300 more, and other countries are expected to buy about 416.[150] Defense Ministry planners, therefore, anticipate that 70 percent of the production will be exported.

The Lavi is a good example of how Israel's arms industry functions as a whole. Initially undertaken to satisfy domestic needs and to reduce reliance on foreign suppliers, the arms industry soon outgrew a domestic base which was too limited to provide the economies of scale necessary for the viable and economical production of major weapons systems. In the early years the IDF was virtually the sole client, but by the early 1980s, over 60 percent of the production was sold abroad.* Increasingly ambitious projects have led to greater pressures to export, with exports assuming a near strategic importance insofar as they make possible an industry that is considered the heart of

---

* Israel's success in recouping the development costs of major weapons systems has been extremely limited. Neither the Arava nor the Kfir have met targets. But even though the production percentage targets have not been met on individual items, export sales enable the country to develop them. Since the government controls the industry and the development of new weapons systems, it can allocate earnings from the industry as a whole as it chooses. (Exports are still mainly of small arms, ammunition, communications, and electronics equipment as well as upgraded obsolete equipment, although according to the U.S. General Accounting Office sales of major weapons systems account for an increasing proportion of the total [U.S. General Accounting Office, "U.S. Assistance to the State of Israel," uncensored draft, Washington, D.C., April 1983, p. 49]).

Israel's security. Paradoxically, it was this strategic dimension that made Israel's arms export policy progressively less tied to political considerations, with the sale of arms being pursued as an end in itself. The consequences of this export policy have been great indeed.

NOTES

1. Stockholm International Peace Research Institute (SIPRI), *World Armament and Disarmament Yearbook 1976* (London: Taylor and Francis, 1976), p. 136.
2. Clifford Wright, "The Israeli War Machine in Lebanon," *Journal of Palestine Studies* 46, no. 2 (Winter 1983): 43.
3. *Jewish Telegraphic Agency*, 29 December 1981.
4. Larry Remer, "Israeli Weapons Industry Goes Boom," *Los Angeles Times*, 29 July 1981.
5. *Ibid.*
6. Richard Goldman and Murray Rubenstein, *Shield of David: An Illustrated History of the Israeli Air Force* (Englewood Cliffs, N.J.: Prentice Hall, 1978), p. 15.
7. *Ibid.*, pp. 69–71.
8. *Israel Government Yearbook, 1969–70* (Jerusalem: Central Office of Information, 1970), p. 115.
9. Nadav Safran, *Israel the Embattled Ally*, 2nd ed. (Cambridge: Harvard University Press, 1979), p. 585.
10. Stockholm International Peace Research Institute (SIPRI), *World Armament and Disarmament Yearbook 1972* (London: Taylor and Francis, 1972), pp. 103–104.
11. *Ibid.*
12. *New York Times*, 9 May 1982.
13. John Fialka, "Israel Bucks Big Leagues in Arms Sales," *Wall Street Journal*, 22 June 1984; Alex Mintz, "The Military-Industrial Complex: The Israeli Case," *Journal of Strategic Studies* 6, no. 3 (September 1983): 118; Efraim Inbar, "The American Arms Transfer to Israel," *Middle East Review*, Fall/ Winter 1982, pp. 40-51.
14. Safran, *Embattled Ally*, pp. 591–592.
15. *New York Times*, 24 August 1981.
16. Eleanor Randolph, "US Halts All Cluster Bomb Aid to Israelis," *Los Angeles Times*, 28 July 1982.
17. *New York Times*, 24 August 1981.
18. *New York Times*, 14 April 1983.
19. *Ibid.*
20. Safran, *Embattled Ally*, pp. 118–122.
21. *Jerusalem Post*, 22 June 1968; *Al Itihad* (Arabic, Jerusalem), 24 June 1968, quoted in *The Palestine Question Yearbook 1968* (Arabic, Beirut: Institute for Palestine Studies, 1970), pp. 416–417.
22. *Ibid.*

23. *Al Hamishmar* (Hebrew), 9 April 1980.
24. Aaron Klieman, *Israeli Arms Sales: Perspectives and Prospects* (Tel Aviv: Jaffee Center for Strategic Studies, 1984), paper no. 24, p. 18.
25. Peter G. Kokalis, "Weapons Wizard—Israel Galil," *Soldier of Fortune*, March 1982, pp. 28–32.
26. *Israel Government Yearbook 1968–69* (Jerusalem: Central Office of Information, 1969), p. 100.
27. Robert Alkor, "Israel's Arms Exports," *Al-Fajr Palestinian Weekly* (Jerusalem), 13–19 April 1981, p. 16.
28. *Israel Government Yearbook 1968–69*, p. 98.
29. *Ibid.*, p. 114.
30. Carl Alpert, "Making and Selling Arms," *Jewish Week*, 13 August 1982.
31. *Israel Government Yearbook 1968–69*, p. 100.
32. Alpert, "Arms."
33. *Davar* (Hebrew, Tel Aviv), 13 September 1967.
34. Safran, *Embattled Ally*, pp. 591–592.
35. *Israel Government Yearbook 1968–69*, p. 98.
36. Yoram Peri and Amnon Neubach, *The Military Industrial Complex in Israel: A Pilot Study* (Tel Aviv: International Center for Peace in the Middle East, 1985), p. 31; Inbar, "Arms Transfer," p. 46.
37. *Ibid.*, Mintz, "Military-Industrial Complex," p. 122.
38. *Israel Government Yearbook 1969–70* (Jerusalem: Central Office of Information, 1970), p. 115.
39. *Times* (London), 17 November 1982.
40. Aaron Klieman, *Israel's Global Reach: Arms Sales As Diplomacy* (McLean, Va.: Pergamon-Brassey's, 1985), p. 55.
41. Mintz, "Military-Industrial Complex," p. 119.
42. *Ibid.*, p. 116.
43. Dan Zarmi, "A Penetrating Self-Examination in the Metal Industry," *Ha'aretz* (Hebrew, Tel Aviv), 7 March 1977.
44. *Al Quds* (Arabic, Jerusalem), 18 March 1983, p. 3.
45. Mintz, "Military-Industrial Complex," p. 116.
46. *Jerusalem Post*, 6 May 1982.
47. Mintz, "Military-Industrial Complex," p. 116.
48. David Lennon, "Israeli Electronics Achieve 16% Growth," *Financial Times*, 26 May 1982.
49. Mintz, "Military-Industrial Complex," p. 110.
50. David Ignatius, *Wall Street Journal*, 17 September 1981.
51. Mintz, "Military-Industrial Complex," p. 110.
52. Ignacio Klich, "Israeli Arms," *South*, April 1982.
53. *Israel Government Yearbook 1969–70*, p. 115.
54. *Ibid.*
55. Stockholm International Peace Research Institute (SIPRI), *World Armament and Disarmament Yearbook 1973* (London: Taylor and Francis, 1973), p. 349.
56. Mintz, "Military-Industrial Complex," p. 118.
57. Safran, *Embattled Ally*, p. 117.
58. Joseph Morgenstern, "High Technology and Economic Independence," *Jerusalem Post*, 30 July 1982.

59. Linda Bernier, "Israel Focuses on High Technology," *Journal of Commerce*, 7 December 1982.
60. SIPRI, *Yearbook 1972*, p. 198, footnote 48.
61. Mintz, "Military-Industrial Complex," p. 112.
62. *Fortune*, 13 March 1978, pp. 72–73.
63. Mintz, "Military-Industrial Complex," p. 117.
64. Peri and Neubach, *Pilot Study*, p. 5.
65. Mintz, "Military-Industrial Complex," p. 115.
66. Peri and Neubach, *Pilot Study*, p. 38.
67. Klieman, *Israeli Arms Sales*, p. 35; Peri and Neubach, *Pilot Study*, p. 78.
68. Moshe Lichtman, "Israel's Weapons Exports," *Monitin*, no. 59 (July 1983): 86–96.
69. Klieman, *Israeli Arms Sales*, p. 35.
70. Mintz, "Military-Industrial Complex," p. 108.
71. *Ibid*.
72. Peri and Neubach, *Pilot Study*, p. 51.
73. Mintz, "Military-Industrial Complex," p. 108.
74. Lichtman, "Israel's Weapons Exports."
75. *Ibid*.
76. Klieman, *Israeli Arms Sales*, p. 26.
77. Zarmi, "Self-Examination."
78. Goldman and Rubenstein, *Shield of David*, p. 78.
79. *The Palestine Question Yearbook 1969* (Arabic, Beirut: Institute for Palestine Studies, 1969), pp. 429–430.
80. U.S. Comptroller General, *U.S. Assistance to the State of Israel* (Washington, D.C.: General Accounting Office), GAO ID 83–51, June 24, 1983, pp. 43–44.
81. Clarence Robinson, Jr., "Israeli Arms Exports Spur Concern," *Aviation Week and Space Technology*, 13 December 1976, pp. 14–17.
82. Goldman and Rubenstein, *Shield of David*, p. 118.
83. *Ibid*.
84. Robinson, "Exports Concern," pp. 14–17.
85. Goldman and Rubenstein, *Shield of David*, p. 119.
86. *Kuwait Times*, 8 November 1981.
87. SIPRI, *Yearbook 1973*, p. 349.
88. Remer, "Israeli Weapons Industry"; Peri and Neubach, *Pilot Study*, p. 31.
89. *Times* (London), 17 November 1982.
90. U.S. Comptroller General, *U.S. Assistance*, p. 45.
91. *Jerusalem Post*, 25 March 1984.
92. Thomas R. Stauffer, "U.S. Aid to Israel," *Middle East Problem Paper*, no. 24 (Washington, D.C.: Middle East Institute, 1983), p. 11; Lawrence Lockwook, "Israeli Superimperialism," *Monthly Review*, January 1983, p. 62.
93. Klieman, *Global Reach*, p. 175.
94. U.S. Comptroller General, *U.S. Assistance*, p. 45.
95. *Ibid*.
96. *Armed Forces Journal*, December 1977, p. 14.
97. *Israel Economist*, August 1971, p. 263.
98. Pinhas Landau, "Elbit Buys 70% of U.S. High Tech Firm," *Jerusalem Post*, 23 October 1984.

99. Michael Dunn, "Israel's Elbit Is a Surprising Leader in Defense Computing," *Defense and Foreign Affairs,* February 1984, pp. 32–33.
100. Esther Howard, "Sorcerer's Apprentice," *MERIP Reports* 13 (February 1983): 20; Robinson, "Exports Concern," p. 15.
101. Robinson, "Exports Concern," p. 15.
102. *Ibid.,* pp. 14–15.
103. Wolf Blitzer, "U.S. Buying Israeli Decoy That Passed Test in Lebanon," *Jerusalem Post,* 19 October 1984.
104. *Israel Economist,* February-March 1972.
105. Howard, "Sorcerer's Apprentice," p. 20.
106. *Ibid.,* p. 21.
107. Robinson, "Israeli Arms Exports Spur Concern," *Aviation Week and Space Technology,* 13 December 1976, p. 14–17.
108. "Ford Denies Israel F–16 Subcontracts," *Aviation Week and Space Technology,* 16 February 1976, p. 14.
109. *Israel Business and Investor's Report,* June 1979.
110. U.S. Comptroller General, *U.S. Assistance,* p. 44.
111. Stockholm International Peace Research Institute (SIPRI), *World Armament and Disarmament Yearbook 1979* (London: Taylor and Francis, 1979).
112. U.S. Comptroller General, *U.S. Assistance,* p. 44.
113. *Ibid.,* p. 46; Howard, "Sorcerer's Apprentice," p. 21.
114. Stephen Zatuchin, "Israel—Armed for Survival," *Jewish Week,* 3 December 1982; *Jerusalem Post,* 12 April 1982.
115. Dan Morgan, "Israel, the Customer, and America, the Armorer, Sway Each Other," *Washington Post,* 21 July 1982.
116. U.S. Comptroller General, *U.S. Assistance,* p. 47.
117. U.S. General Accounting Office, *U.S. Assistance to the State of Israel* (uncensored draft [made available by the Arab American Anti-Discrimination Committee], Washington, D.C., April 1983), p. 41.
118. U.S. Comptroller General, *U.S. Assistance,* p. 48.
119. Ronald Slaughter, "Israel Arms Trade Cozying Up to Latin America," *NACLA Report* 16 (January-February 1982): 50; *Fortune,* 13 March 1978, p. 73.
120. *Davar,* 13 May 1984.
121. *World Business,* 27 July 1981.
122. "Israeli Jet Sets LA–NY Record," *Jerusalem Post,* 4 October 1984, p. 3.
123. Robinson, "Exports Concern," p. 15.
124. *Israel Economist,* August 1971, p. 263.
125. *New York Times,* 14 January 1972.
126. Hirsh Goodman, "U.S. Navy Gets Its First Three Kfirs," *Jerusalem Post,* 20 September 1984.
127. U.S. General Accounting Office, *U.S. Assistance,* uncensored draft, p. 43.
128. *Ibid.,* p. 11; Howard, "Sorcerer's Apprentice," p. 20.
129. Howard, "Sorcerer's Apprentice," p. 20.
130. Joshua Brilliant, "Missile Boat Planned," *Jerusalem Post,* 22 February 1982.
131. U.S. Comptroller General, *U.S. Assistance,* p. 42.
132. *Ibid.,* p. 43.
133. *Ibid.,* p. 52–53.
134. Fialka, "Israel Bucks Big Leagues."

135. *Aviation Week and Space Technology,* 5 November 1984, p. 20.
136. U.S. General Accounting Office, *U.S. Assistance,* uncensored draft, p. 84.
137. *Aviation Week and Space Technology,* 10 January 1983, pp. 20–22.
138. *Jewish Telegraphic Agency,* 5 February 1982.
139. Peri and Neubach, *Pilot Study,* p. 56.
140. Howard, "Sorcerer's Apprentice," p. 21.
141. *Boston Globe,* 18 April 1983, p. 6.
142. Fialka, "Israel Bucks Big Leagues."
143. *Aviation Week and Space Technology,* 10 January 1983.
144. *Aviation Week and Space Technology,* 27 November 1983, p. 22.
145. Hirsh Goodman, "IAI Expects Major Boost from Weinberger Today," *Jerusalem Post,* 17 October 1984.
146. *Aviation Week and Space Technology,* 21 May 1981.
147. *Ibid.*
148. Fialka, "Israel Bucks Big Leagues."
149. *Aviation Week and Space Technology,* 3 December 1984, p. 155.
150. Hirsh Goodman, "Fighter in a Fog," *Jerusalem Post,* 19 February 1982.

CHAPTER THREE

Israel and Latin America

D uring the last decade Latin America was undisputedly Israel's largest market for arms, accounting for approximately 50 to 60 percent of its total military exports.[1] According to the Stockholm International Peace Research Institute (SIPRI), one-third of Israel's total arms sales of $1.2 billion in 1980 went to Argentina and El Salvador alone.[2] Recently, Israeli arms to Asia and Africa have increased, partly as a by-product of Israel's success in regaining some of its old friends, particularly in Africa. Nevertheless, Latin America continues to be a primary market,* accounting for one-third to one-half of Israel's total arms sales.[3] It is no coincidence that Israeli military sales literature continues to come out in two languages, English and Spanish.[4]

History of Israeli-Latin American Relations

Apologists for Israel's arms export policy have often dwelled upon the political and security dimensions of arms sales, which, at least initially, were subordinated to larger foreign policy goals. While this was doubtless true for Asia and sub-Saharan Africa, the situation in Latin America was different from the very beginning. Given the existence of diplomatic ties with virtually all Latin American countries from Israel's very creation, there was no need to use arms sales to gain a foothold as was the case in countries unwilling or unable to maintain formal relations. Latin America's support of Israel in United Nations forums also made it unnecessary to proffer weapons as an inducement for political backing. Moreover, given the distance separating Israel from Latin America, there was no direct strategic interest or geographical security to be derived as in other cases where Israel was "leaping beyond the immediate wall of Arab hostility"[5] to nearby or adjacent areas to break its isolation. It is not surprising, then,

---

* According to the U.S. General Accounting Office report, "U.S. Assistance to the State of Israel," (uncensored draft, Washington, D.C., April 1983), p. 43. Latin America is Israel's "prime market for military exports."

Figure 1.   Map of Latin America

that Israeli arms sales to Latin America have been on the whole remarkable for what appears to be their largely commercial character.

No region outside of Western Europe and North America has been, as a bloc, as supportive of Israel as Latin America, even predating the establishment of the state. Largely Western in orientation, in the 1940s the Latin American countries tended to identify more with the essentially European Zionists than with the non-European indigenous population of Palestine that opposed the growing Jewish political power. Latin American sympathy for Zionist aspirations found expression in the role played by the heads of Latin American delegations during the diplomatic maneuvering at the United Nations that led to the creation of Israel in May 1948. Guatemala* and Uruguay, especially, made significant contributions to advancing the Zionist cause at the United Nations Session on Palestine and as members of the UN Special Committee on Palestine (UNSCOP) which was set up in the spring of 1947. Latin America was instrumental in the passage of the partition plan, without which Israel would not have been created, because at that time Jews were only 35.1 percent of the population of Palestine and owned only 7 percent of the land.[6] In addition to mobilizing other countries to vote for the resolution, the Latin American delegates provided thirteen of the thirty-three votes in favor of partition. Cuba was the only Latin American country to vote against the resolution.† (See Table 5 for Latin American voting on the Palestine question.) The Latin American bloc of eighteen countries also voted unanimously in favor of

---

* The "compromise boundary plan" of Jorge Garcia-Granados became the one basically adopted by UNSCOP. According to Edward Glick, had it not been for Garcia's intervention "the entire partition recommendations would have been in jeopardy." Meanwhile, Benno Weiser of the Jewish Agency's Latin American Department asserted that the idea and much of the final form of the UNSCOP partition plan were "directly traceable to Garcia-Granados and Rodriquez Fabregat [of Uruguay]" (*Latin America and the Palestine Problem* [New York: Theodore Herzl Foundation, 1958], p. 73).

† The vote on partition was thirty-three in favor, thirteen against, and ten abstentions. For a lengthy discussion of Latin America's role in the creation of Israel, see Glick, *Latin America and the Palestine Problem*.

Table 5. Latin American Voting on the Palestine Question at the UN

Resolution Number	181	3210	3236	3237	3375	3376	31/20 †	32/40		33/28			34/65				ES-7/2	ES-7/3	35/168				
								A	B	A	B	C	A	B	C	D			A	B	C	D	E
Argentina*	A	Y	Y	–	Y	Y	–	Y	A	Y	Y	A	Y	A	Y	A	Y	Y	Y	A	Y	A	Y
Bahamas	Y	–	A	A	A	A	A	A	A	A	A	Y	A	Y	Y	Y	A	A	A	A	Y	Y	Y
Barbados	–	A	A	Y	A	A	A	Y	Y	Y	Y	Y	Y	Y	Y	Y	Y	Y	Y	A	Y	Y	Y
Bolivia*	Y	N	N	N	A	A	A	A	A	Y	Y	Y	Y	A	Y	Y	Y	Y	Y	A	Y	Y	Y
Brazil	Y	Y	–	Y	–	–	–	A	A	Y	Y	Y	Y	Y	Y	Y	Y	Y	Y	A	Y	Y	Y
Chile	A	–	N	N	Y	A	A	A	A	A	A	A	Y	A	Y	Y	Y	Y	A	N	Y	A	Y
Colombia	A	A	A	A	Y	A	Y	–	–	N	A	A	Y	N	Y	A	Y	Y	A	A	Y	A	Y
Costa Rica	Y	A	N	N	N	N	N	A	N	A	A	A	Y	N	Y	Y	Y	Y	A	A	Y	Y	Y
Cuba*	N	Y	Y	Y	Y	Y	Y	Y	Y	Y	Y	Y	Y	Y	Y	Y	Y	Y	Y	Y	Y	Y	Y
Dominica													–	–			–		–	–	–	–	–
Dominican Republic	Y	N	–	–	A	A	A	A	N	A	Y	Y	Y	N	Y	Y	N	A	N	N	A	A	A
Ecuador	Y	A	A	–	Y	N	A	A	A	A	A	A	Y	A	Y	Y	Y	Y	Y	A	Y	Y	Y
El Salvador	A	Y	A	–	A	Y	A	A	A	A	Y	A	Y	A	–	–	Y	Y	A	A	Y	Y	Y
Grenada*	–	–	A	Y	Y	Y	A	–	–	–	–	–	Y	Y	Y	Y	Y	Y	Y	Y	Y	Y	Y

Guatemala	Y	A	A	–	A	A	A	N	N	A	N A A A A
Guyana*	Y	Y	Y	Y	Y	Y	Y	Y	Y	Y	Y A A Y Y
Haiti	A	A	A	A	N	Z	Z	Z	A	A	A A Y Y Y
Honduras	A	–	A	A	N	A	N	N	A	A	A Y A Y Y
Jamaica	Y	Y	Y	Y	Y	Y	Y	Y	Y	Y	Y A Y Y Y
Mexico	A	Y	N	Y	N	N	Y	A	Y	Y	Y Y Y Y Y
Nicaragua*	Y	A	Y	N	Y	Y	Y	Y	N	–	Y Y Y Y Y
Panama*	Y	Y	N	Y	N	Y	A	A	–	Y	Y A Y A Y
Paraguay	Y	A	A	A	A	A	A	Y	A	N	A A A Y Y
Peru*	Y	Y	A	A	Y	Y	Y	Y	A	Y	Y A Y A Y
Saint Lucia											
Saint Vincent											Y A – –
Suriname*	A	A	A	A	A	Y	A	Y	Y	A	Y – – – –
Trinidad & Tobago*	Y	Y	Y	Y	Y	Y	Y	Y	Y	Y	Y A Y Y Y
Uruguay	Y	A	A	A	A	A	Y	N	A	A	Y N Y A Y Y
Venezuela	Y	Y	Y	A	Y	Y	Y	Y	A	Y	Y A Y Y Y

Source: "Latin America and the Middle East," *Middle East Economic Digest, Special Report*, September 1981, p. 22. Reprinted with permission of the *Middle East Economic Digest*.

Notes: (Y) in favor; (N) against; (A) abstention; (–) absent; ( ) not a member of the UN; (*) full member status of the Non-aligned Movement summit meeting in Havana (1979).

† Versions of resolutions.

Israel's admission to the United Nations as its fifty-ninth member.* Within a year twenty Latin American countries had extended diplomatic recognition.[7] By the end of 1956, in contrast, Israel had succeeded in gaining the recognition of only ten of the more numerous Asian countries. The Latin American countries were also the only states, aside from the Netherlands, that agreed to set up their primary diplomatic missions in the disputed city of Jerusalem. A study of bloc voting patterns on Israel at the UN General Assembly reveals that in the 1950s the Western bloc was the most supportive, followed by Latin America and sub-Saharan Africa. In the 1960s the Latin American bloc became the most supportive, followed by the Western and Black African blocs.[8] Even with the erosion of support in the 1970s, Latin America remained Israel's largest supporter among third world groups, and, except for Cuba and Nicaragua, disagreements have always stopped short of rupture. According to a Foreign Ministry official, Israel has "relied on Latin American countries to blunt Arab calls for Israel's expulsion from UN Specialized Agencies."[9] (For Latin American voting patterns on Israeli issues at the UN, see Table 6.)

Doubtless this consistent support freed Israel from the need to curry favor in the region; therefore, Latin America did not loom large in Israel's foreign policy considerations in the first decade after its establishment. During that time, Israel needed secure sources of military supplies and economic aid, which were clearly not to be expected from Latin America. Even after the 1955 Bandung Conference† branded Israel as a "bridgehead of Western colonialism,"[10] Israel's efforts to buttress its international position and seek general political support were focused on sub-Saharan Africa and Asia. In 1958 Israel embarked upon its

---

* The countries that voted against Israel's admission were: Afghanistan, India, Pakistan, Burma, Iran, Saudi Arabia, Egypt, Iraq, Syria, Ethiopia, Lebanon, and Yemen. Those that abstained were: Brazil, Denmark, Sweden, Greece, Turkey, Belgium, and Britain (U.N., G.A.O.R., Third Session, Part II, Plenary, p. 330).

† This conference of Asian and African countries was important for its strong opposition to colonialism. It marked the formation of the nonaligned movement.

Table 6.   Latin American Voting on Israeli Issues at the UN

Resolution	Year	Y	(TY)	N	(TN)	A	(TA)
181 (1)	1947	13	(33)	1	(13)	6	(10)
3210 (2)	1974	11	(105)	2	(4)	9	(20)
3236 (3)		6	(89)	4	(8)	14	(37)
3237 (4)		9	(95)	4	(17)	8	(19)
3375 (5)	1975	13	(101)	3	(8)	9	(25)
3376 (6)		10	(93)	5	(8)	10	(27)
31/20 (7)	1976	7	(90)	4	(16)	13	(30)
32/40A (8)	1977	11	(100)	–	(12)	14	(29)
B (9)		6	(95)	5	(20)	14	(26)
32/28A (10)	1978	10		4		12	
B (11)		14		2		10	
C (12)		9		2		15	
34/65A (13)	1979	23		1		3	
B (14)		3		8		16	
C (15)		24		–		1	
D (16)		21		–		4	
ES-7/2 (17)	1980	22	(112)	2	(7)	4	(24)
ES-7/3 (18)		23	(112)	1	(5)	3	(26)
35/169A (19)		16	(98)	1	(16)	10	(32)
B (20)		4	(86)	3	(22)	22	(40)
C (21)		26	(121)	–	(3)	2	(23)
D (22)		23	(121)	–	(4)	5	(23)
E (23)		26	(143)	–	(1)	2	(4)

Source: "Latin America and the Middle East," *Middle East Economic Digest, Special Report*, September 1981, p. 24. Reprinted with permission from *Middle East Economic Digest*.

Notes: Y in favor; (TY) total in favor; N against; (TN) total against; A abstention; (TA) total abstention.

1. Plan of partition.
2. First invitation to the Palestine Liberation Organization (PLO) to participate in debate on question of Palestine.
3. Recognition of the PLO and affirmation of Palestinian national rights.
4. Observer status for the PLO.
5. Invitation to the PLO to participate in Middle East peace efforts under UN auspices.
6. Establishment of UN committee on exercise of the inalienable rights of the Palestinian people (UNCIR).
7. Approval of recommendations of first report by UNCIR as a basis for the solution of the question of Palestine.
8. Appreciation of UNCIR's work and new endorsement of its recommendations.
9. Establishment of a special unit on Palestinian rights at the UN Secretariat.
10. Reaffirmation that all agreements aimed at solving the Palestine question should be within the framework of UN charter and resolutions.

(continues)

Table 6. *(continued)*

11. Appreciation of UNCIR's work.
12. Call to strengthen special unit on Palestinian rights.
13. Recognition of the PLO and reaffirmation of invitation to participate in Middle East peace efforts.
14. Condemnation of Camp David agreements.
15. Appreciation of UNCIR's work.
16. Redesignation of special unit on Palestinian rights as division for Palestinian rights, and organization of four seminars in 1980–81.
17. Recognition of the PLO, reaffirmation of Palestinian rights, invitation to PLO to participate in Middle East peace efforts, call for Israeli withdrawal from all occupied territories, and Israeli compliance with UN resolutions on Jerusalem.
18. Appreciation of UNCIR's work.
19. Recognition of PLO, reaffirmation of Palestinian national rights including UNCIR recommendations on implementation.
20. Rejection of accords which infringe on Palestinian rights without specific mention of Camp David accords.
21. Appreciation of UNCIR's work.
22. Strengthening special unit on Palestinian rights.
23. Censure of Israel's Basic Law on Jerusalem.

International Cooperation Program to "launch, centralize, and direct its aid to developing countries."[11] The aim was to broaden and normalize foreign relations and to counteract Arab accusations of colonialism and imperialism.[12] Once again, Latin America was largely ignored, and Asian and African nations were recipients of initial aid programs.

It was not until the 1960s, when relations with Argentina soured following the kidnapping of Adolph Eichmann and fear of radicalization swept the area in the wake of Castro's victory in Cuba, that Israel began to turn its attention to Latin America.[13] An Israeli-sponsored conference in Montevideo, Uruguay, in February 1961 broached the need to improve relations,[14] and officials from the Israeli ministries of foreign affairs and agriculture were subsequently dispatched to study possibilities for providing technical assistance. Technical cooperation agreements, the first signed with Bolivia in 1961, followed, and by 1973 there were agreements with eighteen Latin American countries.[15] Nonetheless, these programs with individual Latin American countries and with the Organization of American States (OAS) never reached the scope and importance that similar programs did in Africa. Similarly, although Latin America became the primary recipient of Israeli aid[16] when twenty-seven African countries severed diplomatic relations following the October 1973 war,[17] the amount of aid was not large by international standards.*

Nor was Latin America ever an important trading partner. Although Israel launched a major export drive in 1981, announcing that a $20-million fund would be established to develop the Latin American market,[18] trade has remained insignificant. By 1984 Israeli exports to Latin America, excluding arms,† were valued at only $94.6 million, or 1.6 percent of Israel's total exports, despite a dramatic jump of 676 percent from 1972 to 1984. Israeli imports from Latin America, excluding oil,‡ reached $139.2 million, only 1.7 percent of Israel's total imports, despite an increase of 399 percent from 1972 to 1984 (see Table 7).

Energy procurement has gained considerably in importance in Israel's Latin American calculations, especially since the return of the Sinai oil fields (which had largely satisfied Israel's domestic needs)[19] to Egypt under the 1975 Sinai II Agreement and the loss of Iran in 1979 as its primary oil supplier, with 60 percent of the total,[20] following the fall of the Shah. As a result of wars with its Arab neighbors and the latter's economic influence, Israel has access to only about 10 percent of the international oil market.[21] While Egypt is a major supplier, Israel has been unsuccessful in obtaining a long-term, binding Egyptian guarantee of oil shipments.[22] Latin America, therefore, has become the largest source of oil, with Mexico supplying 42 percent in 1982.[23] Moreover, while Mexico is the only Latin American country that publicly

---

* Israel's total aid disbursement in 1980, which was a record high, was only $9 million. Even though three-fourths of multilateral contributions went to the Inter-American Development Bank, this sum in 1980 reached only $1.6 million (Organization for Economic Cooperation and Development [OECD], *1981 Review of Development Cooperatives,* cited in *Kidma,* no. 25, p. 40).

† Israeli exports to Latin America are mainly transport equipment, electrical products, electronics, and chemical and agricultural products (M. Livnat, "Trade with Developing Countries," *Israel Government Yearbook 1978* [Tel Aviv: Israel Publishing Ltd., 1978], p. 180).

‡ Israeli imports from Latin America are mainly foodstuffs and raw materials ("Latin America and the Middle East," *Middle East Economic Digest, Special Report,* September 1981, p. 22).

Table 7. Latin America in Israel's Foreign Trade

	Imports			Exports		
Year	Israel's Total ($U.S. in	From Lt. Am.* millions)	Lt. Am. % Share	Israel's Total ($U.S. in	To Lt. Am.† millions)	Lt. Am. % Share
1972	$1,983.0	$ 34.9	1.76%	$1,149.0	$ 14.0	1.2%
1973	2,989.0	75.0	2.51	1,445.0	23.3	1.6
1974	4,215.0	59.2	1.4	1,825.0	45.0	2.5
1975	4,171.0	101.3	2.43	1,941.0	51.1	2.6
1976	4,132.0	54.4	1.32	2,415.0	73.7	3.1
1977	4,845.0	78.7	1.6	3,082.0	56.0	1.8
1978	5,832.0	88.2	1.5	3,922.0	56.5	1.4
1979	7,471.0	161.8	2.2	4,553.0	75.21	1.7
1980	8,027.3	140.4	1.8	5,537.5	173.1	3.1
1981	7,992.8	161.2	2.0	5,664.2	183.0	3.2
1982	8,116.1	155.9	1.9	5,281.5	130.3	2.5
1983	8,587.4	141.5	1.6	5,111.7	85.4	1.7
1984	8,411.4	139.2	1.7	5,782.8	94.6	1.6

Sources: *Israel Foreign Trade Statistics:* vol. 24, no. 12, Dec. 1973, pp. 35–37; vol. 26, no. 12, Dec. 1975, pp. 21–23; vol. 27, no. 12, Dec. 1976, pp. 18–20; vol. 28, no. 12, Dec. 1977, pp. 18–20; vol. 29, no. 12, Dec. 1978, pp. 21–23; vol. 30, no. 12, Dec. 1979, pp. 19–21. Central Bureau of Statistics, *Monthly Bulletin of Statistics* 32 (June 1981): 32. Central Bureau of Statistics, *Statistical Abstract of Israel, 1982* (Jerusalem: Hed Press Ltd., 1982), p. 204. Central Bureau of Statistics, *Statistical Abstract of Israel, 1984* (Jerusalem: Zohar, 1984) pp. 224–27. Central Bureau of Statistics, *Statistical Abstract of Israel, 1983* (Jerusalem: Hed Press, 1983) pp. 217–220. Central Bureau of Statistics, *Monthly Bulletin of Statistics* 36 (March 1985): 30.

* These figures do not include oil purchase from Latin America.

† These figures do not include arms sales to Latin America.

acknowledges selling oil to Israel, Venezuela and Ecuador are doing so as well.*

---

* In 1978, when the fate of the Shah of Iran became increasingly uncertain, the director-general of the Israeli Prime Minister's Office, Eliahu Ben-Elissar, visited Venezuela in quest of oil ("What Bad News," *The Economist*, 3 March 1979, p. 68). Although no official announcement was made, Venezuela has been a supplier since the late 1970s (*Latin America Regional Reports, Andean Group*, 22 January 1982, p. 1). Concerning Ecuador, see Chapter 4, p. 120.

Overview of Arms Sales

Nonetheless, the most important aspect of Latin American-Israeli relations is arms sales. By the end of 1984, at least eighteen Latin American countries had purchased military equipment—all, indeed, but Guyana, Suriname, French Guyana, and Uruguay. Export items run the gamut from sophisticated electronic gadgetry, fighter bombers, missile systems, and patrol boats, to small arms and ammunition, reconditioned surplus stock items, and captured Palestine Liberation Organization (PLO) weapons. Latin American air forces possess forty-eight of the fifty-six Kfir jet fighters Israel has exported[24] and all but a handful of the some eighty Arava STOLs (short take-off landing transport planes).[25] According to Edy Kaufman, head of the Truman Institute at Hebrew University in Jerusalem, Latin America is not only Israel's major foreign market for arms, it also differs qualitatively from other markets because sales include aircraft and large armaments as well as communications and electronic equipment.[26] These larger sales, including missile systems, patrol boats, and jet aircraft, have generally been made to the more advanced armed forces of South America (see Table 8). Although exports to Central America, mainly of small arms, communications and electronics equipment, and counterinsurgency aircraft, have been more modest in absolute terms, Israel's relative importance as a supplier and military advisor has been far greater given the smaller size and lesser sophistication of the Central American forces (see Table 9).

Israel's arms transfers to Latin America have not been subordinated to foreign policy goals. If anything, the traditional pattern of using arms sales to assist diplomacy has been reversed, and diplomacy appears to be in the service of arms sales. Thus, arms exports have been high, if not at the top of the agenda of virtually every high-level Israeli visit to Latin America in recent years: President Ephraim Katzir to Guatemala in December 1977; Deputy Defense Minister Mordechai Zipori to Chile in January 1979; Foreign Minister Yitzhak Shamir to Mexico in March 1981, to Ecuador in September 1981, and to Argentina and Costa Rica in

Table 8. Israeli Arms Exported to South America

Item	Comments	Reference Source
Argentina		
26 Mirage-5 Dassault fighters	Delivered 1978 and 1979 from Israeli air force stock	Stockholm International Peace Research Institute (SIPRI), *World Armament and Disarmament Yearbook 1979*, pp. 204–205.
26 Mirage-3C (Dagger)	Delivered 1980	SIPRI, *Yearbook 1982*, p. 207.
16 Mirage-3C (Dagger)	Ordered and delivered 1981	*Ibid.*
4 Dabur-class patrol boats		*New York Times*, 9 May 1982, p. 6; *The Middle East*, September 1981; "Armas Israelies Contra America Latina," *OLP Informa* (Mexico City), February 1982, p. 9; SIPRI, *Yearbook 1982*, p. 406.
Small arms Military electronics		*The Middle East*, September 1981.
Antiaircraft shells		Penny Lernoux, "Who's Who of Dictators Obtain Arms from Israel," *National Catholic Reporter*, 25 December 1981.
18 Gabriel-2 Missiles	Ordered 1975	SIPRI, *Yearbook 1978*, p. 258; *Yearbook 1979*, pp. 204–205.
22 Mirage-3C (Dagger)	According to President General Galtieri, bought during the Falklands/Malvinas War	*Washington Post*, 16 December 1982; Edward Schumaker, "Argentina Buying New Arms," *New York Times*, 6 June 1982; *Latin America Weekly Report*, 24 December 1982, p. 10.
24 U.S.-made A–4 Skyhawks	Confirmed by the general command of the Argentina navy July 1983; value put at $70 million	*Washington Post*, 7, 16 December 1982; *Jewish Telegraphic Agency*, 26 August 1982; *Al-Quds* (Jerusalem), 13 June 1983, p. 8; according to Aaron Klieman, *Israel's Global Reach*, 1985, p. 137, Israel sold 30 Skyhawks.

Table 8. (continued)

Item	Comments	Reference Source
22 Kfir fighters		*Ibid.*
Gabriel missiles Shafrir missiles	Unknown quantities sold prior and after the Falklands/Malvinas War	Ronald Slaughter, "Israel Arms Trade Cozying up to Latin Ar- mies," *NACLA Report* 16 (Jan- uary-February 1982): 50; *Latin America Weekly Report*, 24 December 1982, p. 10; *Econo- mist*, 12 June 1982; Schumaker, *New York Times*, 6 June 1982.
4 Arava STOL planes		*Excelsior*, 11 August 1982.
External fuel tanks for Mirage planes Aircraft spare parts	Delivered during the Falklands/Malvinas War	*Economist*, 12 June 1982.
Tank guns Other unidentified weapons		Schumaker, *New York Times*, 6 June 1982.
"Weapons and other 'instruments' for the Secret Po- lice."		Israel Shahak, unpublished document.
Mobile field hospitals		Aaron Klieman, *Israel's Global Reach*, 1985, p. 137.
Parachutes		*Ibid.*
Military uniforms and gear		*Ibid.*
Fire control systems		*Ibid.*
Bolivia		
6 201–IAI Arava planes	Delivered 1976: a $5.5 million deal with spare parts, technical sup- port, and crew training	SIPRI, *Yearbook, 1977*, p. 311.
Gabriel missiles Electronic and com- munication equip- ment		*Aurora* (Tel Aviv), 2 January 1975, Quoted in *Palestine Question Yearbook 1975*, p. 597.

(continues)

Table 8.   (continued)

Item	Comments	Reference Source
24 Kfir fighter planes		Klieman, *Israel's Global Reach*, p. 137.

Brazil

8 Iroquois helicopters		*Latin America Weekly Report*, 24 December 1982, p. 11.
Gabriel missiles		Klieman, *Israel's Global Reach*, p. 137.

Chile

150 Shafrir air-to-air missiles	Ordered 1976; delivered 1977	SIPRI, *Yearbook 1978*, p. 260.
6 Reshef class fast patrol boats	Ordered 1979; delivered 1979–81	SIPRI, *Yearbook 1981*, p. 219.
Antitank missiles		*Excelsior*, 29 December 1977.
1 radar system		U.S. Congress, House, Committee on Foreign Affairs, *Economic and Military Aid Programs*, 96th Cong., 1st sess., 1979, p. 84.
Uniforms and steel helmets		*Yediot Ahronot*, 25 January 1979; Eric Hooglund, *Israel's Arms Exports*, 1982, p. 10.
Parts for U.S.-made C–120 transport planes		*Latin America Weekly Report*, 16 May 1980, p. 10.
1,500 Shafrir air-to-air missiles	Ordered after M. Zippori's visit to Chile 1979	*The Middle East*, September 1981; SIPRI, *Yearbook 1982*, p. 410.
Light arms and ammunition		Klieman, *Israel's Global Reach*, p. 137.
Mobile field hospitals		*Ibid.*
Fire control systems		*Ibid.*

Table 8.   (continued)

Item	Comments	Reference Source
Colombia		
3 201-Arava STOL planes	Delivered in 1980	SIPRI, *Yearbook 1981*, p. 219.
12 Kfir fighter bombers	Armed with air-to-air and air-to-surface missiles; first delivery March 1982.	SIPRI, *Yearbook 1982*, p. 210.
Shafrir missiles	Unconfirmed	*Ibid.*; "Colombia Goes It Alone on Middle East Policy," *Latin America Regional Reports—Andean Group*, 22 January 1982, p. 1.
Modified Centurion tanks	Unconfirmed	*Ibid.*
Soltam artillery		
Light arms	Israel proposed sale in 1972	*Newsweek*, 16 October 1972, quoted in *Palestine Question Yearbook 1972*, p. 444.
Gabriel missiles		Klieman, *Israel's Global Reach*, p. 137.
Airplane maintenance equipment		*Ibid.*
Ecuador		
15 201–IAI Arava planes	Delivered 1975–79	SIPRI, *Yearbook 1977*, p. 314; SIPRI, *Yearbook 1979*, pp. 210–211; *Latin America Weekly Report*, 16 May 1980, p. 10.
24 Nesher jets		*Latin America Weekly Report*, 1 January 1982, p. 3; *El Nacional*, 4 July 1977, quoting the French magazine, *Defense Interarmées*.
24 Kfir-C2	First 12 bought 1981-82; other 12 first reported purchased January 1986	*Armed Forces Journal*, October 1981; SIPRI, *Yearbook 1982*, p. 211; *Hatzofeh*, 30 January 1986.

(continues) ·

Table 8.   (continued)

Item	Comments	Reference Source
Rockets Explosives Ammunition	Delivered 1974–77	U.S. Congress, House, Committee on Foreign Affairs, *Economic and Military Aid Programs*, p. 84.
3 Gabriel MKII missiles		*Latin America Weekly Report*, 16 May 1980, p. 10.
Logistical material for air force Ammunition High impact bombs		*New York Times*, 27 May 1982; *Jewish Telegraphic Agency*, 27 May 1982.
Uzi submachine guns		Spotted by the author at various locations in Quito, Ecuador, August 1982.
Spare parts	For jet fighters sold, according to Ariel Sharon	*Jerusalem Post*, 30 May 1982.
Field kitchens		Klieman, *Israel's Global Reach*, p. 137.
Armored personnel carriers		*Ibid.*
Barak antimissile missiles		*Ibid.*

Paraguay

6 201–IAI Arava planes	Delivered 1977; over a $7 million deal with spare parts and crew training	SIPRI, *Yearbook 1977*, p. 332.

Peru

Military communication and other equipment		Edy Kaufman, Yoram Shapiro, and Joel Barromi, *Israel-Latin-American Relations*, 1979, p. 107.
Parachutes Radio equipment Ammunition Small arms	Delivered 1974–77	U.S. Congress, House, Committee on Foreign Affairs, *Economic and Military Aid Programs in Europe and the Middle East*, Hearings and Markup Before the Subcom-

Table 8.   (continued)

Item	Comments	Reference Source
		mittee on Europe and the Middle East, 96th Cong., 1st sess., 1979, p. 84.
Radar systems		*Latin America Weekly Report*, January 1982, p. 3; interview with Raoul Borja, journalist, Quito, Ecuador, 26 August 1982.

Venezuela

Item	Comments	Reference Source
3 IAI–201 Arava planes	Ordered 1979; delivered 1980. An earlier delivery of an unspecified number was made to the National Guard	SIPRI, *Yearbook 1981*, p. 242.
2 IAI–201 Arava planes	Delivered August 1981 unannounced	SIPRI, *Yearbook 1982*, p. 237.
25 multiple artillery rocket launchers	First batch delivered January 1983	*Nuevo Diario*, 21 July 1982, p. 3; *Latin America Weekly Report*, 30 July 1982, p. 12.
Tactical communications equipment Rockets Bombs	$8.2 million value delivered 1974–77	U.S. Congress, House, Committee on Foreign Affairs, *Economic and Military Aid Programs*, p. 84.
24 Kfir fighter planes		Klieman, *Israel's Global Reach*, p. 137.
Rubber boats		*Ibid*.
2 IAI–201 Arava	Ordered 1981; delivered 1983	SIPRI, *Yearbook 1984*, p. 261.
LAR missile system	Israeli experts helped army install and test system with 88 pound fragmentation rockets fired from multibarreled rocket launchers. Permanent launch pads to be constructed along borders with Guyana, Colombia and Brazil	*Israeli Foreign Affairs*, June 1985, p. 3.

Table 9.   Israeli Arms Exported to Central America

Item	Comments	Reference Source
Costa Rica		
Small arms National guard training		Aaron Klieman, *Israel's Global Reach*, 1985, p. 135.
Dominican Republic		
9-mm Uzi sub-machine guns	Delivered 1974–77	U.S. Congress, House, Committee on Foreign Affairs, *Economic and Military Aid Programs in Europe and the Middle East*, 96th Cong., 1st sess. 1979, p. 84.
El Salvador		
25 IAI–201 Arava planes	Ordered September 1973; delivered 1974–1979. Unit cost $0.7 million	Stockholm International Peace Research Institute (SIPRI), *World Armament and Disarmament Yearbook 1979*, pp. 212–213.
6 Fouga Magister trainers	Licensed production in Israel. Ordered 1973; delivered 1975	SIPRI, *Yearbook 1976*, p. 274.
18 refurbished Dassault Ouragan fighters	Ordered 1973; delivered 1975. From Israeli air force stock	*Ibid.*, p. 275.
200 80-mm rocket launchers	Delivered 1974–77	U.S. Congress, House, Committee on Foreign Affairs, *Economic and Military Aid Programs*, p. 84.
200 9-mm Uzi sub-machine guns	Delivered 1974–77	*Ibid.*
Ammunition Spare parts		*Ibid.*
"Security" equipment		"Armas Israelis Contra America Latina," *OLP Informa* (Mexico City), February 1982, p. 8.

Table 9. (continued)

Item	Comments	Reference Source
Galil assault rifles		Penny Lernoux, "'Who's Who of Dictators Obtain Arms from Israel," *National Catholic Reporter*, 25 December 1981.
4 Mystere B–2 bombers	Ordered and delivered 1981; unconfirmed	SIPRI, *Yearbook 1982*, p. 213.
Armored vehicles		Interview with "Miguel," nom de guerre, International Relations Department of the Salvadoran FMLN, Managua, Nicaragua, 17 August 1982; interview with "Santiago," International Relations Department of the Salvadoran Communist Party, Managua, Nicaragua, 17 August 1982.
3 Arava STOL planes	Sold in 1982	*Latin America Weekly Report*, 17 December 1982, p. 6.
Napalm bombs		*Hadashot*, 2 October 1984, p. 13.

Guatemala

Item	Comments	Reference Source
7 201–IAI Arava planes	Ordered and delivered 1976	SIPRI, *Yearbook 1977*, p. 316.
10 201–IAI Arava planes	Ordered 1977; delivered 1977–78	SIPRI, *Yearbook 1978*, p. 262; SIPRI, *Yearbook, 1979*, pp. 214–215.
5 troop-carrying Asimo helicopters		"Growing Arms Race in Central America May Heat up Region," *Christian Science Monitor*, 28 October 1981.
10 RBY MK armored cars	Delivered 1974–77	U.S. Congress, House, Committee on Foreign Affairs, *Economic and Military Aid Programs*, p. 84.
5 field kitchens	4 delivered 1974–77	*Ibid.*; Klieman, *Israel's Global Reach*, p. 135.

(continues)

Table 9. (continued)

Item	Comments	Reference Source
50,000 Galil assault rifles	15,000 delivered 1974–77	*Christian Science Monitor,* 28 October 1981.
1,000 machine guns		*Ibid.*
3 naval coast guard ships (Dabur boats)	Talks started in 1978	Mauricio Goldstein, "Con Armas Israelis Asesinan al Pueblo Guatemalteco," *Punto Final Internacional,* August 1981, p. 14; interview with "Emilcar," nom de guerre, high ranking official in the Political Wing of the Guatemalan EGP, Managua, Nicaragua, 18 August 1982.
Grenade launchers 81-mm mortars 120 tons of ammunition	Arrived in Guatemala's Santo Tomas de Castilla port 3 months after suspension of U.S. military aid	Goldstein, *Punto Final Internacional,* August 1981, p. 14; *Nuevo Diario,* 28 September 1981.
Bulletproof vests Military tents		*Ha'aretz,* April 1979, quoted in Ignacio Klich, "Guatemala's Back-Door Arms Deals," *8 Days,* 13 March 1982.
Shields Tear gas Gas masks	Bought by Interior Minister Donaldo Alvarez in 1980 visit to Israel	Interview with Emilcar.
Fire ejectors	Used to burn bushes and people. Captured by EGP from government troops	*Ibid.*
Tactical transmission system	Cover the whole country. Bought 1977 or 1978	*Ibid.*; "Israel Aliado de la Dictadura Guatemalteca," *OLP Informa* (Mexico City), April 1982, p. 8.
Radar system	Has 5 receivers. Bought end 1980. Israeli controlled and directed	*Ibid.*; *News from Guatemala* 3 (October 1981): 1.
High-tech products: • Radar • Intelligence information computing		*Latin America Weekly Report,* 5 September 1980, p. 8; *El Dia,* 8 May 1982: interview with Emilcar; John Rettie,

Table 9. (continued)

Item	Comments	Reference Source
and communications equipment • Radar circuits to detect guerrillas smuggling arms		*Manchester Guardian Weekly,* 10 January 1982.
Helmets		*Le Monde,* 25 January 1979.
5 million rifle bullets	Bought in 1977 for $1.8 million through David Marcus Katz	*Excelsior,* 18 July 1977, p. 2A; interview with Emilcar.
Shipload light arms	65 tons delivered 1977	SIPRI, *Yearbook 1980,* p. 144.
10,000 105-mm HEAT (high-explosive anti-tank) ammunition	Supplied 1981–82 to the army for $6 million	SIPRI, *Yearbook 1982,* p. 188.
Kfir fighters	Unspecified number	Klieman, *Israel's Global Reach,* p. 135.
Haiti		
600 9-mm Uzi submachine guns	Delivered 1974–77	U.S. Congress, House, Committee on Foreign Affairs, *Economic and Military Aid Programs,* p. 84.
106-mm recoilless rifles		*Ibid.*
24 Kfir-C2 fighter/ ground attack Ammunition	Ordered 1983, unconfirmed	SIPRI, *Yearbook 1984,* p. 238
Honduras		
12 Dassault Super Mystere fighters	French-made, Israeli-refurbished. Ordered 1976 and 1977. From Israeli air force stocks	SIPRI, *Yearbook 1977,* p. 317. *Yearbook 1978,* p. 262. *Yearbook 1979,* pp. 214–215; Richard Goldman and Murray Rubenstein, *Shield of David* 1978, p.80 [These planes served in the Israeli air force for 19 years (Goldman et al., p. 81)].
8 Dassault Super Mystere fighters	Ordered 1977	*Latin America Weekly Report,* 17 December 1982, p. 6.

(continues)

Table 9. (continued)

Item	Comments	Reference Source
6 Arava STOL transport aircraft	Ordered and delivered 1976	U.S. Congress, House, Committee on Foreign Affairs, *Economic and Military Aid Programs*, p. 84; Klieman, *Israel's Global Reach*, p. 135.
1 Westwind reconnaissance plane	Delivered 1974–77	*Ibid.*
14 RBY MK armored cars		*Ibid.*
106-mm recoilless rifles		*Ibid.*
Mortars, 4.2 in. (107 mm)		*Ibid.*
600 AN/PRC radios		*Ibid.*
5 fast patrol boats	Unconfirmed	SIPRI, *Yearbook 1981*, p. 222; Klieman, *Israel's Global Reach*, p. 135.
12 Kfir fighters	Sharon deal signed during his December 1982 visit. According to some sources the sale never materialized due to Honduras' lack of funds. The information has not been confirmed elsewhere	*Guardian* (US), 26 January 1983; *Israeli Foreign Affairs*, October 1985; interview with Jane Hunter, editor of *Israeli Foreign Affairs*, Washington, D.C., 6 February 1986.
RBY armored cars Galil assault rifles Radar equipment Military replacement parts	Sold 1982	*Latin America Weekly Report*, 24 December 1982, p. 10; *The Observer*, 12 December 1982; *Latin America Weekly Report*, 17 December 1982, p. 6.
Missiles	Sold 1982	*Latin America Weekly Report*, 17 and 24 December 1982.
Tanks Self-propelled guns Rocket launchers	Captured from PLO 1982 Unconfirmed	*Latin America Weekly Report*, 24 December 1982, p. 10.
Uzi submachine guns		Klieman, *Israel's Global Reach*, p. 135.

Table 9. (continued)

Item	Comments	Reference Source
M–4 Sherman MT	Ordered 1983, unconfirmed part of Kfir deal	SIPRI, *Yearbook 1984*, p. 239.
Mexico		
25 201–IAI Arava planes	Ordered 1973. Unit cost $650,000	SIPRI, *Yearbook 1976*, p. 275; *Latin America Weekly Report*, 16 May 1980, p. 10.
10 201–IAI Arava planes	Ordered 1977. Records indicate these have been delivered	SIPRI, *Yearbook 1978*, p. 271. *Yearbook, 1979*, pp. 226–227.
4 Westwind reconnaissance planes		*Jerusalem Post*, 12 January 1981.
Uzi submachine guns	Used by Mexico's federal security	*Press release*, Partido Socialista de los Trabajadores (PST), Mexico City, Mexico, 9 September 1978.
Electronic wirefences Radars		*Excelsior*, 15 March 1977.
Telecommunication equipment Flying ambulances		*Excelsior*, 14 March 1982.
14 201–IAI Arava planes	No indication if this is a new order	
Armored cars and troop carriers		Klieman, *Israel's Global Reach*, p. 135.
Nicaragua		
14 201–IAI Arava planes	Ordered 1973. 5 delivered 1974, the rest 1975–77. Unit cost $650,000	SIPRI, *Yearbook 1974*, p. 282, *Yearbook, 1975*, p. 240, *Yearbook, 1977*, p. 330.
4 armed patrol boats	Only one or two are left. Somoza loyalists used the rest to flee	*Newsweek*, 20 November 1978, p. 68; Interview with Marwan Tahbub, PLO Ambassador, Managua, Nicaragua, 15 August 1982.

(continues)

Table 9. (continued)

Item	Comments	Reference Source
1 light military transport plane	Most likely Westwind	*Le Monde*, 4 July 1979.
67 tactical radios	Delivered 1974–77. Valued at $0.3 million	U.S. Congress, House, Committee on Foreign Affairs, *Economic and Military Aid Programs*, p. 84.
Helicopters Small patrol boat Heavy mortars Machine guns	Delivered 1978	*Latin America Weekly Report*, 16 May 1980, p. 10.
Heavy combat tanks Light artillery Missile launchers Patrol vehicles Helicopters	Old Sherman tanks delivered May 1975. Other cargo ships were in route	*Ha'aretz*, 10 May 1978; interview with Ambassador Tahbub.
2–3 radars	Delivered to Somoza but no time to set them up	Interview with Ambassador Tahbub.
Trucks Flack jackets Mortars		*Newsweek*, 20 November 1978, p. 68.
Missiles	Anti-aircraft, surface-to-surface missiles and ground-to-ground missiles. Delivered secretly by two Israeli planes	*Ibid*.; *New York Times*, 19 November 1978; *Excelsior*, 8 June 1979, p. 20A.
500 Uzi submachine guns 500 Galil assault rifles		*Newsweek*, 20 November 1978, p. 68; *Haolam Haze*, 4 October 1978.
5 plane loads of arms	Delivered November 1978. Planes landed at a private track in Montelimar, east of Managua	*El Sol*, 18 November 1978.
2 plane loads of arms	Delivered at Las Mercedes Airport November 1978. Other sources indicated there were 3 planes	*Jerusalem Post*, 15 November 1978; *Newsweek*, 20 November 1978, p. 68.

Table 9. (continued)

Item	Comments	Reference Source
Sea-to-sea missiles		*World Business,* 6 October 1980.
T–54 and T–55 tanks		Klieman, *Israel's Global Reach,* p. 135.
Panama		
1 1123 Westwind reconnaissance plane	Bought 1975 for $1.6 million	SIPRI, *Yearbook 1976,* p. 275; *Excelsior,* 25 February 1977.
Radar and communications systems		U.S. Congress, House, Committee on Foreign Affairs, *Economic and Military Aid Programs in Europe and the Middle East,* 96th Cong., 1st sess., 1979, p. 84.

December 1982; and Defense Minister Ariel Sharon to Honduras in December 1982.

Arms sales to Latin America, however, have reaped few benefits diplomatically. On the contrary, far from advancing Israel's cause, large-scale arms sales have coincided with a significant erosion of support in Latin America. By the end of 1979, eleven Latin American countries had become members of the nonaligned movement, traditionally critical of Israeli policies.* This change is easily seen in UN voting patterns (see Table 5). Guatemala alone has been unwavering in its support of Israel,†

---

* These countries were: Argentina, Bolivia, Cuba, Grenada, Guyana, Jamaica, Nicaragua, Panama, Peru, Suriname, and Trinidad and Tobago.

† In December 1985 Guatemala's civilian president-elect announced that he was planning to order an investigation of Israel's role in arming the Guatemalan army (*Haaretz,* 10 December 1985).

never going beyond an occasional abstention in anti-Israeli votes. The others have checkered voting patterns, and most recognize the PLO as the sole legitimate representative of the Palestinian people, as well as the rights of the Palestinians. Five Latin American countries, including Mexico and Brazil, voted in favor of the 1975 General Assembly resolution equating Zionism to racism; eleven abstained.[27] All of the Latin American countries, with the exception of Guatemala and the Dominican Republic (which abstained) voted in favor of the 1980 censure of Israel's Basic Law of Jerusalem, which reaffirmed the 1967 annexation of the Arab part of the city, and which precipitated the flight of all twelve Latin American missions from Jerusalem to Tel Aviv.* While there is no doubt that these setbacks were keenly felt, particularly the Zionism equals racism vote, these votes never interfered with Israel's prompt and expeditious delivery of arms orders.

Emergence of Latin America as Israel's Major Arms Market

Many factors led to Latin America's emergence as a primary market for Israeli arms. This region is beyond question the largest potential market. Israel's friends in Western Europe either manufacture their own weapons or utilize interlocking, complementary weapons systems as part of NATO policy. The Soviet bloc is off-limits. Many third world countries are dependent on Middle Eastern oil and hence are sensitive to pressures from the Organization of Petroleum Exporting Countries (OPEC); others lean toward the Arab states for historical or cultural reasons. Furthermore, although arms production in Latin America is growing, the region continues to meet most of its weapons needs through foreign markets.

---

* As of January 1986 the embassies of Costa Rica, Honduras, and El Salvador had been moved back to Jerusalem (*Jerusalem Post*, 11 January 1986).

Regional Factors

Territorial Disputes and Internal Strife. Powerful factors in Latin America stimulate the potential of this market. First, because few regions are as rife with not only unresolved territorial but a variety of other disputes (see Table 10), the area is marked by an unusually high demand for weapons. Argentina is at odds with Great Britain over the Malvinas/Falklands, with Uruguay over territorial waters, and until recently with Chile over the Beagle Channel Islands. Bolivia is quarreling with Chile over water usage and with Brazil over territory in the Amazon jungle. Ecuador claims the Amazonian triangle seized by Peru, and Peru has irredentist designs on its former southern province of Arica which was seized by Chile in the last century. Venezuela claims territory belonging to Guyana and is at odds with Colombia. In Central America Honduras and El Salvador are in dispute over borders, Guatemala claims Belize, and all are pitted against Nicaragua. Although most of these disputes have been largely confined to academic debates or have been evoked in occasional UN speeches, the rising tide of nationalism and the influx of sophisticated weaponry into the region have renewed enthusiasm for the recovery of lost territories by military means.[28] A number of these quarrels have erupted into open conflict in recent years: Argentina with Britain; Ecuador with Peru; and Honduras with El Salvador and with Nicaragua. In the case of the latter, U.S. involvement has exacerbated local tension.

While territorial disputes have unquestionably fueled the arms buildup in the region (Argentina and Chile spent more than $1 billion each for new weapons and deployed forces along their borders in the late 1970s)[29], most of the weapons procured in Latin America have been used in suppressing internal dissent. Uruguay, Peru, Paraguay, Colombia, Chile, Argentina, Brazil, Bolivia, Honduras, Guatemala, and El Salvador have all had to deal with guerrilla movements, and the instability and economic duress of other countries make the threat of insurgency real. Reflecting the increased use of the military in an internal security

Table 10.   Territorial and Border Disputes in Latin America

Participants	Description of Dispute
Argentina—Britain	Argentina claims the British colony of the Falkland Islands off its southeast coast. They fought a war over the islands in 1982.
Argentina—Chile	In May 1985 the two countries signed a Vatican-mediated pact that ended their dispute over the possession of three islands in the Beagle Channel. Both countries sought control over the 200-mile economic zone and its potential oil and gas resources. The new treaty gave Chile sovereignty over the islands but limited its maritime rights to the Cape Horn area.
Argentina—Uruguay	Territorial limits in the waters of the River Plate have been the source of a dispute that flared to near confrontation in 1973.
Bolivia—Brazil	In 1973 Brazil took a small strip of territory in Santa Cruz, leading some to believe that Brazil wants to expand across the Abuna River, Bolivia's northern boundary.
Bolivia—Chile	Bolivia broke diplomatic ties with Chile in 1962 over the use of Rio Lanca water. In 1975 ties were resumed, but broken again in 1978, when negotiations for an outlet to the Pacific for Bolivia broke down. A military buildup on the borders followed.
Colombia—Nicaragua	Nicaragua claims a chain of islands now ruled by Colombia. In 1979 Nicaragua renounced the 1928 treaty under which the archipelago was awarded to Colombia.
Guatemala—Belize	Until recently, Guatemala claimed sovereignty over all of Belize, but now only wants ownership of the southernmost fifth.
Haiti—Dominican Republic	The security of the 193 miles of shared border, particularly the narrow valleys that provide access from Haiti, has been a source of much tension.
Honduras—El Salvador	A boundary over which a brief war was fought in 1969.
Nicaragua—Honduras	The border was closed in April 1981 following clashes. The major conflict is the presence of defeated Nicaraguan former National Guardsmen in Honduras under the protection of the Honduran military. The guardsmen have used Honduran territory to attack the Sandinistas in Nicaragua.

Table 10.   (continued)

Participants	Description of Dispute
Peru—Chile—Bolivia	During the War of the Pacific in 1879, Peru lost its southern province of Arica to Chile, and Bolivia lost its only access to the sea to Chile. Bolivia and Peru have often threatened to redeem their national honor.
Peru—Ecuador	Ecuador claims a large part of the Amazon which was lost to Peru in 1941. Border clashes flared up in 1981.
Suriname—Guyana	A dispute over 6,000 square miles of bauxite-rich land that resulted in an armed clash in 1969.
Venezuela—Colombia	Dispute over territorial waters that are likely to have oil reserves.
Venezuela—Guyana	Venezuela claims over 58,000 square miles (over half of Guyana). Published documents in the 1950s led many Venezuelans to believe that the arbitration team of 1899 was tainted by bribery and, hence, that the current border is not binding.
Venezuela—Trinidad and Tobago	Territorial fishing rights dispute.

Sources: *Washington Post*, 3 May 1985, p. 20; *New York Times*, 14 January 1983, p. A5; *Jerusalem Post*, 18 July 1982; *Boston Globe*, 30 May 1982, p. 11; 6 March 1983, p. 9; 18 April 1983, p. 13; Andrew Pierre, *Global Politics of Arms Sales* (Princeton, N.J.: Princeton University Press, 1982), pp. 235–236; and Gay Hammerman, ed., *Almanac of World Military Power*, 5th ed. (San Rafael, Calif.: Presidio Press, 1980), pp. 57, 74, 113, 130, 132, 137, 164–165, 168, 303, 358.

role, the strength of the army in South America overall has increased by 50 percent over the past two decades, while that of the army, navy, and air force combined has increased by only 30 percent.[30]

The Role of the Military. Even without potential conflicts, external or internal, the salience of the military in Latin American politics would itself predispose the region to weapons procurement. Governments dominated by the military are inevitably more attentive to the needs of their defense establishments and inclined to acquire arms that are perceived to add to the military's institutional dignity.[31] The only countries with strong civilian traditions are Mexico, Costa Rica, and to a lesser extent Venezuela. All the others either are or have been controlled by the military, either directly or through the exercise of a kind of veto power. Argentina, Brazil, Uruguay, Bolivia, and Peru recently emerged from long years of direct military rule, but political and economic uncertainties and the history of the military coup d'etat as a tool for change make it impossible to take the new civilian rule for granted.

In any event, the critical role of the military in the region has worked in favor of the intensification of Israel's relations with Latin American governments.[32] Aside from professional admiration for Israel's military exploits and an affinity of world view, or at least common understanding shared by professional military men, the Latin American military is fervently anticommunist and tends to perceive Israel as the guardian of Western civilization in the face of leftist terrorists and Soviet-backed Arab regimes. Some Israeli authors have called attention to the Latin American military establishment's tendency to see an analogy between Latin American revolutionaries on the one hand, and the leftist elements of the Middle East that Israel is dedicated to eradicate on the other.[33]

Beyond this natural affinity, Israel has been nurturing relations with the military establishments of Latin America since the early 1960s. At that time the Kennedy administration, alarmed at Castro's victory in Cuba and the boost it gave to leftist movements in the region, asked Israel to implement its "civic action" programs[34]—primarily military-agricultural projects of the Nahal type* and paramilitary youth organizations†—to counterbalance

---

* Israel's Nahal experience was based on the notion that agricultural training should be an integral part of military service. The idea is "to turn the army into a constructive force, which though capable of combat operation, would in times of peace be interwoven within the national creativity" (Israel Ministry of Defence, *Nahal, Pioneering Fighting Youth* [Tel Aviv: Ministry of Defence, 1963], p. 1). Thus, the military was to participate in a variety of social services for the civilian population, in most cases a public relations measure.

† Israel's paramilitary youth movement, Gadna, educates young people between the ages of 14 and 18 "to be ready, both morally and physically, to answer the call of their country—to serve it both in war and peace" (Israel Ministry of

this influence.[35] Using funds from the U.S. Agency for International Development (AID),[36] Israel offered specialized instruction in how to organize paramilitary youth groups and Nahal programs for high-ranking officers and other officials of twelve Latin American countries.* These countries also sent selected youths to Israel for training.[37] The programs, though ostensibly nonmilitary in nature, were significantly under the direction of a special unit within the Israeli Defense Ministry called the Department for Cooperation and Foreign Liaison.[38] The programs were enacted when, according to Kaufman et al., "Israel successfully promoted the idea of using the military as a factor in national development."[39] While these civic action programs in most cases did not leave a lasting legacy, they did involve direct interaction between Israeli military personnel and the Latin American military establishment at a time when bilateral relations in other areas were not active.[40]

Building on these contacts, in 1964 Israel initiated a policy of promoting visits by Latin Americans to Israeli military bases, defense industries, and related installations.[41] Kaufman et al. note 160 such visits between 1964 and 1971, representing eighteen Latin American countries.[42] The Israeli government spent lavishly on military visitors,[43] many of whom were high-ranking officers, including chiefs of staff (Bolivia in 1964 and 1974, Chile in 1967, Peru in 1970, Guatemala in 1971, Venezuela in 1971, Ecuador in 1974), chiefs of naval forces (Venezuela and Chile in 1970), a chief of the air force (Guatemala in 1971), ex-defense ministers and retired chiefs of staff (Bolivia, Chile, Colombia, El

---

Defence, *Gadna Youth Battalions* [Tel Aviv: Ministry of Defence, 1963], p. 2). It promotes civic consciousness, patriotism, and the spirit of service, and trains youth in such skills as aviation, seamanship, signals, and marksmanship. The first replica of this program in Latin America was successfully conducted in Costa Rica in the mid-1960s, though, given the dissolution of the country's army, the program reportedly stressed the civic aspects, promoting a sense of national purpose through such activities as tree planting and the construction of schools, community facilities, and roads (Edy Kaufman, Yoram Shapiro, and Joel Barromi, *Israel-Latin American Relations* [New Brunswick, N.J.: Transaction Books, 1979], p. 105).

* Uruguay, El Salvador, Ecuador, Bolivia, Guatemala, Costa Rica, Venezuela, Mexico, Panama, Peru, Chile, and Colombia. (*Israel Government Yearbook 1970–71* [Jerusalem: Central Office of Information, 1971], p. 105).

Salvador, Venezuela, and Uruguay), and key military personnel holding nonmilitary cabinet posts. A number of these visitors later became heads of state. Alfredo Ovando Candia, for example, visited Israel in 1964 as commander-in-chief of the armed forces and became Bolivia's president in 1968.[44] Kjell Laugerud Garcia visited Israel as chief of staff in 1971 and again just before he took office as Guatemala's president in 1974.[45] During his last visit, Laugerud Garcia pledged to expand cooperation with Israel. João Baptista Figueiredo, president of Brazil until the country's return to democracy, spent six weeks in Israel when he was a general in the army.[46] Moreover, a stream of Israeli military officials regularly visited their counterparts in Latin America.

Thus, by the time the Israeli defense industries had outgrown their domestic base and were in need of foreign markets for their surplus, contacts facilitating sales in Latin America had long been in place.

The Marketing of Israeli Arms

Nevertheless, Israel was a latecomer to the arms market which was already heavily saturated by the major arms suppliers. The United States had a near monopoly on weapons sales to Latin America until the mid-1960s, after which it increasingly had to share the market with France (in second place) and the Soviet Union (in third). As a result of U.S. arms policies under President Carter, the Soviet Union pulled into first place in 1977, and France fell back to third. Other important suppliers to the region include Italy, the Federal Republic of Germany, and the United Kingdom.[47]

Indeed, given the competition and the newness of the Israeli arms industry, it is remarkable that Israel has penetrated the market to the extent that it has. This has happened due to the excellence of Israeli products and their suitability to Latin American needs, its "total package" approach with a range of support services, and its reliability as a supplier regardless of the circumstances. The penetration of the market has also been due to fortuitous circumstances beyond Israel's control, such as President Carter's human rights policy, as well as to its skillful use of opportunities.

The Marketing Network. Before discussing the advantages offered by Israeli products, a knowledge of how the market network functions is helpful. The Israeli government controls all arms exports, at the highest level through the Ministerial Committee on Weapons Transfers, and at the operational level through the Defense Ministry Defense Sales Office (SIBAT), which is structured along geographical lines and has a special section for Latin America. In principle, SIBAT's South American section coordinates the activities of the various elements of the arms marketing network, including those of the military and diplomatic missions in most Latin American states; the regional offices or representatives of the major arms producing companies such as Israel Aircraft Industries (IAI), Israel Military Industries (IMI), and Tadiran (or the special marketing companies such as Koor's "Koor Sachar"); the independent dealerships such as the Eisenberg Group, Elul Technologies, Sherwood, Eshborn, and Gal Yoatzim, which are often owned by or associated with former Israeli Defense Forces (IDF) officers or government officials;[48] and finally, the private arms merchants.

According to the *New York Times,* there are about 300 private Israeli arms agents operating worldwide.[49] The *National Catholic Reporter* identifies twenty such merchants in Latin America.[50] Whatever their number, private agents are extremely active. And although theoretically the government (through SIBAT) must supervise all arms negotiations, in practice it is content to approve the final sale with few questions asked about how the sale was made. Bribes and irregularities are said to be rife, and commissions in Latin America reportedly reach 25 percent, as opposed to the 5 to 10 percent which is customary elsewhere.[51] This is not to say that the activities of the arms merchants are not controversial. The Defense Ministry at various times has tried to put an end to "unnecessary" intermediaries, agents, and arms merchants and to conduct business in a "more centralized way."[52] Defense Minister Ariel Sharon, in particular, wanted more centralization and was concerned about the inordinately high commissions paid to middlemen, which he termed "blackmailing the state."[53] David Marcus Katz has been singled out by the Hebrew press as one of the best known of the arms merchants. He operates out of Mexico City and is said to represent seventeen arms manufacturers including TA'AS. The accusation has been made that Katz's high fees have cost Israel large deals in Central America that otherwise would have gone through.[54] When Ezer Weizman was defense minister, there was a move to curb Katz's activities. However, Deputy Foreign Minister Yehuda Ben Meir and Education Minister Zeveloon Hammer, both members of the National Religious Party to which Katz contributes generously (he is also, according to *Davar*, a generous contributor to Gush Emunim[55]), reportedly put pressure on Weizman to stop the effort.[56] According to *Davar*, Katz "has the backing of political circles, including those close to the Prime Minister."[57] Other private dealers are said to be similarly well connected in Jerusalem.

But the private agents have not been given free rein only because of their friends in high places, but rather because they succeed. The private arms merchants account for as much as one-third of Israel's total arms sales contracts worldwide.[58] They bring in huge deals obtained by their vast networks of personal contacts with the ruling elites of the countries in which they operate. David Marcus Katz, for example, was a close personal friend of Anastasio Somoza and has lines to virtually every leader of importance in Latin America. Private dealers often act as middlemen between official Israeli channels and the potential client states; for example, the arms talks between Defense Minister Sharon and the Honduran government in December 1982 took place in Katz's presence. However, the connection works both ways, and the fact that private dealers are identified with the Israeli government facilitates their success. Levi Tsur, another of the top arms merchants in South America, described in an interview with *Ma'ariv* how he is received "like a king" in South America, as "representing the victorious Israeli empire."[59] Tsur is a former senior air force officer who uses the connections acquired during his years as Israeli military attache in Venezuela and Ecuador to sell weapons manufactured by small companies as well as IDF surplus. He further stated that "a lot depends on you. But I won't deny that Israel's reputation saves you a lot of effort."[60] As an example of how the private merchants and government officials can cooperate on a deal, *Ma'ariv* recounted an incident in which an independent agent negotiating the sale of Arava STOL (short take-off landing) transport planes to Argentina almost lost out to competitors from well-known Western companies. The salesman confided to *Ma'ariv* that the deal was saved by the minister of commerce and industry, Yigael Horowitz, who hinted to the Argentines that there could be "difficulties" in Israeli meat purchases from Argentina. Six Aravas were sold.[61]

Suitability of Products. Israel's range of export items is well suited to the Latin American market. The long-simmering but generally low-level territorial disputes of the region necessitate the procurement of weapons, but not necessarily those on the cutting edge of technology. Indeed, many of Israel's larger, if not most prestigious, sales to the area fall under its retrofit-for-export program. Tanks, fighter bombers, antisubmarine aircraft, armored vehicles, and other systems that are no longer functional in the highly competitive arena of the Middle East but are adequate for Latin American needs, are overhauled, refurbished, updated, and sold at considerably less cost than new systems. Israel also has a program for upgrading weapons systems currently used by a client's armed forces; a recent example is the IAI's upgrading of fifteen Mirage V planes for Colombia to make them resemble Kfirs.[62] In a similar category are Israel's sales of captured PLO or other Arab stocks, such as the Soviet-made multiple rocket launchers it sold to Venezuela in July 1982 after the Lebanon invasion[63] and the PLO stocks supplied to Central America shortly thereafter. Israel is, in fact, the second largest exporter of Soviet-made equipment in the world.[64]

A number of Israel's own products are well suited to Latin American priorities such as counterinsurgency and internal security. According to SIPRI, a substantial percentage of Latin America's arms imports has been counterinsurgency equipment for coping with internal security problems.[65] In recent years, in keeping with its market, Israel has given greater emphasis to such items at international arms bazaars. At the 1981 Air Show at Le Bourget, France, the centerpiece of its exhibit was the EL/ M–2121 Intelligence Battlefield Surveillance Radar. The device detects small infiltrating guerrilla units, locates them, and can even classify targets moving on the ground from as far away as 75 miles.[66] The system weighs approximately 40 pounds and can be easily assembled in the field.[67]

Aside from electronic surveillance and radar equipment, Israel manufactures a host of weapons with counterinsurgency uses. The most popular export item is probably the Uzi submachine gun, which can be fired full or semi-automatic rifle, from the hip or shoulder and which is used by security forces and police throughout the region. The Galil assault rifle, which fires standard NATO ammunition and can be used either as an automatic or semi-automatic rifle, is also widely used by various kinds of military forces. Another very popular export is the Arava STOL which has been used to bomb rebel targets and villages in Central America and is in service in most air forces in Latin America. The Arava, which is advertised as a "rugged, versatile, economical" aircraft with a "proven capability to function in remote areas, under adverse conditions, from unprepared strips, in extremes of climate and terrain," can carry as many as twenty-four fully-equipped paratroopers. Its "low speed control and maneuverability" make it ideal for low-level strafing and bombing. It can be fitted with two fixed-firing, 0.50-inch machine guns with the option of a third gun installed in the rear of the fuselage.[68]

In deference to this market, which lacks a high degree of technological sophistication, Israel has taken pains to keep its products simple. The Uzi, for instance, is an extremely reliable and easy-to-handle weapon. It can be field-stripped and reassembled in a matter of minutes and can operate effectively even if sand has been poured into it.[69] The need for simplicity was a major priority in the IAI's development of the Arava aircraft in the early 1970s. In an interview with *Aviation Week and Space Technology*, an industry official noted that IAI clients were generally "unsophisticated in the operation of modern aircraft," their experience often being limited to surplus World War II equipment so that "in many cases [they had] to jump a generation or two in technology and operational procedures even to operate the Arava." Ease of handling, ruggedness of construction, and unsophisticated maintenance requirements are continually stressed in the sales literature. Even Israel's Kfir fighter bomber is billed as being less complex to operate and maintain than comparable aircraft.[70]

Simplicity of operation in no way implies a loss of efficiency or reliability. After all, most Israeli products were developed for use by the Israeli Defense Forces and have been battle-tested. Advertising appearing in military trade publications makes full use of this fact.* The Shafrir air-to-air missile "was very successful in the 1973 Yom Kippur War," while the Gabriel sea-to-sea missile is "the only such battle-tested system in the West." The Israel Aircraft Industry (IAI) "has a front-line position in Israel's security and defense industry with an impressive listing of product breakthroughs that are integral parts of the country's defense posture" and has experience "coping with a wide variety of combat environments." An IAI advertisement headlined "Israel: Experience for Export" notes, "in the direct defense field, Israel has proved a reliable testing ground with interplay between soldiers on the front line and the men who make their equipment. At IAI there is a constant dialogue between pilots flying fighters . . . and the engineers and scientists who take their input from field use to improve and design the next generation of equipment."[71] Israel's military prowess also serves as advertising

---

* These advertisements appeared in a number of defense-related publications, e.g., *Military Technology and Electronics*, May, August, and November 1982; *International Defense Review*, nos. 7 and 9, 1982; and *Aviation Week and Space Technology*, 27 December 1982.

in itself. In fact following the invasion of Lebanon in 1982, there was talk of discontinuing advertising as an unnecessary expenditure of funds: "Nowadays, when the entire world can see how our bombs do exactly what they are supposed to do, the Israeli Military industry could save itself the cost of its advertisements."[72] A few months later, however, with news reports that the USSR's most advanced tank, the T–72 had fared badly against the Israeli Merkava in Lebanon,[73] *The Christian Science Monitor* reported that Israel was launching a new advertising campaign to capitalize on the publicity surrounding its weapons superiority.[74]

Intangible Advantages of "Buying Israeli." For U.S. arms clients seeking alternate suppliers, either to diversify or because of U.S. restrictions on their arms purchases, Israeli weapons are a good substitute. Sales literature emphasizes that Israeli products are "oriented to the latest Western technology" and "compatible with U.S. systems." In a special advertising section of *Aviation Week and Space Technology,* care was taken to emphasize the "vast amount of U.S. made parts and material in the Kfir, from its engines, made here under license, to the aluminum in the body." Elsewhere it mentions that because "a high percentage of the finished product is actually U.S. or European manufactured . . . the purchasing country is committing itself to Western systems which will need the necessary infrastructure to support them— meaning more future sales."[75] While the last statement is obviously a bid for Western tolerance of Israeli competition, there is a message for the third world buyer as well: While diversifying arms sources, it can remain firmly in the Western camp as far as weapons compatibility is concerned and can rest assured of the technological superiority of the product. From a political standpoint, too, Israeli arms are a good substitute. The fact that most third world regimes are fervently anticommunist makes acquisition of Soviet bloc arms out of the question.[76] Consequently, Israel's reputation as a bulwark against revolutionary leftist governments also stands it in good stead. In some cases Israel's special relationship with the United States is an advantage because buyers hope to use cooperation with Israel to gain respectability with Israel's friends in Congress or to help advance their case with a U.S. administration.*

Economic Advantages. Of great importance to the economically hard-pressed regimes of Latin America, Israeli weapons are a good buy. In addition to being cheaper than comparable Western products†—Israeli skilled labor and research and development cost less than in the West—they have the versatility that increases their cost effectiveness. The Kfir jet performs "both fighter attack and interceptor missions which would *otherwise require an inventory of two or more specialized aircraft*" (emphasis added).[77] Marketing campaigns for the aircraft also stress that it can perform a variety of missions: in addition to its "primary task of attack in supporting land force advances and in destroying surface-to-air missile batteries and radars," it also has the "capability to fight in air combat and be fitted for reconnaissance." Its "low speed maneuverability in dog fighting will aid precision in ground attack missions." Elsewhere, the Kfir is billed as a

---

* According to Aaron Klieman, "Israeli diplomats are not above suggesting the purchase of its military goods as an acceptable and fair *quid pro quo* for using the near legendary strength of the pro-Israeli lobby in the Congress and its influence with the American Jewish community on behalf of the arms client" [*Israel's Global Reach: Arms Sales as Diplomacy* McLean, Va.: Pergamon-Brassey's, 1985, p. 41]. There have been a number of examples of the expectation, if not the suggestion. According to the *Washington Post* (13 August 1983) El Salvador hoped its close ties with Israel would induce the pro-Israel lobby in the United States to lend a "discreet hand" in congressional debates to push for higher U.S. military aid levels. Similarly, according to Israel Shahak (*Israel's Global Role: Weapons for Repression* [Belmont, Mass.: Arab-American University Graduates Inc., 1982], p. 20), the Chilean regime hoped that published photos of General Pinochet with high-ranking Israelis such as former Chief of Staff Mordechai Gur, along with Gur's statements that press reports of Pinochet's excesses were "not commensurate with reality," would help its standing with the United States. For Costa Rica see Shahak, *Israel's Global Role,* p. 199.

† According to Michael Shorr, general manager of Israel Military Industries (TA'AS), Israel has successfully competed with foreign arms manufacturers because it offers lower prices. However, the International Monetary Fund reports that low labor productivity and wage increases have resulted in a 28 percent rise in unit labor costs since 1979, which has had an impact on prices, making Israeli products less competitive than previously (cited in Klieman, *Israel's Global Reach,* p. 67).

"multi-role fighter-interceptor and attack weapons platform" with "versatile on-board avionics that *make possible immediate conversion from one mode to another*" (emphasis added). Similarly, sales literature for the Arava STOL notes that it "performs a variety of missions better and more economically than other aircraft," and that it is an effective substitute for a helicopter in many instances. After stressing its military capabilities, the advertisements add that it is "quickly convertible to transport configuration, and can accommodate 20 passengers in airliner comfort."[78] Aside from passenger service, other civilian functions mentioned are cargo transport, disaster relief, agricultural missions, search and rescue missions, flying clinic, and fighting forest fires. Similarly, the Westwind executive jet, essentially a long-range passenger plane, can be modified for marine reconnaissance, signal intelligence, antisubmarine warfare, or as an air-to-sea missile platform.[79]

The "Total Package" Approach and Other Benefits. The excellent performance of Israeli arms is not the entire story. The customer does not merely buy a weapon, but an entire package, the kind of personalized service less likely to be offered by the major suppliers. IAI prepares "heavy packages of support" for its products, including training pilots and mechanics both in Israel and in the client's country, organization of a maintenance system from scratch, development of stocking plans for spare parts, and demonstration of how the aircraft could be used in both military and civilian roles.[80] Sales contracts include on-call service on a long-term basis. Upon delivery, an area representative is assigned to assist in introducing a new system. As the sales literature points out, "These qualified personnel provide the operator with a source for nearby—and when necessary on-site—assistance in technical matters affecting operation and maintenance." The line between assistance in installation and orientation to new systems and advisory services is sometimes rather blurred. This works to Israel's advantage by reinforcing the notion that the purchaser of Israeli weapons also acquires Israeli experience and know-how— "Experience for Export" as the advertisement says. It is here that Israel's reputation for no-nonsense and effective solutions to internal unrest and terrorism as well as its own expertise in counterinsurgency methods serves its arms sales well. Even in certain Latin American countries known for their anti-Semitism and persecution of local Jews, Israel's macho image makes Israeli arms salesmen welcome.[81] The Israeli daily *Ma'ariv*, for example, quotes an arms merchant who "tells with pleasure about the welcome he and Brigadier General Yosef Kastel received in Paraguay after the Entebbe operation."[82] In contrast to the United States, which is perceived as overly fastidious and soft on communism, Israel is seen as knowing how to handle tough situations. The Contra leader, Adolfo Calero, making known his preferences concerning foreign assistance for the Nicaraguan rebels, stated: "We think the Israelis would be best because they have the technical experience."[83] More to the point, and reflecting an attitude widespread among the more hard-line elements of Latin America, a Salvadoran colonel in charge of counterinsurgency operations in northern El Salvador argued for an Israeli rather than a U.S. role, remarking: "The Americans know nothing. Don't forget they lost in Vietnam. The Israelis do know."[84]

A willingness to meet the special needs of customers is a hallmark of Israeli arms sales. Besides training and advisory services, other inducements to buy Israeli equipment include a willingness to share military technology and to enter into coproduction agreements. Thus, in April 1983 when Brazil was negotiating with Israel for the purchase of sophisticated missiles similar to France's Exocet, Israel offered the transfer of the technology contained in the weapon. According to Maximiano da Fonseca of Brazil, "this would include . . . the possibility for us to open up the missile and look inside,"[85] a situation that certainly would not have been available with the purchase of the French-made Exocet. Similarly, to induce Argentina to commit itself to the new Lavi fighter, Israel offered a co-production agreement for the plane.[86] Although the deal did not materialize, Argentina would not have received a similar offer from other leading arms producers. In another case IAI's maintenance and repair division, Bedek Aviation, won a $25 million contract for the maintenance of the Colombian air force's Mirages in the face of stiff competition from French and Spanish companies not only because its offer was cheaper,[87] but because it included the added incentive of providing for some local input.[88]

Israeli efficiency and ability to meet deadlines is also considered a valuable benefit. According to the Colombian daily *El Siglo*, it was mainly Israel's speed of delivery that was responsible for Colombia's decision to buy a squadron of Kfirs rather than French Mirage-5s.[89] Given Colombia's border conflict with Venezuela, and the latter's 1981 acquisition of twenty-four U.S. F–16s, the Colombian air force was under pressure to strengthen its defense capability. While France insisted upon nine months to satisfy the terms of the proposed contract, Israel offered to deliver the Kfirs in only two.[90]

Finally, Israel's no-questions-asked approach to arms sales and its absolute reliability as a supplier regardless of circumstances are also notable benefits. With the exception of discreet inquiries on behalf of the Jewish communities resident in Latin American countries, it has never displayed any wish to interfere in the local politics of the regimes to which it sells arms. As Israeli General Rahav'am Ze'evi remarked in 1977 when asked about sales to Latin American countries with serious human rights infractions: "the regimes in the various countries are the exclusive concern of the nations who live there."[91] More recently, when asked about El Salvador's human rights record, an Israeli Foreign Ministry spokesman said: "Israel doesn't distinguish between good governments and bad ones."[92] Thus, where other governments may hesitate to supply arms because of reluctance to be associated with countries having a history of human rights violations (Chile, Argentina, El Salvador, Guatemala, Paraguay, or Uruguay) or because of hesitancy to contribute to an arms escalation in a volatile situation (Argentina and Chile, Peru and Ecuador, Honduras and Nicaragua), Israel has no such constraints. "We sell to everyone," Foreign Minister Yitzhak Shamir declared. "That is, we don't sell to our enemies or to the Soviet bloc. Besides these exceptions, we have our own activities in the international markets alongside the Europeans and the Americans. We sell to governments—legal governments."[93] Thus, Israel's penetration of the Latin American market is closely connected to its ability to seize the opportunities created by international politics, notably U.S. human rights policies of the late 1970s and the arms embargo on Argentina following the Falklands/Malvinas War.

Constraints on Market Growth

Israel's Latin American customers, who are military-dominated, avowedly anticommunist, and far removed from the Arab-Israeli conflict, are less subject to the political considerations that affect certain customers elsewhere (such as Iran under Khomeini, the Phalangists of Lebanon, Colonel Mengistu's Ethiopia, and other sub-Saharan African states). This freedom from political constraints is particularly evident in the right-wing military dictatorships and the "pariah states." Romeo Lucas Garcia of Guatemala, Pinochet of Chile, and the military junta of Argentina did not seek international or domestic approbation. However, this situation is changing, not only with the growth of the debt crisis which makes nations more sensitive to international factors, but especially as the Latin American states return to democracy and civilian rule. Indeed, the effects of these changes are already being felt.

The greater risk of political fallout affecting arms sales in a democratic country with a free and vocal press and opposition can be seen in the case of Mexico. Despite Israel's energetic efforts to promote military cooperation,* its arms exports to Mexico have remained limited and not at all commensurate with the market's potential. The political delicacy surrounding the issue of Israeli arms transfers in a country that prides itself on its progressive,

---

* In 1977, for example, Israel mounted a major "industrial" exhibition in Mexico City showing products of fifty Israeli companies (*El Sol*, 7 March 1977). Its primary focus was military hardware, the IAI alone occupying more than 60 percent of the grounds, and the bulk of the "industrial equipment" ranged from planes to electronic and sophisticated military equipment (*Excelsior*, 29 December 1976; *El Sol*, 26 April 1977). The show was inaugurated by Mexican President José Lopez Portillo, and was followed by a special demonstration of various products for Mexico's military leaders (*Excelsior*, 27 April 1977).

revolutionary past was demonstrated in the uproar caused by the discovery of an IAI sales office in Mexico City in September 1978. The Mexican Socialist Workers Party (PST), after verifying information concerning the existence of the office which it had received from Marwan Tahbub (at the time, PLO representative in Mexico City),[94] convened a press conference to denounce the "IAI's Permanent Mission to Latin America." The sales office, which was completely staffed and guarded by Israelis (including a retired Israeli army general)[95] and equipped with thick electronic doors and closed-circuit television,[96] was discreetly set up in a quiet residential district of Mexico City.* The Mexican Foreign Ministry and other federal agencies claimed to have been unaware of its existence.[97] In the furor which followed, *Excelsior*, a leading Mexican daily, charged in a September 13, 1978 editorial entitled "Mexico: A Trampoline, Reinforcer of Dictatorships" that the IAI mission had been established "over the shoulders of the high court" and that it was arranging sizeable arms sales for Latin America's unpopular governments.[98] Although the Israeli embassy in Mexico initially denied any knowledge of the office,[99] it was obliged in the face of compelling evidence to acknowledge it. The embassy pointed out, however, that the office had no connection with the Israeli government† [100] and that it was the responsibility of David Marcus Katz, a private arms merchant operating out of Mexico.‡ Shortly thereafter, the office disappeared and the political storm subsided.[101]

Similarly, Mexico's last-minute decision against buying twenty-four Kfirs in January 1981,[102] ostensibly because they were "too costly and too difficult to maintain,"[103] in fact, is believed to have been politically motivated. As Israeli officials

---

* The address was 124 de las Calles de Horacio, Col. Palanco, Mexico D.F. (business card of Yohay Remetz).

† As noted in Chapter 2, Israeli arms sales must be approved by the government. The Ministerial Committee on Weapons Transfers reviews and approves on behalf of the government "every single arms package for export" (Klieman, *Israel's Global Reach*, p. 99).

‡ See the section, The Marketing Network, in this chapter for a discussion of Katz's activities.

pointed out at the time, "the Kfir is the cheapest aircraft of its kind in the world."[104] Moreover, Mexican Defense Minister General Felix Galvan had headed a sixteen-member delegation including the deputy chief-of-staff and senior army officers to inspect the Kfir and other equipment as guests of Prime Minister Menachem Begin.[105] The general was reportedly "very satisfied with what he had seen."[106] During a dinner in his honor, he expressed confidence that Israel and Mexico could cooperate in joint projects important for Mexico's national security.[107] However, internal political opposition to the proposed deal was reportedly strong.[108] Mexico could ill afford the publicity that would have resulted from having been the first country to buy the Kfir, running the risk of harming its relations with the Arab countries.[109] The dozen U.S. F-5 supersonic jet fighters purchased instead[110] did not involve the same political risks and were therefore preferable.

It was, likewise, for political as well as economic reasons that Israel's laborious six-year negotiations with Mexico for the building of a joint aircraft industry in the state of Yucatan broke down.[111] The plant was to overhaul Israeli-built aircraft in Latin America, service other aircraft, assemble the Arava, and manufacture spare parts.[112] The high-level negotiations, which even involved Mexico's President Luis Echeverria, began in 1973 and reached an advanced stage before they were ended when Mexico signed an agreement with Spain to assemble the Aviocar C-212 transport aircraft domestically—again, a less controversial choice of partner.

As the largest regional arms market, Latin America is an appropriate place to study Israel's arms export policy. By focusing on three cases in the region—Ecuador, Argentina, and Central America—each of which provides a different perspective, the factors contributing to the rise of Israel's weapons sales, as well as the vulnerability of its arms policy and the constraints on further growth are clearly demonstrated. By illustrating the impact of U.S. policy (thwarting, inhibiting, or facilitating) on Israel's arms sales, these cases also bring into sharp relief the extent to which Israel's success or failure depends on the United States.

NOTES

1. *La Opinion*, 27 March 1974; *El Dia*, 16 November 1978; *World Business*, 6 October 1980; Dan Goodgame, "Israel Asks U.S. to Finance Sales to Latin America," *Miami Herald*, 13 December 1982.
2. Edward Cody, "Sharon to Discuss Arms Sales to Honduras," *Washington Post*, 7 December 1982.
3. *The Israel Economist*, August 1982, cited in Aaron Klieman, *Israel's Global Reach: Arms Sales As Diplomacy* (McLean, Va.: Pergamon-Brassey's, 1985), p. 132.
4. Daniel Southerland, "Israeli Economy Said to Depend Heavily on Export of Weapons," *Washington Post*, 22 March 1985.
5. Aaron Klieman, *Israeli Arms Sales: Perspectives and Prospects* (Tel Aviv: Jaffee Center for Strategic Studies, 1984), paper no. 24, p. 17.
6. Walid Khalidi, *From Haven to Conquest* (Beirut: Institute for Palestine Studies, 1971), p. 841.
7. Jorge Garcia-Granados, *The Birth of Israel: The Drama As I Saw It* (New York: Alfred A. Knopf, 1948), pp. 288–289.
8. Edy Kaufman, Yoram Shapiro, and Joel Barromi, *Israel-Latin American Relations* (New Brunswick, N.J.: Transaction Books, 1979), pp. 184–185.
9. *Jerusalem Post*, 16 December 1982.
10. D.V. Segre, "The Philosophy and Practice of Israel's International Cooperation," in *Israel in the Third World*, eds. Michael Curtis and Susan Aurelia Gitleson (New Brunswick, N.J.: Transaction Books, 1976), p. 11.
11. *Israel Government Yearbook, 1969–70* (Jerusalem: Central Office of Information, 1970), p. 239.
12. Segre, "Philosophy and Practice," p. 10.
13. Kaufman et al., *Latin American Relations*, p. 117.
14. *Ibid.*, p. 97.
15. *Ibid.*, p. 118.
16. *Ya* (Madrid), 14 December 1974, p. 16.
17. *Ibid.*
18. *Latin America Weekly Report*, 9 October 1981, p. 8.
19. Bishara Bahbah, "Israel and the Need for Secure Oil Suppliers," *Al-Fajr Palestinian Weekly*, 28 September 1984, p. 6.
20. *Petroleum Intelligence Weekly* (PIW), 28 May 1979, p. 10.
21. *Financial Times* (London), 24 October 1980, p. 12. The British Government, for example, reaffirmed, in 1982, its refusal to sell oil to Israel [*Jewish Telegraphic Agency*, 11 February 1982].
22. *Oilgram*, 18 January 1980, p. 2.
23. *Jerusalem Post*, 27 October 1982; *Latin America Weekly Report*, 24 December 1982, p. 11.
24. Klieman, *Israeli Arms Sales*, p. 45.
25. Goodgame, "Israel Asks U.S.," pp. 1A, 14A.
26. Kaufman et al., *Latin American Relations* p. 105.
27. *The Palestine Question Yearbook, 1975* (Arabic), (Beirut: Institute for Palestine Studies, 1976), pp. 588–89.
28. *Boston Sunday Globe*, 30 May 1982, p. 11.

29. Andrew Pierre, *The Global Politics of Arms Sales* (Princeton: Princeton University Press, 1982), p. 235.

30. Stockholm International Peace Research Institute (SIPRI), *World Armament and Disarmament Yearbook 1982* (London: Taylor and Francis, 1982), p. 404.

31. Pierre, *Global Politics of Arms Sales*, pp. 235–236.

32. Kaufman et al., *Latin American Relations*, p. 51.

33. *Ibid.*, p. 50.

34. Ignacio Klich, "Guatemala's Back-Door Arms Deals," *8 Days*, 13 March 1982.

35. Israel Ministry of Foreign Affairs, *Israel and Latin America: A Summary of the International Cooperation Program*, (Jerusalem: Ministry of Foreign Affairs, 1970), cited in *Le Monde Diplomatique*, October 1982.

36. *New York Times*, 15 October 1962, cited in *Le Monde Diplomatique*, October 1982.

37. Kaufman et al., *Latin American Relations* p. 107.

38. *Le Monde Diplomatique*, October 1982.

39. Kaufman et al., *Latin American Relations*, p. 104.

40. *Ibid.*

41. *Ibid.*, p. 108.

42. *Ibid.*

43. Penny Lernoux, "Israeli Arms Aimed at Terrorists," *National Catholic Reporter,* 25 December 1981, p. 23.

44. Kaufman et al., *Latin American Relations*, p. 108.

45. Klich, "Guatemala's Back-Door Arms Deals."

46. David Markus, "Brazil's President Says He Holds Israel in High Esteem," *Jewish Telegraphic Agency*, 19 April 1982.

47. SIPRI, *Yearbook 1982*, pp. 396–397.

48. Moshe Lichtman, "Israel's Weapons Exports," *Monitin*, July 1983.

49. *New York Times*, 7 February 1982.

50. Lernoux, "Who's Who of dictators obtain arms from Israel," *National Catholic Reporter,* 25 December 1981.

51. Lichtman, "Weapons Exports."

52. Edy Kaufman, "The View from Jerusalem," *Washington Quarterly* 7 (Fall 1984): 46.

53. Lichtman, "Weapons Exports."

54. *Ibid.*

55. *Davar*, 13–14 November 1979, cited in Israel Shahak, *Israel's Global Role: Weapons for Repression* (Belmont, Mass.: Association of Arab-American University Graduates, Inc., 1982), p. 17.

56. Lichtman, "Weapons Exports."

57. *Davar*, 13–14 November 1979, cited in Shahak, *Israel's Global Role*, p. 17.

58. Klieman, *Global Reach*, p. 118.

59. Emmanuel Rosen, "Lonely Wolves in the Arms Jungle," *Ma'ariv*, 12 August 1982.

60. *Ibid.*

61. *Ibid.*

62. Klieman, *Global Reach*, p. 124.

63. *Latin America Weekly Report*, 24 December 1982, p. 10.

64. Southerland, "Depend on Export."
65. Stockholm International Peace Research Institute (SIPRI), *World Armament and Disarmament Yearbook 1981* (London: Taylor and Francis Ltd., 1982), p. 114.
66. *Jerusalem Post,* 29 May 1981.
67. *Jerusalem Post,* 23 May 1982.
68. Richard Goldman and Murray Rubenstein, *Shield of David: An Illustrated History of the Israeli Air Force* (Englewood Cliffs, N.J.: Prentice Hall, 1978), pp. 115–116.
69. *New York Times,* 7 February 1982.
70. "Israeli Paratroopers Increase Mobility with C-130 Training," *Aviation Week and Space Technology,* 23 February 1976, pp. 22-23; *Aviation Week and Space Technology,* 19 July 1976, p. 118.
71. "Israel: Experience for export," Special advertising section, *Aviation Week and Space Technology,* 8 October 1979.
72. Amnon Abramovich, "Israel Stops Its Arms Advertisements," *Ma'ariv,* 20 October 1982.
73. *Jerusalem Post,* 13 June 1983.
74. *Christian Science Monitor,* 27 December 1982.
75. "Experience for export," *Aviation Week and Space Technology,* 8 October 1979.
76. Pierre, *Global Politics of Arms Sales,* p. 243.
77. IAI advertisement, *Aviation Week and Space Technology,* 9 July 1976, p. 118.
78. *Aviation Week and Space Technology,* 26 July 1976, pp. 22-23.
79. Klieman, *Global Reach,* p. 75.
80. *Aviation Week and Space Technology,* 23 February 1976.
81. Emmanuel Rosen, "Lonely Wolves in the Arms Jungle," *Ma'ariv,* 12 August 1982.
82. *Ibid.*
83. *Los Angeles Times,* 16 April 1984.
84. *Le Monde,* 19 February 1985, cited in *Israeli Foreign Affairs* 1, no. 5 (1985); also cited in Reuters radio broadcast on Latin America (Buenos Aires) 1424 GMT, 22 January 1985.
85. *Boston Globe,* 18 April 1983, p. 20.
86. *Al-Quds* (Arabic, Jerusalem), 15 May 1983, p. 8.
87. *Latin America Weekly Report,* 5 September 1980, p. 7.
88. *Latin American Regional Reports, Andean Group,* 22 January 1982, p. 1.
89. *Jewish Telegraphic Agency,* 31 December 1981.
90. *Ibid.*
91. *Yediot Ahronot* (Hebrew, Tel Aviv), 1 April 1977.
92. *Excelsior,* 4 August 1983, cited in *Israeli Foreign Affairs,* January 1985, p. 2.
93. Larry Remer, "Israeli Weapons Industry Goes Boom," *Los Angeles Times,* 29 July 1981.
94. Marwan Tahbub, former PLO representative in Mexico City, Mexico and PLO Ambassador to Managua, Nicaragua, interview 9 and 15 August 1982.
95. Mexican Workers Socialist Party (PST), press release, 9 September 1978; *El Dia,* 14 November 1978.
96. *El Dia,* 14 November 1978.

97. *Ibid.*, PST, press release, 3 September 1978.
98. *Excelsior*, 13 September 1978.
99. *Yediot Ahronot*, 10 September 1978; *Ma'ariv*, 17 September 1978.
100. Tahbub interview.
101. Silvia Sandoval, member of the Central Committee responsible for the international relations of the PST, Mexico City, 3 August 1982.
102. *Jerusalem Post*, 16 January 1981.
103. *Jerusalem Post*, 26 January 1981.
104. *Ibid.*
105. *Jewish Telegraphic Agency*, 13 January 1981.
106. *Jerusalem Post*, 16 January 1981.
107. *Ibid.*
108. Sandoval interview.
109. *Latin America Weekly Report*, 10 April 1981, p. 6.
110. *Ibid.*
111. Kaufman et al., *Latin American Relations*, p. 106.
112. *Financial Times*, 14 June 1977, p. 7; "Latin America and the Middle East," *Middle East Economic Digest* (MEED), *Special Report*, September 1981, p. 23; *Latin America Weekly Report*, 9 October 1981, p. 8.

CHAPTER FOUR

South American Case Studies: Ecuador and Argentina

E cuador is one of Israel's oldest friends in Latin America. In 1963 Ecuador and Bolivia were the first Latin American countries to adopt Israel's Nahal-type military-agricultural programs, which introduced the use of armed forces for agricultural tasks. The program was intended to provide a model for civic action and a way of tackling national problems. More importantly, since the military had recently ousted the constitutional government, the program's aim of building a positive and constructive image of the armed forces was particularly relevant.[1] Seven years after the program was inaugurated, an Ecuadoran military publication wrote of the Nahal program:

> The State of Israel, through the Units of Nahal, shows us a new road in military organization and philosophy. It is showing us that the armed forces can widen the scope of their activities, for the benefit of the rural population, with a humanitarian mission . . . and even more, it has demonstrated to us that the soldier-farmer is the one who defends his farm with greater eagerness and heroism, and while defending his land, his family, he is defending his fatherland.[2]

High-level military visits to Israel began in the mid-1960s, and Ecuador was among the twelve Latin American countries that sent youths to Israel for training. The entire graduating class of Ecuador's elite military academy went to Israel in 1965.[3] Senior defense officers visited in 1971, the chief of staff in 1974,[4] and the defense minister in May 1984.[5] Ecuadoran officers also attended Nahal officer courses in Israel, and in January 1970 the Israeli and Ecuadoran defense ministries co-sponsored a conference in Quito on "The Role of the Military in Agricultural Development," which was attended by representatives of twelve Latin American countries.[6] That same year, Ecuador's General Gustavo Banderas declared: "For us small countries, Israel is an inspiring example of courage and faith, of ability and high moral standards."[7]

Ecuador has had a military regime only intermittently, but the influence of the military remains preponderant even during periods of civilian rule. In this country, with a particularly unstable history in the twenty-three years between 1925 and 1948, there were no less than twenty-two heads of state, none of whom completed a full term in office. As a result, the military has stepped in on a number of occasions. The junta that seized power in 1963 stayed in power for three years and that which came to power in 1972[8] ruled until "el retorno," the restoration of civilian rule in 1979. Since then, the military has continued to keep a close watch on the country's affairs. Following strikes and rioting over government-imposed price increases in October 1982, it was reported that only stern warnings from the United States prevented another military coup.[9] Nonetheless, Ecuador differs from its neighbors, Colombia and Peru, in an absence of serious guerrilla activities and a general lack of political extremism.

The armed forces of Ecuador are comprised of approximately 40,000 men, of whom some 30,000 are in the army, which includes several infantry brigades, one armored brigade, and one special forces brigade. Since 1960, the military share of the budget has more than doubled,[10] reflecting a trend toward militarization that is characteristic of the area and which is encouraged by Ecuador's long-simmering dispute with Peru. The armed forces are supplied mainly by the United States (heavy tanks and armored vehicles, submarines, patrol boats, support ships), France (combat aircraft, light tanks), and West Germany (submarines, fast patrol boats with surface-to-surface missiles).[11]

Israel has sold Ecuador arms since the 1970s. In 1976 official sources in Quito indicated that over a three-year period the country had bought Israeli arms, including rockets, explosives, ammunition, and Uzi submachine guns, worth up to $200 million,[12] a substantial amount when compared to Israel's other arms exports at the time. Deliveries of Israeli-built Arava planes began in 1975, and fifteen in all were supplied by 1979. Israeli supplies also included Gabriel MK–III missiles (see Table 8).

The sale that attracted the most attention occurred in 1976. Frustrated in efforts to obtain permission to buy U.S. Northrop F–5s,[13] Ecuador became the first country to order the Kfir, the

first Israeli-designed and produced jet fighter, which was completed in 1974. But the fact that the plane was equipped with U.S.-
designed General Electric J–79 engines, which were built in
Israel under a G.E. license, made the proposed $150 million deal
subject to U.S. governmental approval under the U.S. Arms
Export Act. In his first major decision on arms controls, President
Carter vetoed the proposed sale as part of his policy to reduce
worldwide conventional arms transfers and to prevent the proliferation of sophisticated military equipment in regions where
they did not yet exist.

Israel's stated aim in producing the Kfir was to avoid overde-
pendence on the United States for front-line fighters. Assurances
were given that there was no intention of exporting the aircraft,
which for the first five or six years was to be used exclusively to
build Israel's own inventory.[14] Nonetheless, Israel professed
shock when Carter blocked the sale.[15]

When the U.S. ban on the proposed sale was announced in
mid-February 1977, IAI President Al Schwimmer flew to Ecuador where he was given until March 15 to persuade Washington to reverse its decision. While he was in Washington for
talks with the Carter administration and the Pentagon, 500 employees of the IAI demonstrated in front of the U.S. embassy in
Tel Aviv[16] carrying placards reading "Bread and Work."[17] Meanwhile, the Israeli daily *Ha'aretz* warned on 7 March 1977 of
massive layoffs if the United States prevented the deal from going
through. According to the article, some 4,000 IAI employees
were working on the Kfir production line, of whom "1,500 were
earmarked for immediate dismissal, if the Americans had not
reached agreement with Israel."[18] To give an idea of the importance Israel attached to the sale, Prime Minister Yitzhak Rabin,
himself, stated at the time: "It is not that we seek to become a
merchant of arms; we need military exports for our own defense
capability."[19]

Later in 1977 Israel appealed the U.S. decision on the
grounds that the USSR was supplying Peru with SU–20 fighters
and surface-to-air missiles. Because "advanced and sophisticated

aircraft" had already been introduced to the region, the Kfir sale should be allowed as well.[20] Despite the emotional atmosphere surrounding the case, the United States held firm. This was disappointing for Israel because it had anticipated brisk sales for the aircraft. IAI officials later claimed that President Carter's action had resulted in a loss of over $1 billion in arms sales to Latin America alone.[21] In an effort to compensate for the loss of the $150 million deal[22] and to mollify Israel's friends in Congress, the president added $285 million in economic assistance to the 1978 U.S. aid package to Israel.[23]

With the Kfir unavailable, Ecuador turned its attention to the purchase of the Israeli-made Nesher, a pre-Kfir modification of the Mirage-3 and -5, which is capable of carrying air-to-air and air-to-ground missiles. Because the Nesher was equipped with a French Atar 3C engine produced in Israel without a license,* there were no export problems. Ecuador ordered twenty-four Nesher jets and began taking delivery in 1977.[24]

With the return to constitutional rule in 1979 and the installation of a democratically elected president, Jaime Roldos, Ecuador's relations with Israel cooled somewhat. Roldos enthusiastically supported Nicaragua's Sandinista government and the opposition in El Salvador and gave his direct personal support to defend human rights in Latin America. During Roldos' presidency Quito became the seat of the newly formed Latin American Association for Human Rights, of which he was the honorary chairman.[25] Roldos was also known to be sympathetic to the Palestinians. Indeed, it was during his term that the Palestine Liberation Organization (PLO) representative in Peru, Issam Bseisso, traveled to Quito to look into the possibility of opening a PLO office there.[26] During his visit, the first by a PLO official, Bseisso met with members of parliament, Foreign Minister Alfredo Pareja, and the undersecretary of state, who told Bseisso

---

* The engine was built from plans obtained from Israeli sympathizers in France and Switzerland. An engineer employed in the Sulzer plant in Switzerland that was building the engines under Snecma license delivered twenty cartons of plans to Israel via West Germany, for which he was paid $200,000. (*Aviation Week and Space Technology*, 16 August 1976).

that he hoped a PLO office would be opened in Quito within a year.[27] As an interesting comment on the army's power even under civilian rule and the strength of Israeli ties with the country's military, a subsequent recommendation by an Ecuadoran parliamentary Foreign Relations Committee to the government that the PLO be authorized to open an information office in the capital was not acted upon.[28] The Ecuadoran National Security Council, which determines foreign policy, blocked the proposal. Although the council is headed by the president (a civilian), and includes the archbishop and the foreign minister, it is dominated by the military, which occupies the majority of the seats and thus has effective veto power. According to members of journalistic circles in Quito, Israel used its considerable influence with the military to block the proposal.[29]

Israeli-Ecuadoran relations were quickly restored to earlier levels with the January 1981 outbreak of armed hostilities between Ecuador and Peru. The territorial dispute between the two countries dates back to the 19th century. Marked by border incidents and quarrels, the situation reached a climax in 1941 when Peru pushed northward and occupied a vast tract of land claimed by Ecuador. Subsequently, a peace conference hastily convened by the United States resulted in the Protocol of Rio, which was guaranteed by the United States, Argentina, Chile, and Brazil. Under the treaty, Ecuador relinquished most of the "Amazonian Triangle," 200,000 square kilometers of dense jungle, to Peru. However, Ecuador considered that it had agreed to the protocol under duress and never really accepted the new frontier. Late in 1980 Ecuadoran troops moved into the disputed area and set up cemented defense positions. On January 22, 1981, the vastly superior Peruvian forces* began strafing the positions. Before a cease-fire was arranged on February 3, over 200 people had died, mainly as the result of air strikes.[30] During

---

* With 95,000 men, the Peruvian army outnumbered Ecuador's by three to one. Peru's military was also considerably better equipped, and its air force possessed 120 combat aircraft, against Ecuador's fifty-five. (Hugh O'Shaughnessy, "Ecuador: Suspicion Behind Foreign Relations," *Financial Times* [London] 10 August 1981.)

the fighting, Israel shipped much-needed arms and ammunition to Ecuador[31] while simultaneously offering to sell Peru sophisticated radar systems.*[32]

This brief war rekindled Ecuador's interest in obtaining its own Kfir jets. In October 1980, several weeks before the U.S. presidential elections, in a move probably not divorced from political considerations, President Carter approved an Israeli request to present the Kfir[33] for sale in Venezuela and Colombia.[34] While not a sales approval, it did signal a possible change in American foreign policy. This initial change of approach became a reality under Carter's successor.

Shortly after President Reagan took office, Israel resubmitted its application for permission to sell Kfirs to Ecuador. The application was approved in record time—less than thirty days[35]—and in March 1981 the State Department quietly notified Israel that it would not object to the transaction. When the sale was finally concluded, it was not made public at the request of the Israeli government,[36] doubtless for fear of offending Peru so soon after the brief war between the two states. Indeed, when Ecuadoran newspapers announced the sale in August, Peru reportedly was indignant. Two months later both U.S and Israeli sources confirmed the sale, which included twelve Kfir fighters with an option to purchase twelve more.†[37] Thus, five years after

---

* According to a number of individuals interviewed by the author in Quito (including a prominent TV journalist, Raoul Borja 30 August 1982. Carlos Rodriguez, president of the *Comite del Pueblo*, 27 August 1982; Jaime Galarza Zavala, noted author, 27 August 1982; and a colonel in the Ecuadoran military), Israel offered to put an undisclosed number of Kfir jets, pilots, and commandos at Ecuador's disposal. When questioned about the report, Antonio Lara, deputy chairman of the Ecuadoran Parliament's Foreign Relations Committee, refused to address the issue of the involvement of any Israeli pilots or commandos but did confirm that Ecuador had rejected the offer of Kfir jets at the time because they were "unreasonably over-priced" (interview, Quito, Ecuador, 27 August 1982)

† According to the *Latin America Weekly Report* (25 September 1981), Israeli Foreign Minister Yitzhak Shamir during his September 1981 visit to Ecuador offered to swap the Kfir fighters for oil. The U.S. General Accounting Office report estimated the purchase price for the twelve Kfirs at $196 million ("U.S. Assistance to the State of Israel," [uncensored draft, Washington, D.C., April 1983], p. 49).

the initial order, Ecuador became the first country to buy the plane, although only half the twenty-four provided for under the original contract were purchased.[38]

Less than a year after the sale of the Kfirs, another Israeli arms transaction with Ecuador received a great deal of publicity. In May 1982 at the height of the Falklands/Malvinas fighting, an Ecuadoran plane carrying high impact bombs and ammunition was seized while refueling in New York. U.S. federal officials had discovered that the permit required under U.S. law to ship military equipment through the United States had not been obtained.[39] Given the widely publicized reports of Israel's role in rearming Argentina,[40] which was under a U.S arms embargo, the presence of Israeli nationals among the crew of the Ecuatoriana flight aroused suspicion, as did the seemingly unnecessary expense of sending arms to Ecuador by plane rather than ship. However, both Israeli Defense Minister Ariel Sharon and Ecuatoriana president Miguel Castillo insisted that the arms were destined for Ecuador,[41] and the plane was allowed to proceed. Although comparatively small in quantity, later arms deals have represented, according to an Ecuadoran Foreign Ministry official, "a great amount of money for Ecuador."[42]

Israeli and Ecuadoran military cooperation extends to a number of other areas. Israel is reported to have a technical assistance agreement to service the Israeli-made weapons in Ecuador's arms inventory,[43] including the Arava, Nesher, and Kfir planes. It also has a contract to service, all the way from Tel Aviv, the aircraft of Ecuador's national airlines company, Ecuatoriana.[44] It was Israel, in fact, that supplied the nucleus of the airline in late 1974 with three Boeing 720 jets reconditioned by the IAI.[45] The sale represented Israel's first major deal with the Ecuadoran Defense Ministry, which has had direct control of the national airline since the early 1970s, and included both maintenance and pilot training. That the servicing contract, which is still in effect, was awarded more for political than for commercial reasons is clear. Prior to Israel's involvement, Ecuatoriana had a profitable maintenance shop in Miami which also serviced planes of other airlines, but the Miami shop closed down after Israel was awarded the contract. According to a former financial vice president of Ecuatoriana, the Ecuadoran Defense Ministry's decision reflected "their lack of genuine concern over whether the airline makes money or not."[46] Israel is also reported to have been involved in Ecuador's arms industry since the mid-1970s. At that time, in what was believed to be an arms-for-oil swap, Israel bid on a contract to build an arms factory in Ecuador, a deal convenient for Ecuador insofar as it had difficulties financing the project.[47]

Although few Ecuadoran officials have discussed military cooperation with Israel, Pablo Yanez, the director of bilateral relations in Ecuador's Foreign Ministry, acknowledged that Israel has provided assistance for one of Ecuador's military industries, Direccion d' Industrias del Ejercito (DINE).[48] Other sources have pointed out Israeli involvement in another arms factory, Fabrica Militar-Ecuatoriana (FAMA)[49] which produces clothing, helmets, small arms, and other necessities for Ecuador's armed forces. Both FAMA and DINE have benefited from Israeli expertise and technology. However, the extent of Israel's involvement in both enterprises is not publicly known.

Ecuadoran sources maintain that the military advisory role of Israel dates back to the 1960s,[50] and that it includes instruction of government security forces[51] and a heavy involvement with the air force.[52] Advisors are also reported to have trained the Ecuadoran military in conventional warfare and counterinsurgency tactics.[53]

The most outstanding incident concerning the Israeli military advisory role reached the press in 1977. On March 22, 23, and 28 the Israeli daily *Ha'aretz*, followed by other publications, reported that a group of Israelis acting in a private capacity had approached a number of Latin American countries, including Ecuador, with an offer to supply ultramodern military equipment and the services of Israeli military advisors to help them combat terrorism. These citizens included Rahav'am Ze'evi, a retired Israeli general; Betzalel Mizrahi, a contractor from Tel Aviv with links to organized crime; Haim Topol, an internationally known actor; and a former Mossad agent. While the reports are unclear as to whether the contacts were initiated by the Ecuadoran government or the Israeli group, General Ze'evi and Haim Topol apparently met with an Ecuadoran minister. General Ze'evi affirmed that he had discussed his intentions with "a great number of involved personalities" in Israel and that Prime Minister Rabin was aware of the project. According to General Ze'evi, any proposed project would be screened by Israeli government officials who would have the right to veto it. In fact, General Ze'evi was still on the government payroll at that time, having recently resigned as the prime minister's advisor on antiterrorism.[54]

As a result of the stir created by the *Ha'aretz* articles, General Ze'evi granted an interview to the newspaper *Yediot Ahronot*, which appeared on April 1, 1977, to explain his motives. In addition to bringing in needed foreign currency, he felt the project would provide employment for security specialists who were having difficulty finding jobs suited to their skills upon completing service with the Israeli Defense Forces (IDF) or with the Security Services (Shin Bet).

Like many countries in Latin America, Ecuador has been hard hit by financial problems. The economic boom of the 1970s collapsed with the sharp decline in oil prices in the early 1980s. Ecuador's foreign debt in 1985 stood at about $7.1 billion[55] while debt servicing was costing the government well over $900 million annually.[56] Considering the high unemployment and gross income disparities, the austerity measures enacted to curb inflation increased the already widespread frustration. In the light of the resulting fear of radicalization and internal unrest (seemingly borne out by the strikes and riots of October 1982 and March 1983), it is not surprising that Ecuador balanced its longstanding friendship with Israel with other needs.

Thus, Ecuador has looked increasingly to its Arab partners in the Organization of Petroleum Exporting Countries (OPEC), which it joined in 1973, for assistance. This option was made easier by the fact that Ecuador, which sees itself as the victim of Peru's territorial aggressions, was disturbed by the aggressive policies of Israeli Prime Minister Menachem Begin[57] and later by the invasion of Lebanon. According to a high-level official in

Ecuador's Foreign Ministry, a decision was reached defining the country's primary interest with the Arab world as being in the financial field.[58] Quito has reportedly been conducting negotiations with a number of Arab countries to arrange for a loan of several hundred million dollars.[59] Kuwait, according to Ecuadoran officials, has shown interest in providing financial support in the area of infrastructure and has also indicated that it is willing to open lines of credit to Ecuador.[60] Finally, Kuwait, along with Shell Oil Co., has reportedly expressed interest in helping Ecuador search for more oil.[61]

Unquestionably, the possibility of this assistance accounts for Ecuador's curious position of denying oil sales to Israel while publicly stating its willingness to do so. Thus, in August 1982 Ecuador's undersecretary of state for political affairs, Ambassador Hernan Veintimilla, stated that Ecuador would sell oil to any country, with the exception of South Africa, willing to pay an equitable price, "whether it was destined to Israel or the Soviet Union."[62] But official records covering the period from 1972 to 1981 of Ecuador's state oil company, Corporacion Estatal Petrolera Ecuatoriana (CEPE), reveal no oil sales to Israel.[63] Ambassador Veintimilla himself indicated that Israel was not buying oil from Ecuador. Discrepancies in the claim are numerous, however. In 1980 the newly appointed Ecuadoran ambassador to Israel expressed his country's willingness to increase its oil shipments to Israel.[64] A few years later, Xavier Lasso, former vice director of CEPE's foreign marketing office, revealed in an interview that Ecuador had been selling oil to Israel through intermediaries,[65] and more specifically in one case through a U.S. company called Fuel Oil Trading, which concluded a three-year contract with Ecuador in February 1980 for the supply of 15,000 barrels a day. In addition, reports indicated the existence of an Ecuadoran-Israeli oil-for-arms-swap in 1977.[66]

Despite improved relations with various Arab states, Israel's ties with Ecuador's military remain strong—especially since the shift to the right that followed President Roldos' death in a plane crash in 1981 and continued with the inauguration of Leon Febres Cordero, leader of the conservative Social Christian Party, in

August 1984. Ecuador's defense minister visited Israel in May 1984.[67] Furthermore, Ecuador's recent arms purchases from Israel have included Barak antimissile missiles for its navy and twelve Israeli Kfir jets, which now constitute the vanguard of the Ecuadoran air force.[68] Domestic tension and fear of an eventual armed insurgency movement (which resulted in increased U.S. military aid for national security or counterinsurgency activities)[69] are among the reasons given for the purchase. The sale may also serve to strengthen Israel's more traditional active role in the country.

Argentina

Whereas arms sales to Ecuador were built on solid relations between the two countries and particularly those between their military establishments, arms sales to Argentina were principally the result of the vicissitudes of international politics. Indeed, it was largely because of U.S. arms policies and the boycott of weapons transfers by the Western powers following the Falklands/Malvinas War that Israel was able to penetrate the Argentine market. By 1981 Israel was supplying 14 to 17 percent of Argentina's total arms imports.[70] Products were chiefly heavy and sophisticated military items such as aircraft and missiles, because Argentina has its own arms industry (ranking seventh among third world arms producers) that manufactures equipment ranging from warships, armored vehicles, and rockets to a wide selection of small arms.[71]

Argentina established diplomatic ties with Israel almost immediately following the creation of the state and was the first Latin American country to open a legation there. Moreover, it has long been Israel's largest trading partner in Latin America, being Israel's "foremost and steadiest supplier of meat since 1948,"[72] with the trade deficit reaching $67 million in Argentina's favor in 1979 compared to $32 million in 1978.[73] But relations were never warm. In fact, they were minimal until Argentina's emergence in the late 1970s as Israel's most important arms client, accounting for 25 percent of its total sales.[74] Indeed, more so than with any other country, these relations could be reduced almost exclusively to the military dimension.

Like many countries in the region, Argentina until recently had an inordinate need for weapons. Dominated by the military even during most periods of nominally civilian rule since the 1930s, the country was also embroiled in taxing territorial disputes and plagued by internal unrest and armed opposition. The 1970s marked an upsurge of activity on both domestic and external fronts, reflected in the growth of Argentine military expenditures by over 50 percent from 1970 to 1980.[75]

Runaway inflation, declining production, and overall economic deterioration (resulting from rapid industrialization at the expense of agricultural development and exacerbated by the demagogic policies of Juan Peron) had given rise to social unrest and political turbulence. After the military relinquished its grip in 1973 and the Peronists returned to power, factionalism and violence reached new heights. Extremists of both the right and left engaged in terrorism, with the government of Juan Peron, and then of his widow Isabel, powerless to stop the violence despite emergency decrees and the declaration of a state of siege. On March 24, 1976, the military intervened for the sixth time in less than a half century in an effort to end the chaos.* A "campaign against terrorism" of unprecedented violence was unleashed. Thousands of "leftist terrorists" were rounded up by Argentine security forces and never heard from again. By 1980 the opposition had been largely silenced, but the number of the *desaparecidos* (the disappeared ones) had reached some 15,000 to 20,000.†[76] Reflecting this massive government effort was the fact that from 1970 to 1980 the number of police and paramilitary forces in Argentina doubled, while the armed forces as a whole increased by only 35 percent.[77]

---

* The Argentine military dislodged constitutional governments in 1930, 1943, 1955, 1962, 1966, and 1976.

† These are the unofficial figures as reported by Amnesty International, Americas Watch, the Washington Office on Latin America, and other human rights groups. The present Argentine government, in civil trials against the former regime, cites the number of *desaparecidos* as 9,000.

Externally, Argentina's longstanding territorial disputes were rekindled during the same period. Argentina had been at odds with Chile over the demarcation of the border dividing the two countries at the southern tip of the continent. In particular, the quarrel involved possession of three islands in the Beagle Channel (claimed by Argentina but under the jurisdiction of Chile) and control of the potential mineral and fishing resources in the maritime economic zone surrounding the disputed islands.[78] In 1971 Argentina and Chile agreed to submit their quarrel to arbitration by the International Court of Justice at The Hague, and the following year signed the General Treaty on the Legal Solution of Disputes. Nonetheless, when the court gave the three islands to Chile under the 1977 arbitration award, which was confirmed by Great Britain as was required under the 1971 arbitration agreement, Argentina rejected the ruling. Both countries deployed their armed forces along their borders and embarked upon a serious armament policy.[79] (The dispute was finally resolved in 1985 by a Vatican-mediated agreement that gave the islands to Chile but limited its maritime rights to the Cape Horn area.)

Just about that time, Argentina was in particular need of weapons, but its relations with the United States, hitherto its largest arms supplier, began to sour. The atrocities attributed to the military junta were such that the newly installed Carter administration with its emphasis on human rights could not but react. In 1978, despite Buenos Aires' anger over what it considered U.S. attempts to influence its internal affairs, President Carter decided to restrict military assistance and sales to Argentina.

For Israel, President Carter's ban on military credits to Argentina and the country's need for weapons for the Beagle Channel dispute could not have come at a better time. Until then, the only major recorded arms transaction with Argentina had been the 1976 sale of eighteen Gabriel MK–II ship-to-ship missiles.[80] After the Carter ban, however, Israel sold Argentina 26 Mirage-5 Dassault fighters, assembled in Israel, followed by 26 Mirage-3C Daggers (see Table 8, section on Argentina).[81] It also sold tank guns and four Dabur patrol boats. Danit, a private Israeli firm headed by former Israeli member of parliament Samuel Flatto-Sharon, also acted as the intermediary in Argentina's acquisition of $1.5 million worth of American-made antiaircraft shells from Pakistan.[82] (The extradition of Flatto-Sharon from Israel was sought by France for embezzling at least $60 million in fraudulent real estate deals in the 1960s and 1970; he was sentenced in absentia to a five-year jail term.) By 1981 Argentina was buying up to 17 percent of its arms from Israel.[83]

The Beagle Channel dispute, similarly, spurred Israel's sales to Chile, which doubled its military expenditures between 1977 and 1980.[84] Israel's success in selling arms to both parties to the conflict, unlike less successful efforts a few years later in the Ecuador-Peru dispute, was undoubtedly due to the fact that Chile, like Argentina, was experiencing difficulties in obtaining arms from other sources. The excesses of Chile, notorious for human rights violations, had forced both the United States and Great Britain to impose arms embargoes (which were strictly enforced).[85] The British embargo was in retaliation for Chile's torture of a British doctor, Sheila Cassidy.[86] The American suspension of military aid was prompted both by Chile's human rights record and by its refusal to extradite high-ranking military officers implicated in the 1976 assassination in Washington of a former Chilean foreign minister in the Allende government.[87]

As the Beagle Channel dispute heated up, General Mordechai Gur, former chief of staff of the Israeli Defense Forces, traveled to both Argentina and Chile in July 1978 with the aim of selling arms. His first stop was Chile, where he announced to President Augusto Pinochet that he "knew the Chilean army is accustomed to victories and hungry for more."[88] The statement, reported in the Buenos Aires press, created a considerable furor in Argentina. It did not, however, affect the welcome accorded to General Gur, who met with General Viola, supreme commander of the Argentine army, and was treated as if he were still chief of staff. In a newspaper interview General Gur confirmed his interest in promoting arms sales: "This is no secret; everybody knows that Israel has emerged as a successful competitor to the long-standing suppliers of arms for the Argentinian army."[89]

General Gur's visit to Chile was followed by that of Deputy Defense Minister Mordechai Zipori in January 1979. During that visit, Chile contracted with Israel to service and to supply spare parts for its U.S.-manufactured C–130 transport planes.[90] More important, the Pinochet regime ordered six Israeli-made, missile-armed fast patrol boats and 150 Shafrir missiles (see Table 8). Concerning the sophisticated infrared Shafrir missiles, it should be noted that a similar sale to Chile in 1976 had drawn considerable U.S. criticism.[91] According to *Aviation Week and Space Technology*, Congress was concerned at the time that in selling the weapons system Israel was actually selling U.S. technology without U.S. approval, since the Shafrirs were basically rebuilt versions of the U.S. Raytheon AIM 9D/G with solid-state components packaged in Israel.[92] Beyond that objection, it had been noted that the introduction of highly sophisticated weapons systems to Latin America was in contradiction to U.S. policy.[93] The 1976 sale nonetheless went through.

Tension over the Beagle Channel eventually abated, and open conflict was averted in 1980 by Vatican mediation to which both sides agreed. In October 1984 after Argentina's transition to civilian rule, the two countries signed a protocol agreeing to a treaty which, according to Argentine Foreign Minister Dante Caputo, "satisfies the interests of both sides."*

Several years after the Beagle Channel crisis, Argentina's territorial dispute with Great Britain erupted into open warfare. The conflict was over a group of islands, known as the Malvinas to Argentina and the Falklands to Britain, about 480 miles northeast of Cape Horn. Although the islands had been under British control, first as a Crown Colony and then as a self-governing dependency, for a century and a half, Argentina never renounced its claim of sovereignty. As successor to Spanish interests in the region, it administered the islands until Britain seized them in 1833, invoking a former sovereignty claim.

---

* Chile retained control of the islands, Argentina got control of the waters on the Atlantic side of the channel, and Chile control of the waters on the Pacific side of the channel.

Argentina's attempt to reassert its sovereignty by invading and occupying the islands on 2 April 1982, was a failure. Britain dispatched its fleet, and by the time Argentina surrendered ten weeks later, 800 to 1000 Argentine and 250 British lives had been lost.[94]

Argentina's arms buildup in the post-1977 period had been carried out primarily with Chile in mind rather than the more highly sophisticated British forces. Thus when the Falklands/Malvinas War broke out, Argentina was not well-stocked in the up-to-date aircraft and equipment needed to challenge the British forces.[95] Under pressure from Britain at the beginning of the war, Israel promised not to sign any new arms deals with Argentina.[96] While Israel was forthright in making clear its intention to deliver items that had already been contracted for, it stated that "absolute non-interference" prevented it from taking new orders.[97]

But sales never stopped. Argentina's heavy losses in combat jets during the war and the need for missiles and spare parts forced the government to search for suppliers. According to the *Jerusalem Post*,[98] Israel's arms sales took place "through numerous subterfuges," and at the height of the war foreign diplomats in Tel Aviv noted two Argentine officers charged with coordinating the dispatches from Israel Aircraft Industries (IAI).[99] According to a number of sources, including Argentina's president at the time, General Leopoldo Galtieri, Israel agreed, albeit not publicly, to sell Argentina twenty-two Mirage-3C Dagger planes while the war was still being fought.[100] The planes were accompanied with spare parts and Israeli technicians to assist in the assembly process.* Other Israeli equipment was circuitously delivered through Europe and other Latin American countries, particularly Ecuador and Peru. This equipment included the air-launched version of the Gabriel sea-skimming missile (similar to the French Exocet missile that sank two British warships), Shafrir air-

---

* According to Argentine accounts, twenty Israeli-built Dagger planes, from an official total of thirty-four aircraft, were lost by Argentina (*Guardian*, 30 July 1982).

to-air missiles, and the Barak missile systems. Even more useful to Argentina were spare parts for aircraft and external fuel tanks for the Mirages that had been bought from Israel. Two fuel tanks had to be jettisoned on almost every flight.[101]

Argentina's defeat and the heavy losses it sustained in materiel, particularly in the air force,[102] marked the beginning of a new and intensive arms buildup. During 1982 Argentina is believed to have spent more than $1 billion on arms purchases.[103] Not only did lost equipment need to be replaced, but also a clear signal was needed to show Britain that despite military defeat, Argentina was not about to sign a peace treaty or renounce its claim to the islands.

British suspicion after the war resulted in persistent pressure on the U.S. and European nations to stem weapons sales to Argentina. Being less vulnerable to British pressure, Israel was eyed by the Argentine government as a key resource in its large and expensive arms-buying campaign.[104] Argentina expected Israel to become a principal supplier of new equipment for its air force for items ranging from combat fighters and radar to spare parts.[105] Indeed, by the end of the year, Israel was reported to have sold Argentina an additional twenty-four U.S.-made A–4 Skyhawks.[106] Argentine press reports claimed that as many as seventy Daggers were sold in all, thirty-five of them before the outbreak of the fighting. However, there was no independent confirmation of this.[107]

Argentina's defeat in the 1982 Falklands/Malvinas War further discredited the military junta and hastened its decision in mid-1982 to embark upon a gradual transition back to democracy. In anticipation of the transfer of power to civilian leaders whom the military feared would question and curtail new arms purchases, the junta was anxious to rearm before the transition was completed.[108] It was thus that Israel's Foreign Minister Yitzhak Shamir in December 1982 was reported to have intended to sign a new arms deal with Argentina.[109] Similarly, the military government was reported by *Aviation Week and Space Technology* to have been considering the purchase of Kfir C2s and C7s in mid-1983.[110] Finally, on the eve of the transfer of power and immediately following the lifting of the U.S. arms embargo in December 1983, the junta purchased several secondhand Electra antisubmarine warfare (ASW) aircraft, originally manufactured by Lockheed, but renovated and upgraded with radar and other equipment for Argentina, presumably for use against British submarines in the South Atlantic.[111]

Israel's arms sales to Argentina, in addition to illustrating how Israel has benefited from international politics to advance its interests, are noteworthy for another reason. Nowhere else in Latin America—perhaps nowhere else in the world—is there a clearer example of Israeli *realpolitik* in arms sales, of the primacy of commercial interests over principles. After all, Argentina was the only country in Latin America that failed to declare war on the side of the Allies during World War II, and it was reportedly only under pressure from the United States that it refrained from overtly joining the Axis. Its German-trained armed forces were penetrated by the Nazis, and there was a strong pro-Axis faction within Grupo de Oficiales Unidos (GOU) which seized power in 1943. Moreover, the U.S. State Department's "Blue Book" on Argentina issued just prior to the elections in February 1946, apparently in the mistaken hope of hurting Juan Peron's chances of victory, contained documentary proof of Peron's Axis ties.[112]

Despite its Jewish community, following the Second World War Argentina hosted a large colony of Nazis. Many known Nazi criminals were given *de facto* asylum, including Edward Roschmann, "Butcher of Riga," who was responsible for the killing of 40,000 Jews in Riga.[113] Argentina refused West Germany's request for the extradition of a number of war criminals, such as Karl Klingenfuss and Dr. Josef Mengele.[114] Argentina also gave refuge to Adolf Eichmann, albeit under an assumed name, in 1950. His kidnapping by Israeli secret service agents in May 1960 considerably strained Israeli-Argentine relations even though Eichmann was stateless and therefore not legally entitled to Argentine protection.[115]

Nor was this legacy of anti-Semitism confined to the war or the immediate postwar era. Indeed, it may have reached its apogee at the time Israel was stepping up its arms export drive to Argentina in the late 1970s. Thus, in 1978 while Jewish prisoners held without charge in Argentine jails were being forced to kneel before pictures of Hitler[116] and tortured to accompanying chants of "Jew! Jew!", Argentina was receiving a series of high-ranking Israeli military officers on "friendly visits" to sell arms.*[117]

Considering that the Argentine junta's anti-Semitic activities were well-known, having been documented by the U.S. Congress, the Catholic Church, and especially the local branch of the American Jewish Committee,[118] it is impossible that Israel was not aware of the situation. Later, in fact, it claimed that its military relations with Argentina had saved hundreds of Jews from military jails.[119] Nonetheless, at the time the Begin government consistently refused, at least publicly, to comment. Reportedly the government even tried to restrain Jacobo Timmerman—the Argentine newspaper publisher whose 1980 *Prisoner Without a Name, Cell Without a Number* recounts the five months of torture and anti-Semitic outrages he endured—in his virulent criticism of the Argentine junta.† The perception expressed in the *Latin America Weekly Report* is widespread: "The Jewish State's concern for the disappeared was subordinated to political and commercial considerations."[120] In a more general sense, Edy Kaufman, associated with the Hebrew University, was obliged to dismiss Israel's claims that arms sales were often undertaken as an insurance to protect local Jews. He added: "so far, commercial considerations seem to have prevailed. Arms are being supplied regardless of the possible consequences concerning the well-being of the recipient country's Jewish community."[121]

The presence of anti-Semitism sets Argentina apart from other examples of Israeli cooperation with repressive regimes. Israel's reported involvement in training Savak, the shah of Iran's notorious secret police, can easily be justified on strategic

---

* These included visits by Lieutenant General Hayim Laskov, former chief of staff of the Israeli Army, in May, General Mordechai Hod and General Motta Gur in July. (See *Ha'aretz*, 10 August 1978, cited in Israel Shahak, *Israel's Global Role: Weapons for Repression*, [Belmont, Mass.: Association of Arab-American University Graduates, 1982], p. 21.)

† See Dan Margaolet, "Israel Silences Jewish Critic of Argentina," *Kol Ha'ir*, 20 November 1981, cited in Eric Hooglund, *Israel's Arms Exports* (Washington, D.C.: American-Arab Anti-Discrimination Committee Research Institute, 1982), p. 10.

grounds given Iran's proximity to Iraq. Its support of the Somoza government, though certainly not strategic, can be defended, as indeed Israel has done, on the grounds of repaying the old debt of Somoza's help to the Zionists before the creation of the state.* Likewise, South African ties with Israel go back to the friendship between Chaim Weizman and Jan Smuts, the assistance extended by South Africa to the early alliance between Britain and Zionism, and South Africa's support of militant Zionism in Palestine since the 1930s.[122] Thus, while Israel's arms sales to South Africa are commercial, they are buttressed by close cooperation in the political, cultural, and scientific (not to mention nuclear and military) domains, frequent exchanges of visits and consultations at the highest level, and even in the pairing of Haifa and Cape Town as "sister cities" in 1975.[123] With Argentina, there are no past debts to justify traffic with a regime large segments of which were known for anti-Semitism. But *realpolitik* in arms sales is not new, one recalls Moshe Dayan's rejoinder in the face of the storm of outrage that followed the discovery in 1959 of the government-sanctioned munitions sales to West Germany: "Germany would become strong with or without Israeli weapons—but would Israel?"[124]

Be that as it may, Israel's first public attempt to intercede on behalf of the Jewish *desaparecidos* in Argentina took place at the end of 1982,[125] after the junta had announced its intention to return the country to democracy and after the human rights situation had shown marked improvement. During his December 1982 visit to Buenos Aires, Israeli Foreign Minister Yitzhak Shamir got Argentine officials to promise to investigate the disap-

---

* When the Haganah had difficulty obtaining weapons on the international market, Somoza's father once in 1939 and again in 1948 purchased arms in his name but then shipped them on to Palestine. Although in the second instance the Zionists paid Somoza $200,000 cash for his trouble (L. Slater, *The Pledge* [New York: Simon & Schuster, 1970], pp. 257–259), and in repayment of the first they had later intervened on his behalf with the Truman administration when he was in disfavor (*Latin America Weekly Report*, 9 March 1984, citing the memoirs of Israeli Ambassador to Nicaragua Moshe Tov), Israel has often invoked its debt towards Somoza's father as the explanation for its being the regime's only arms supplier in the months preceding its collapse (see *Israeli Foreign Affairs*, December 1984, p. 3).

pearance of some 1,000 Jews, including thirty Israeli citizens,[126] who had disappeared between 1976 and 1979.[127]

Nor did the provision of Argentina with much-needed arms translate into any political or diplomatic benefits for Israel. Argentina joined the non-aligned movement in 1979 and voted with increasing frequency against Israel at the United Nations. The chief of the Argentine junta, General Reynaldo Bignone, sharply criticized Israel's invasion of Lebanon and raised the diplomatic status of the Arab League in Buenos Aires, for which Israel unsuccessfully requested an explanation.[128] In the wake of the September 1982 Sabra and Shatila massacres in Lebanon, Argentina reduced the level of its diplomatic representation in Tel Aviv.[129] Foreign Minister Shamir attempted during his December 1982 visit to get assurances that the PLO would not be allowed to open an office in Buenos Aires. Scarcely two weeks later, the Argentine vice minister of foreign affairs announced that Argentina would consider the opening of a PLO office in the capital.[130] Moreover, Foreign Minister Shamir was not accorded treatment befitting his station during his visit. His counterpart, Argentine Foreign Minister Juan Aguirre Lanari, was "too busy" to meet him at the airport and sent his adjunct instead.[131] During the three days Shamir spent in Buenos Aires, he met with Lanari for only an hour and a half and was accorded only a "brief talk" with the president.[132] Part of the explanation for Argentina's almost cavalier treatment of Israel perhaps lies in the fact that Israel's need to sell weapons to Argentina exceeds Argentina's need to buy them from Israel.

Nonetheless, there was a definite convergence of interests between the two countries in the military domain, with many examples of cooperation. Argentine planes were caught transporting Israeli arms to Guatemala[133] and to Khomeini's Iran.[134] Israeli and Argentine advisors together train security forces in Guatemala[135] and help the anti-Sandinista forces operating out of Honduras.[136] A CIA report seized at the U.S. embassy in Tehran in March 1979 indicates that the Israeli intelligence and security force Mossad carried out training missions in Argentina and shared information with the Argentine army.[137] Finally, Israel also agreed to receive a "planeload of documents" which Argentine air force officers "spirited out of the country" when power was transferred to the civilian president, Raul Alfonsín, in December 1983.[138]

The return to constitutional rule has marked a decrease in Israel's arms exports to Argentina. The debt crisis—ignored by the military junta which financed purchases in the wake of the Falklands/Malvinas War by paying only the interest due on its $40 billion foreign debt and refinancing the principal—has caught up with Argentina.[139] The weapons contracted for by the junta are being paid for, sometimes with frozen Argentine beef.[140] The 1985 defense budget has been slashed drastically in comparison to the 1983 level. Nevertheless, Israeli military cooperation with Argentina continues. According to BBC World Service, Argentina and Israel signed a military pact in the latter part of 1985. The agreement was for joint production of a missile-firing, medium-sized tank. The tank, which will be called TAM, will have among its components an Israeli-built gun with a range of twenty miles.[141] On the diplomatic front, and contrary to most expectations, Argentina's ties with Israel have shown improvement since the advent of President Alfonsín to power. In September 1984 he informed a delegation from the American Jewish community that his country would take a more even-handed approach vis-à-vis Israel in international forums.[142] A year later Israel and Argentina signed a memorandum of economic and commercial cooperation. The memorandum stated that both countries would take action to increase significantly the volume of mutual trade. In addition, Argentina and Israel committed themselves to increased economic, commercial, technological, and scientific cooperation.[143]

NOTES

1. Edy Kaufman, Yoram Shapiro, and Joel Barromi, *Israel-Latin American Relations* (New Brunswick, N.J.: Transaction Books, 1979), p. 104.
2. *Ibid.*, p. 49–50.
3. *Ibid.*, p. 107.
4. *Ibid.*

5. *Jerusalem Post*, 3 May 1984.
6. *Palestine Question Yearbook 1970* (Beirut: Institute for Palestine Studies, 1971), p. 736.
7. Kaufman et al., *Israel-Latin American Relations*, p. 48.
8. Interview with a prominent TV journalist, who asked not to be identified, Quito, Ecuador, 30 August 1982.
9. Jackson Diehl, "Ecuadorans Picked Leader to Tackle Economic Woes," *Washington Post*, 8 May 1984.
10. Stockholm International Peace Research Institute (SIPRI), *World Armament and Disarmament Yearbook 1982* (London: Taylor and Francis, 1982), p. 413.
11. *Ibid.*, pp. 412–413.
12. *El Sol*, 10 February 1977; interview with Pablo Yañez, Director of Bilateral Economic Relations, Foreign Ministry, Quito, Ecuador, 24 August 1982.
13. *Aviation Week and Space Technology*, 14 February 1977, p. 24.
14. *Aviation Week and Space Technology*, 13 December 1976, pp. 14–17.
15. *Ibid.*
16. *Aviation Week and Space Technology*, 14 March 1977, p. 24.
17. Israel Shahak, *Israel's Global Role: Weapons for Repression* (Belmont, Mass.: Association of Arab-American University Graduates, Inc., 1982), p. 38.
18. *Ha'aretz*, 7 March 1977, cited in Shahak, *Global Role*, p. 38.
19. *Aviation Week and Space Technology*, 13 March 1977, p. 24.
20. *Aviation Week and Space Technology*, 4 July 1977, p. 14.
21. *Armed Forces Journal International*, August 1977, p. 12; *Fortune Magazine* 13 March 1978, p. 73, cited in Ronald Slaughter, "Israel Arms Trade: Cozying Up to Latin Armies," *NACLA Report on the Americas*, January-February 1982, pp. 49–54.
22. *Le Monde*, 15 March 1977.
23. *New York Times*, 8 February 1977, p. 1.
24. *Latin America Weekly Report*, 1 January 1982; *El Nacional* (Mexico City), 4 July 1977.
25. Hugh O'Shaughnessy, "Ecuador: Suspicion Behind Foreign Relations," *Financial Times* (London), 10 August 1981.
26. *Latin America Weekly Report*, 1 January 1982, p. 3.
27. Interview with Raoul Borja, journalist, Quito, Ecuador, 26 August 1982.
28. Interview with Jaime Galarza Zavala, author and political activist, Quito, Ecuador, 27 August 1982.
29. Borja interview; Galarza interview; interview with Antonio Lara, deputy chairman of the Parliament's Foreign Relations Committee, Quito, Ecuador, 27 August 1982.
30. SIPRI, *Yearbook 1982*, p. 412.
31. SIPRI, *Yearbook 1982*, pp. 412–413.
32. Borja interview.
33. Gregory Orfalea, "Arms Build-Up in the Middle East," *Link* 14 (September-October 1981): 6.
34. Edward Cody, "U.S. Lifts Veto on Israeli Jet Sales to Ecuador," *Washington Post*, 21 March 1981.
35. *Ibid.*
36. *Armed Forces Journal*, October 1981.

37. SIPRI, *Yearbook 1982*, p. 211.
38. U.S General Accounting Office, "U.S. Assistance to the State of Israel," GAO ID 83–51, uncensored draft, Washington, D.C., April 1983, p. 43.
39. Aaron Klieman, *Israeli Arms Sales: Perspectives and Prospects* (Tel Aviv: Jaffee Center for Strategic Studies, 1984), p. 46.
40. *New York Times*, 27 May 1982.
41. *Ibid.; Jewish Telegraphic Agency*, 27 May 1982.
42. *Latin America Regional Report—Andean Group*, 22 January 1982, p. 1; SIPRI, *Yearbook 1982*, p. 219.
43. Interview with Nabil Zanbenah, political activist, Quito, Ecuador, 24 August 1982.
44. Interview with Samson Jijon, former financial vice president of Ecuatoriana, Quito, Ecuador, 28 August 1982.
45. Kaufman et al., *Israel-Latin American Relations*, p. 131, note 52.
46. Jijon interview.
47. *Yediot Ahronot*, 25 May 1976.
48. Yañez interview.
49. Zanbenah interview.
50. Borja interview.
51. *Excelsior*, 13 September 1978.
52. Jaime Reibel, "Israeli-U.S. Competition for Mexican Jet Sale," *Jewish Telegraphic Agency*, 29 December 1980.
53. Interview with Marwan Tahbub, PLO ambassador, Managua, Nicaragua, 9 and 15 August 1982.
54. This section is based on the following sources: Matty Golan, "General (reserves) Ze'evi and actor Topol Offered Ecuador Sophisticated Equipment," *Ha'aretz*, 22 March 1977; *Ha'aretz*, 23 March 1977; Matty Golan, "Our Man in Ecuador," *Ha'aretz*, 28 March 1977; *Yediot Ahronot*, 1 April 1977; *El Sol*, 23 March 1977; *Chicago Tribune*, 17 April 1977, p. 14; Shahak, *Global Role*, p. 22.
55. Don Kirk, "Debtor Nations: Ease the Burden," *USA Today*, 31 July 1985, p. 4a.
56. *Latin America Weekly Report*, 24 September 1982, p. 6.
57. O'Shaughnessy, "Ecuador."
58. Edward Glick, *Latin America and the Palestine Problem* (New York: Theodore Herzl Foundation, 1958), p. 46.
59. Interview with a high level official, who asked not to be identified, at the Central Bank of Ecuador, Quito, Ecuador, 24 August 1982.
60. Yañez interview.
61. O'Shaughnessy, "Ecuador."
62. Interview with Ambassador Herman Veintimilla, undersecretary of state for political affairs, Ministry of Foreign Relations, Quito, Ecuador, 24 August 1982.
63. Unpublished document provided by Corporacion Estatal Petrolera Ecuatoriana (CEPE) in August 1982.
64. *Middle East Economic Digest, Special Report*, September 1981, p. 22.
65. Interview with Xavier Lasso, former vice-director of CEPE's Foreign Marketing Department, Quito, Ecuador, 13 August 1982.
66. *Ibid.*

67. *Jerusalem Post*, 3 May 1984.
68. *Yediot Ahronot*, 9 April 1984; *Hatzofeh* (Hebrew, Jerusalem), 30 January 1986.
69. Diehl, "Ecuadorans Picked Leader."
70. *Jerusalem Post*, 29 April 1982; *Al-Fajr* (Jerusalem), 4–10 June 1982.
71. SIPRI, *Yearbook 1982*, p. 196.
72. Tahbub interview.
73. Interview with Silvia Sandoval, member of the Central Committee responsible for the international relations of the Mexican Worker's Socialist Party (PST), Mexico City, Mexico, 3 August 1982.
74. Esther Howard, "Israel: The Sorcerer's Apprentice," *MERIP Reports* 13 (February 1983): 24; *Christian Science Monitor*, 12 December 1982.
75. SIPRI, *Yearbook 1982*, p. 406.
76. *Philadelphia Inquirer*, 14 December 1982; *New York Times*, 15 December 1982; Eric Hooglund, *Israel's Arms Exports* (Washington, D.C.: American-Arab Anti-Discrimination Committee, 1982), p. 9.
77. SIPRI, *Yearbook 1982*, p. 406.
78. *Ibid.*, p. 410–411.
79. *Ibid.*
80. Stockholm International Peace Research Institute (SIPRI), *World Armament and Disarmament Yearbook 1979*, pp. 204–205.
81. For the Mirage-5 Dessaults, see SIPRI, *Yearbook 1979*, pp. 204–205 and *Yearbook 1982*, p. 207; and for the Mirage-3C Daggers, see SIPRI, *Yearbook 1982*, p. 207.
82. Ignacio Klich, "Israel et l'Amérique Latine: Le Pari d'un engagement accru aux côtés de Washington," *Le Monde Diplomatique*, February 1983.
83. *Jerusalem Post*, 29 April 1982; *Al-Fajr* (Jerusalem), 4–10 June 1982.
84. SIPRI, *Yearbook 1982*, p. 410.
85. *Excelsior*, 13 October 1978.
86. *Middle East Magazine*, September 1980.
87. Hooglund, *Israel's Arms Exports*, pp. 10–11.
88. Penny Lernoux, "Israeli Arms Aimed at 'Terrorists,'" *National Catholic Reporter*, 25 December 1981.
89. Shahak, *Israel's Global Role*, p. 21.
90. *Latin America Weekly Report*, 16 May 1980, p. 10.
91. *Excelsior*, 29 December 1977.
92. Clarence Robinson Jr., "Israeli Arms Exports Spur Concern," *Aviation Week and Space Technology*, 13 December 1976, pp. 14–17.
93. *New York Times*, 15 January 1977, p. 1; *Latin America Weekly Report*, 16 May 1980, p. 10.
94. *Jerusalem Post*, 19 October 1984.
95. Edward Schumaker, "Argentina Buying New Arms," *New York Times*, 6 June 1982.
96. *Financial Times*, 5 May 1982.
97. Borja interview.
98. *Jerusalem Post*, 6–12 June 1982.
99. Klich, "Israel et l'Amérique Latin," p. 17.
100. *Washington Post*, 16 December 1982.
101. Schumaker, "Argentina Buying."

102. *Ibid.;* Aaron Klieman, *Israel's Global Reach: Arms Sales as Diplomacy* (McLean, Va.: Pergamon-Brassey's, 1985), p. 156. Some of these weapons were sold through arms dealers, (*The Economist*, 12 June 1982).
103. *Washington Post,* 16 December 1982.
104. *Christian Science Monitor* (Boston), 27 December 1982.
105. *Washington Post,* 16 December 1982.
106. *Washington Post,* 7 and 16 December 1982; *Jewish Telegraphic Agency,* 26 August 1982. For more information on the subject see: *The Times* (London), 10 December 1982; *Jerusalem Post,* 14 December 1982.
107. Klieman, *Global Reach,* p. 165.
108. *Washington Post,* 16 December 1982.
109. *Salt Lake Tribune,* 16 December 1982, p. 10.
110. David North, "Budget, Politics, Hamper Equipment," *Aviation Week and Space Technology,* 25 July 1983, p. 34.
111. Claudia Wright, "South Atlantic: Hunting Season," *New Statesman* 106 (16–23 December 1983): 19.
112. *Encyclopedia Britannica,* 14th ed., s.v. "Argentina."
113. Lernoux, "Israeli Arms."
114. Hannah Arendt, *Eichmann in Jerusalem: A Report on the Banality of Evil* (New York: Penguin, 1982), p. 265.
115. Ibid., pp. 236–240.
116. Amnesty International, cited in Shahak, "Israel's Global Role," p. 20.
117. Lernoux, "Israeli Arms."
118. *Jerusalem Post,* 27 January 1984, cited in *Israeli Foreign Affairs* 1 (April 1985): 8.
119. *Ha'aretz,* 10 August 1978.
120. *Latin America Weekly Report,* 17 February 1984, p. 15, cited in *Israeli Foreign Affairs* 1 (April 1985): 8.
121. Edy Kaufman, "The View from Jerusalem," *Washington Quarterly* 7 (Fall 1984): 46.
122. Shahak, *Israel's Global Role,* p. 25.
123. *Israeli Foreign Affairs* 1 (March 1985): 8.
124. Klieman, *Israeli Arms Sales,* p. 12.
125. *Jerusalem Post,* 15 December 1982.
126. *Washington Post,* 16 December 1982.
127. *Excelsior,* 13 October 1978, cited by the Observer News Service.
128. Klich, "Israel et l'Amérique Latine," *Le Monde Diplomatique,* February 1983.
129. *Ibid.; Israeli Foreign Affairs* 1 (April 1985): 3.
130. Klich, "Israel et l'Amérique Latine."
131. *Ibid.*
132. *Ibid.; New York Times,* 15 December 1982.
133. *Yediot Ahronot,* 3 November 1980.
134. *New York Times,* 24 August 1981.
135. Haim Baram, *Ha-Olam Ha-Zeh* (Hebrew), 12 April 1984; *The Guardian,* 10 December 1982.
136. *Washington Post,* 14 November 1984.
137. Klich, "Israel et l'Amérique Latin," p. 17.
138. *Buenos Aires Herald,* 18 December 1983; *Latin America Weekly Report,* 17 February 1984, cited in *Israeli Foreign Affairs* 1 (April 1985): 8.

139. *New York Times*, 6 June 1982.
140. *Middle East*, March 1985, cited in *Israeli Foreign Affairs* 1 (April 1985): 8.
141. *Israeli Foreign Affairs* 1 (May 1985): 7; *Israeli Foreign Affairs* 1 (November 1985): 1, 8; interview with Jane Hunter, editor, *Israeli Foreign Affairs*, Washington, D.C., 5 February 1986.
142. *Al Anba* (Arabic, Jerusalem), 4 September 1984.
143. Israeli Government, Press Office Press Bulletin, Jerusalem, 27 November 1985.

CHAPTER FIVE

The Central American Experience

Perhaps no Israeli military connection has attracted more attention than that in Central America. In absolute terms, Israeli arms sales to the area have been modest,* not at all comparable to those made to Argentina, for example. However, relative to the size of the countries involved and their limited armed forces, Israel has been a major supplier with its weapons sales occasionally rivaling those of the United States.

With the exception of Nicaragua, which has purchased no weapons from Israel since the overthrow of the Somoza government, all the countries of the region are important clients and have signed military agreements with Israel. At the end of 1982, the *New York Times* quoted U.S. officials as saying that Israel was the largest supplier of infantry equipment to El Salvador and Guatemala, and had a "comparable role" in Honduras and Costa Rica.[1] Israel's role in the region goes beyond the provision of weapons and military communications and electronics equipment to include a broad range of military assistance, such as training, counterinsurgency and intelligence advice, and military-agricultural development projects based on the Nahal-type projects of the 1960s. Moreover, Israeli-Central American military ties are fraught with a political significance which by and large has been lacking elsewhere in Latin America.

Perhaps as a result of Israel's importance as a supplier, the governments of Guatemala, Honduras, El Salvador, and Costa Rica have been more forthcoming in their support of Israel than those of any other region. Guatemala, like Nicaragua under Somoza, has not supported a single UN resolution critical of Israel; Honduras has supported only four, and El Salvador and Costa Rica seven (Venezuela and Peru each supported eighteen anti-Israeli votes; Argentina 14; Mexico 13; Brazil and Bolivia 11 each; and Ecuador, 10). All the Central American states except Guatemala voted for the 1980 UN resolution condemning Israel's

---

* According to *Time* magazine (28 March 1983), sales of military hardware reached only $45 to $50 million in 1982.

"Basic Law of Jerusalem" and subsequently moved their embassies from Jerusalem to Tel Aviv. Honduras, Costa Rica, and El Salvador, however, returned their embassies to Jerusalem several years later. The only countries to have done so, they incurred the anger of the Arab states.*[2]

These Central American countries are also less reticent in expressing admiration for Israel and acknowledging its help. While Argentina, Ecuador, and indeed most Latin American countries were highly critical of Israel's invasion of Lebanon in June 1982, Costa Rica's Foreign Minister Fernando Volio publicly stated that he "understood Israel's motives,"[3] and Guatemala's Defense Minister Benedicto Lucas Garcia expressed admiration for Israel's military decisiveness and willingness to stand up to Washington.[4] Former Guatemalan President Garcia stated that Israel is "a model and an example to follow,"[5] while his successor's chief of staff called Israel "our main purveyor of arms and Guatemala's number one friend."[6] El Salvador's interim President Alvaro Magaña stated that "Israel is the only country with the possibility of helping us."[7]

As a region, Central America has all the characteristics traditionally associated with Israeli arms clients—longstanding, entrenched traditions of military rule, right-wing orientation, high incidence of territorial disputes and internal strife, and a tendency toward human rights violations—which make procurement of arms at desirable levels from other countries difficult. But what makes the area particularly interesting from the standpoint of Israeli arms exports is the light it sheds on the complex relationship between these sales and the actions or policy of the

---

* When Costa Rica announced its decision to move its embassy back to Jerusalem in 1981, only Saudi Arabia, Kuwait, and the United Arab Emirates broke off relations (*Le Monde Diplomatique*, February 1983). But when El Salvador followed suit several years later, the Arab reaction was directed at both countries. Egypt and Lebanon broke off relations with both. The Jerusalem Committee of the Islamic Conference meeting in Morocco in April 1984 (including Morocco, Saudi Arabia, Syria, Iraq, Lebanon, Guinea, Niger, Mauritania, Jordan, the PLO, Pakistan, Bangladesh, Indonesia, and Senegal) passed a series of resolutions, including the total boycott of El Salvador and Costa Rica (*Israel Foreign Affairs*, January 1985).

United States. Indeed, the American presence in the area is so overwhelming as to make Israel's actions essentially reactive, with its role expanding and contracting as a function of U.S. policy—expanding as a result of the human rights policies of the late 1970s and contracting as the U.S. reclaimed its place as the preeminent supplier and restored its former levels of aid in the early 1980s.

Although Israel has maintained close relations with all the Central American states, it did not become a major arms supplier to the region until the mid-1970s. As elsewhere, by turning international politics to its advantage (e.g., territorial disputes and U.S. human rights policies), Israel was able to break into a market that until the mid-1970s had been dominated by the United States.

Territorial Disputes

Israel's first large sale to Central America in recent times (it had sold $1.2 million worth of arms to Nicaragua and $1.5 million to the Dominican Republic in the 1950s)[8], was to El Salvador in the early 1970s as part of the country's arms buildup in the wake of its 1969 "soccer war" with Honduras. The war, in which 2,000 people died and 100,000 were made homeless,[9] broke out as a result of a longstanding border dispute exacerbated by demographic pressures from land-hungry El Salvador (with 500 inhabitants per square mile) on sparsely populated and underexploited Honduras, which has only fifty persons per square mile.[10] The arms contract signed in 1973 included forty-nine military planes, including twenty-five Arava STOL counterinsurgency aircraft, six Fouga Magister trainer aircraft, and eighteen refurbished Dassault Ouragan fighter aircraft, all of which were delivered by 1975 (see Table 9).

Honduras, which had enjoyed aerial superiority in the 1969 war with El Salvador, reacted angrily to the sales and accused Israel of supporting the adversary.[11] But in 1975 Israel concluded a $57 million arms deal with Honduras,[12] so that when the dispute between the two countries flared up again in 1976, Israeli weapons were in arsenals on both sides of the border.

Later that year, Israel agreed to sell Honduras six refurbished Dassault Super Mystere jets, thereby introducing supersonic aircraft into the region (see Table 9).[13] The deal was controversial, however.[14] The U.S. government saw the sale as undercutting its policy of refusing to sell sophisticated military equipment to Latin America, and noted that relations between Honduras and El Salvador had not been fully restored since the 1969 fighting.*[15] Moreover, Israel had neglected to obtain U.S. permission for the sale, required under the U.S. Arms Export Control Act since Israel had upgraded the French fighter jets by outfitting them with U.S.-manufactured Pratt and Whitney engines. This was the first time the issue of the retransfer of weapons containing U.S. components covered by the 1976 act was tested. Although Israel was found in violation of the law, Washington subsequently accepted Israeli Ambassador Simcha Dinitz's explanation that the affair had been a "misunderstanding."[16] Shortly thereafter, the United States allowed Israel to sell an additional fourteen Super Mystere jets to Honduras. Further sales of military equipment followed, ranging from fast patrol boats and Arava planes to armored vehicles and rifles.

Guatemala, too, was involved in a territorial dispute, although it never erupted into open warfare. Its claims on the British colony of Belize (which was slated for independence and became independent in 1981), caused Great Britain in 1975 to pressure the Ford administration to withhold shipments of offensive weapons to Guatemala.[17] The following year, Israel delivered its first shipment of four Arava STOL planes, followed by another ten in 1977. Israel's first arms deal with Guatemala was signed in

---

* Indeed, at the time of publication the quarrel is still not resolved and a peace treaty has never been signed. Although the two countries agreed in 1979 to hold five years of direct talks, the period ended without resolution. Deep-seated suspicion, especially on the part of Honduras, remains and has become even more acute with the upgrading of the Salvadoran army into an effective fighting force through U.S. training. (Joanne Omang and Edward Cody, "Honduras Wary of U.S. Policy," *Washington Post*, 24 February 1985, p. 24.)

1974,[18] and involved ten RBY armored cars, four field kitchens, and Galil assault rifles (see Table 9).

U.S. Human Rights Policy

The Carter administration's human rights policy inaugurated in 1977 had the greatest impact on Israel's sales to Central America, particularly to El Salvador, Guatemala, and Somoza's Nicaragua, all of which had been accused of gross and systematic violations of human rights. During the five-year period following the U.S. ban on military credits to El Salvador, Israel was most active in the country, delivering rocket launchers, Uzi submachine guns, Galil assault rifles, ammunition, spare parts and "security" equipment, and the last shipments of the Arava STOL counterinsurgency aircraft. Israel reportedly supplied El Salvador with an average of 80 percent of its weapons needs prior to 1980.[19]

Guatemala responded to President Carter's new policy by rejecting U.S. military aid altogether rather than complying with the human rights standards set by Congress. Three months after the U.S. suspension of military assistance, a cargo load of Israeli grenade launchers, Galil rifles, Uzi submachine guns, 81-mm mortars, and 120 tons of ammunition arrived at the port of Santo Tomas de Castilla.[20] According to opposition figures, by the end of 1977 the Guatemalan army had switched from Garaud M–1 rifles to Israeli-made Galils.[21]

Meanwhile, Israel agreed to sell Guatemala an additional ten Arava STOL planes, which were delivered that year and during 1978.[22] Five troop-carrying helicopters were also sold.[23] Although Israel initially denied that it was supplying weapons to Guatemala, which was coming under increasing international censure for its human rights violations, the situation came into the open on 28 June 1977, when an Argentine plane carrying twenty-six tons of arms and ammunition from Israel to Guatemala was confiscated in Barbados.[24] According to the *Excelsior*, quoting the Israeli daily *Ha'aretz*, the government of Barbados lodged an official protest to Israel on the grounds that the arms would end up being used against Belize, although the newspaper added that the arms shipments had received the blessings of "various countries."[25] In December Israeli President Ephraim Katzir visited Guatemala and signed a military assistance agreement with President Kjell Laugerud Garcia for the modernization of Guatemala's military and the training of officers in Israel.[26] The country's defense minister, General Otto Spiegler, was subsequently sent to Israel "to study the purchase of arms for the armed forces."[27] Despite the purchase of large items such as helicopters and Aravas,* most of Guatemala's military purchases from Israel have actually been small arms (see Table 9). Talks for the Kfir were initiated in July 1979, but the agreement was thwarted by the refusal of the United States to authorize the sale.[28] Under a $6 million contract in 1980, an additional 10,000 Galils were purchased,[29] and in 1981 it was estimated that practically all of the 25,000 men in the Guatemalan army, including the artillery units, used some type of Israeli weapons.[30] Several years later, an incident was reported in which U.S. customs agents in Florida impounded 12,000 illegally imported Israeli-made rifles destined for Guatemala.[31]

Israeli arms sales to the Somoza regime likewise received an important boost from the Carter administration's policy. Even before the United States cut off economic and military aid to Nicaragua in November 1978,[32] Israeli weapons had become critical to the regime's survival (see Table 9). The Nicaraguan National Guard's supply of weapons and ammunition was severely depleted after the September 1978 popular insurrection,[33] and without reinforcements the government forces were not expected to be able to hold out long against the guerrillas.[34] By 13 October

---

* In July 1979 Guatemala approached Israel with a request to buy the Kfir jet. However, due to the U.S. refusal to grant Israel permission to sell the Kfir, the deal fell through. When the United States lifted the ban, Guatemala signed an agreement in 1981 to buy one squadron of these Kfir jets (*Latin America Weekly Report*, 16 May 1980, p. 10; *Al-Fajr Palestinian Weekly*, 4–10 December 1981, p. 4; Stockholm International Peace Research Institute [SIPRI], *World Armament and Disarmament Yearbook 1979*, [London; Taylor and Francis, 1979] p. 188).

1978, the Mexican daily *Excelsior* wrote that Uzis, Galils, and Aravas "will determine the fate of Somoza" and that the victory "would be a victory for Israel because it will show that Israeli-manufactured weapons are reliable and trustworthy."[35] Until the regime's collapse in July 1979, Israel was Somoza's sole weapons supplier,* delivering helicopters, heavy combat tanks, patrol vehicles, mortars, Galil rifles, Uzi submachine guns, and even missiles. According to *Newsweek*, the shipments were unloaded by night from unmarked Israeli planes under the supervision of Somoza's son.[36] Israeli technicians installed an antiaircraft defense system around the president's residence, reportedly as protection not only against the Sandinistas but against Venezuela and Panama, outspoken foes of Somoza.[37] In response to pressure from the United States and Latin American countries, Israel finally terminated supplies several weeks before Somoza's fall and ordered home two cargo ships loaded with two Dvora missile boats and a number of armored vehicles[38] (the arms had been prepaid in cash, which Israel did not return to the successor government on the pretext that Somoza owed some money).[39] By that time, however, Israeli arms were so ubiquitous as to have become synonymous with the Somoza dictatorship: the Galil assault rifle was brandished as a symbol of triumph before television cameras by Sandinista soldiers celebrating their victory.[40]

Fallout of the Sandinista Victory

The Sandinista victory totally changed the situation. The low-level insurgencies and civil wars endemic in this area of poverty and severe income disparities received a tremendous moral boost from the success of the new Sandinista regime in Nicaragua. This, in turn, helped spark military buildups and in general drew the region into an era of escalating violence. Former Somoza National Guardsmen moved into the border areas of

---

* Although a $2 million order for arms was placed with Argentina, it probably was not delivered (*Israeli Foreign Affairs* [March 1985]: 6).

hitherto relatively peaceful Honduras from which they launched attacks into Nicaragua.[41] Former Sandinistas who had broken with the new Nicaraguan regime launched harassment operations from Costa Rica,[42] the only traditionally nonmilitarist country in the region. El Salvador, too, though to a much lesser extent, hosted anti-Sandinista forces while still embroiled in its own decades-old civil war that intensified in 1979 despite a so-called "revolutionary coup" in 1979 and the presence of a civilian as the nominal head of the junta.* Only Guatemala, separated from Nicaragua by greater physical distances, has no anti-Nicaraguan forces on its soil. However, it was the scene of a guerrilla challenge of its own and the government waged a war against what it termed "Marxist subversion" and those attempting to bring about land reform.†

El Salvador

The Sandinista victory also brought Central America back to the very center of U.S. policy considerations, causing a reassessment of its human rights policies in the interests of staving off what it perceived as the spread of communism. Where possible, the United States resumed military assistance. On 28 July 1982, less than two years after the government of General Carlos Humberto Romero was overthrown, President Reagan certified that El Salvador had made significant progress on human rights. This was done even though Amnesty International, the American Civil Liberties Union, and the UN Permanent Commission on Human

---

* According to the Stockholm International Peace Research Institute (SIPRI), between the revolutionary coup of 1979 and 1983, 45,000 Salvadorans were killed, 200,000 left homeless, and 300,000 emigrated (*World Armament and Disarmament Yearbook 1984* [London: Taylor and Francis, 1984], p. 520).

† On 1 July 1982, Lucas Garcia, shortly after seizing power in Guatemala in a military coup d'etat, declared a state of siege and launched a counterinsurgency offensive against the leftists. Within six months, some 3,000 to 5,000 people had been killed, 250,000 had been displaced from their homes, 30,000 had fled to Mexico, and 80,000 had been put into civil patrols. (SIPRI, *Yearbook 1984*, p. 520; Alan Riding, "The Central American Quagmire," *Foreign Affairs* 61, no. 3 (1982): 654.

Rights had concluded that violations were escalating and that the major responsibility lay with the government security forces or paramilitary groups operating with government acquiescence. According to the legal aid office of the Roman Catholic Archdiocese of San Salvador, a total of 12,501 people in El Salvador were murdered by the army, national guard, or various police forces and paramilitary groups during 1981.[43] Improvement of human rights has been certified by the Reagan administration regularly since then, and the landslide victory at the polls of Christian Democrat José Napoleon Duarte in May 1984 has assured continuing congressional support for the government.

With the resumption of U.S. involvement in El Salvador on a large scale,* Israel's role has decreased, but it continues as an important weapons supplier, the second largest source of arms after the United States.[44] In 1981 Israel was reported to have sold El Salvador an additional four Mystere B-2 bombers and in 1982 three Arava STOLs, along with less important items, including napalm.† In August 1983 a delegation headed by Ernesto Magaña, son of interim president Alvaro Magaña, visited Israel to inquire about counterinsurgency help. They met with Defense Minister Moshe Arens and were taken to see Israeli military installations and Israel Aircraft Industries (IAI) plants. During the visit the decision to relocate the Salvadoran embassy in Jerusalem was announced, fueling speculation about what El Salvador would receive in return.[45]

Israel has also been accused of installing and operating electronic surveillance and data systems in El Salvador. According to

* U.S. aid levels reached $196 million in 1984, most of which was used to buy U.S. equipment and supplies (*Washington Post,* 28 January 1985), leaving Israel little chance to compete.

† While Salvadoran air force commander Col. Rafael Bustillo affirmed the purchase of napalm from Israel, he maintained that it had not been used since 1981, when the accuracy of U.S. A-37 bombers made its use "unnecessary." However, repeated reports of napalm use, some based on examinations by a Harvard burn specialist (*New York Times,* 30 September 1984), led to the U.S. ambassador to El Salvador's affirmation that the Salvadoran military did have napalm, "probably of Israeli origin" (*Newsweek,* 8 October 1984, cited in *Israeli Foreign Affairs,* December 1984).

Arnaldo Ramos, the U.S. representative of Frente Democratico Revolucionario (FDR), Israel has set up a computer system that monitors 1,000 phone calls simultaneously and pinpoints heavily used phones. Another system monitors people's movements,[46] and computer terminals, some manned by Israelis, have reportedly been set up at military checkpoints. According to former Salvadoran Vice Minister of the Interior Colonel Francisco Guerra y Guerra,* the Israelis began installing a computer system for surveillance purposes in 1978.[47]

In recent years Israel's advisory role has been more important than military hardware, especially since the United States has been limiting the number of advisors it will have in the country at any one time to fifty-five.[48] An estimated 100 to 200 Israeli military advisors have been training the Salvadoran military in counterinsurgency tactics,[49] arms maintenance,[50] and intelligence services.[51] Israelis have also been training local air force pilots[52] as well as security personnel.†[53] U.S. intelligence sources have confirmed that Israeli advisors were used to combat Salvadoran insurgents. According to Colonel Francisco Guerra y Guerra, Israeli military advisors were "very active" helping ANSeSaL, the Salvadoran internal security agency, as of the mid-1970s.[54] Israeli advisors are believed to be involved in agricultural development, as well as in the establishment of citizens defense committees (recruited through forced conscription in rebel areas), the creation of which was approved by El Salvador's Constituent Assembly in July 1984. Francisco Jose Guerrero, former presidential minister and presently attorney general in the Duarte government, speaks admiringly of Israel's ability to set up "civilian defense systems on farms in endangered areas."

---

* A member of the first junta that overthrew the Romero government in October 1979, Guerra resigned in January 1980 with the "coup within a coup" that moved the country to the right.

† According to Jorge Handal, leader of the Salvadoran Communist Party, Salvadoran army and air force officers have been trained in Israel for a number of years, both in counterinsurgency (*Excelsior*, 10 October 1979) and as pilots (interview by author with Miguel, nom de guerre, International Relations Department of the Salvadoran FMLN, Managua, Nicaragua, 17 August 1982).

Salvadoran Deputy Defense and Public Security Minister Colonel Reynaldo Lopez Nuila, who is believed to have been an important force in the establishment of the citizens defense committees, visited Israel in March 1985.[55] Finally, Colonel Sigifredo Ochoa, one of the leading figures of the campaign against the guerrillas, acknowledged that his civic action strategy involving the citizens defense committees and forced resettlement programs was based on the Israeli model.[56]

Honduras

Neither Honduras nor Costa Rica was subject to U.S. human rights restrictions. Both are relatively peaceful countries with virtually no guerrilla movement and, hence, significantly less government killing and repression than have characterized their neighbors. However, with the disruptions that followed the Sandinista victory, Honduras and Costa Rica have been drawn increasingly into the regional turmoil by virtue of their geography. This has had important ramifications for Israel's military ties with both countries.

Honduras, which shares a 500-mile border with Nicaragua and hosts tens of thousands of Salvadoran refugees and ex-Somoza National Guardsmen, inevitably became an important staging area for clandestine U.S.-sponsored operations against the Sandinista government and the theater of military activities aimed at disrupting supply lines from Nicaragua to the guerrillas in El Salvador. These twin goals were enthusiastically embraced by Honduran Armed Forces Chief of Staff General Gustavo Alvarez.* Fearing that Honduras would be the next target for

---

* Overt military rule in Honduras ended with the 1981 election of Roberto Suazo, the first popularly elected president in over twenty years. Nonetheless, the military continued to wield power, especially in security matters and foreign policy, where Alvarez was reportedly in charge (*New York Times*, 10 October 1982). This situation has changed somewhat since Alvarez was ousted in March 1984 and replaced by a more liberal and less high-handed group of officers, but the military's preeminence persists.

"international communism," in mid-1982 General Alvarez launched what was termed a "preventive war" against Honduran leftists, who had been gaining ground as a result of the country's high unemployment and severe strains on the economy caused by a sharp decline in exports. At the same time, Alvarez was deeply involved in the organization of the Somocista forces, the anti-Sandinista Contras grouped into the Nicaraguan Democratic Force (FDN) operating from Honduras.[57] In his desire for Honduras to take a more active role in combat operations with the Contras against Nicaragua and with the El Salvadoran government against the Salvadoran guerrillas, Alvarez embarked upon an arms buildup of his own. In order to upgrade the Honduran air force by replacing the aging Israeli Mysteres, he approached the United States for F–5s and France for Mirages. He was rebuffed in both attempts. According to the *Washington Post*, neither Washington nor Paris was willing to make so visible a sale in light of the Honduran quarrel with the Sandinistas and Sandinista charges of hostile Honduran activities from its territories.[58]

Against this background Israeli Defense Minister Ariel Sharon arrived in Honduras in early December 1982 at the head of a delegation which included General David Ivri, the head of the Israeli air force, who one month later was named president of the Israel Aircraft Industries. In the course of the three-day visit, General Sharon was flown to La Ceiba on the Atlantic Coast where the Hondurans wanted to build a major military base. Sharon was also taken to two other bases in the center of the country to assess Honduran military needs.[59]

The result of this visit was an agreement signed by General Sharon and General Alvarez which U.S. intelligence sources said would escalate Israel's involvement in Honduras to an unprecedented degree.[60] The agreement was reportedly worth $25 million[61] and covered the acquisition of armored tanks, rocket launchers, Galil rifles, radar equipment, military replacement parts, and, most important, twelve Kfir jet fighters (see Table 9). According to the *Christian Science Monitor*, a second phase of the agreement was to involve missiles.[62] Although Honduras initially denied such an agreement, maintaining that the "conversations were limited to possible future economic and technology agreements,"[63] it was learned that two weeks prior to the visit the Honduran Congress had approved a constitutional amendment empowering General Alvarez to conclude armament and military training agreements.*[64]

Since Sharon's visit, the United States has stepped up its involvement in Honduras with the approval of $72.5 million in security assistance for 1985.[65] Furthermore, some 150 diplomatic and 1,300 U.S. military personnel are permanently stationed there. The latter number has swelled to 5,000 as a result of joint military maneuvers which have continued virtually nonstop since February 1983.[66] American forces have built bases and airfields in Honduras and set up a regional military training center where U.S. Green Berets train Honduran and Salvadoran troops in counterinsurgency techniques.†[67]

As in the case of El Salvador, Israeli military sales and involvement in Honduras have suffered from the heightened U.S. role, although Israel has since sold Honduras rebuilt super Sherman M–4 Al–E3 and M–4 Al–E8 tanks as well as artillery and Picket antiarmor weapons.[68]

Honduras has also been the conduit through which Israel channels aid to the Nicaraguan Democratic Force (FDN), the former Somoza National Guardsmen operating from Honduran territory. Early in 1983 while on a secret visit to a CIA training center in Virginia, General Alvarez reportedly inspected samples of weapons that Israel had seized from the Palestine Liberation

---

* Because Honduras lacked the funds to finance the proposed arms deal, the Sharon visit failed to produce the planned weapons procurement (Ze'ev Schiff, "Israeli Tracks," *Ha'aretz*, 29 June 1983). According to the PLO ambassador in Nicaragua, Marwan Tahbub, at least thirty-five Israeli military advisors were active in various departments of the Honduran air force in 1980, and this number increased dramatically between 1981 and 1982 when Honduras "was actively preparing for war against the Salvadoran guerrillas and the Sandinista regime in Nicaragua." The deal also reportedly included provision of some fifty Israeli military advisors (interview, Managua, Nicaragua, 15 August 1982).

† Five thousand Salvadorans were trained at the school up until September 1984 when Honduras, alarmed at the growing military might of a traditional enemy, insisted that no more Salvadorans be trained there (*Washington Post*, 24 March 1985).

Organization (PLO) in Lebanon. According to U.S. officials quoted in the *New York Times*, at the request of the United States Israel had begun to supply Honduras with captured PLO weapons including machine guns, artillery pieces, mortar rounds, hand grenades, and ammunition "for eventual use by Nicaraguan rebels."[69] According to FDN sources, a shipment of 2,000 AK–47 rifles was received from Israel in October 1983. Six months later, NBC News reported that one-fourth of the FDN forces had been armed with AK–47s which Israel had seized from the PLO. Israel also offered equipment from the PLO stocks for Honduran use, provided it pay the transportation costs.[70]

With the 31 March 1984 ousting of General Alvarez by a group of officers who were less eager to cooperate with the United States, Honduras has been trying to keep as far out of regional military politics as is possible. With the uncertainties over the future funding of the Contras, fears of "Lebanonization" and the destabilizing potential of 14,000 armed Somoza National Guardsmen on Honduran soil are increasingly evoked.

Costa Rica

Costa Rica, the only country in Central America with a deeply rooted democratic tradition, was, like Honduras, drawn into the conflict because of its 320-mile border with Nicaragua. Lacking a national army, which was abolished by constitutional amendment in 1949[71] and replaced by a 10,000-man force divided into rural and civil guards,[72] it is ill-equipped to enforce its tradition of neutrality. Following the installation of the Sandinista government in Nicaragua, Costa Rica has been the somewhat reluctant host of Eden Pastora's Revolutionary Democratic Alliance (ARDE), a group of former Sandinistas, some of whom had used Costa Rica as a base in their struggle against Somoza before falling out with the current Nicaraguan government.[73] The country's strong antimilitarist tradition has kept it from becoming, like Honduras, a full-fledged staging area for attacks on Nicaragua. Still, ARDE has set up its political headquarters in San José and uses Costa Rican territory as a military base. Moreover, the spillover from the regional turmoil fueled the domestic social unrest which arose from a deteriorating economic situation in the early 1980s, leading to demonstrations, strikes, and threats of work stoppage.[74] Thus, in the early 1980s Costa Rica for the first time had become the scene of limited, but nonetheless real, terrorist activities.[75]

By the time Luis Alberto Monge was elected president in February 1982, fear of further escalation caused Costa Rica increasingly to consider strengthening its meager security capabilities.[76] Israel was a logical place to look for help,* especially since direct U.S. military aid to a country which had disbanded its army might have occasioned U.S. congressional opposition. Moreover, Costa Rica had long maintained warm relations with Israel, and in the mid-1960s had successfully replicated Israel's Gadna program.[77] President Monge, a former ambassador to Israel, explicitly said he would "prefer Israel's advice in security matters to that of others."[78]

Several months after assuming office, President Monge met Prime Minister Menachem Begin in Washington in June 1982,[79] immediately after the Israeli invasion of Lebanon. According to *Le Monde Diplomatique,* Begin introduced Monge to leading members of the American Jewish Committee and the B'nai B'rith Anti-Defamation League.[80] They promised to support Costa Rica in its negotiations with sixty-six U.S. banks to reschedule its $4 billion debt and to do everything possible to help Costa Rica get American credits on good terms to finance development projects.[81] During the meeting Prime Minister Begin indicated that Israel was "very willing to help" in Costa Rican security matters.[82] Then immediately after the meeting President Monge announced the transfer of Costa Rica's embassy from Tel Aviv to Jerusalem.

---

* According to PLO Ambassador to Nicaragua, Marwan Tahbuo, Israel had offered Costa Rica arms and military advisory services in the late 1970s, following an attack by Somoza's National Guards in retaliation for its support of Sandinista rebels. Costa Rica reportedly turned down the offer on the grounds that building a strong military could be construed as reviving the army.

This pledge was reiterated in October when Israeli Foreign Minister Yitzhak Shamir visited Costa Rica.[83] He promised assistance for the security forces,[84] including arms and "advisors on security matters,"[85] without specifying the number or length of stay.[86] The following month, the Israeli daily *Ha'aretz* reported[87] that Israel was ready with Washington's go ahead to set up an electronic detection system along the Nicaraguan border.[88]

In January 1983 Costa Rica's Public Security Minister Angel Solano Calderon paid a follow-up visit to Israel as the guest of Defense Minister Sharon.[89] The two men signed an agreement on 11 January 1983 in which Israel promised to provide instruction in antiterrorist techniques, and police and presidential security force training.[90] In addition, Israel was also called upon to increase the efficiency of Costa Rica's information services.[91] Since then, Israel has cooperated with the United States in conducting training programs for Costa Rica's security forces.[92]

In addition to supplying intelligence teams, security and communications specialists, and military training personnel,[93] Israel provides some weapons to Costa Rica, specifically Galil rifles,[94] mortars, and communications gear.[95] Costa Rica was also made the same offer that was made to Honduras: Israel would supply military equipment captured from the PLO in Lebanon, provided Costa Rica pay the transportation costs.[96]

The most ambitious project in which Israel, in cooperation with the United States, is involved in Costa Rica is a $500 million defense and settlement plan in the north of the country. The project, which is being carried out in the zone along the Nicaraguan border, involves land clearance, road building, and creation of settlements. According to a Jack Anderson column in the *Washington Post*,[97] the border project, combined with the military buildup in Honduras, is designed to "create a giant strategic pincer physically isolating Nicaragua by land."[98] The plan was reportedly discussed by President Reagan and President Monge in June 1982.[99] Later that year, a special task force composed of Costa Ricans, Americans, and Israelis was set up to undertake detailed planning. Financing was to be provided by the U.S. Agency for International Development (AID), at least initially, while Israel would provide the technical expertise "presumably based on its experience with settlements in the West Bank."[100] A $19 million loan agreement for the project was signed in September 1983.[101] According to *Le Monde Diplomatique*, some thirty Israeli advisors were in the region carrying out the plan as of October 1984.[102] Latin America expert Edy Kaufman, while not mentioning the project specifically, wrote that toward the end of 1984 Israel had about 100 experts in Costa Rica working in "different spheres of development aid."[103]

But criticism in Costa Rica was mounting for what was seen as a departure from its traditional neutralism and a shift toward Washington. The example of Honduras, ever more mired in the military plans of the United States and faced with the specter of 14,000 jobless and armed former National Guardsmen on its territory in the event of a U.S. policy change, was not reassuring. So in November 1983 President Monge took advantage of the resignation of his anticommunist foreign minister, Fernando Volio,*[104] to proclaim "the perpetual, active and unarmed neutrality" of Costa Rica to be enshrined in the constitution.[105]

Shortly thereafter, Costa Rica turned down a U.S. offer to build, at U.S. expense, a network of roads and bridges giving access to the more isolated areas along the Nicaraguan border.[106] The project, which was separate from but complementary to the U.S.-Israeli-Costa Rican settlement project,[107] was rejected because it could be "considered a provocation against Nicaragua."[108] Distrust of American intentions can be seen in the reaction to the arrival in Costa Rica of U.S. Army Special Forces advisors to train Civil Guard officers. According to a senior Costa Rican security official, there was a "widespread perception in the country that the United States was pressing Costa Rica to militarize" and that it wanted the country to take a "more militant stand toward Nicaragua."[109] The U.S. advisors were reportedly

---

* Volio was the chief proponent of the faction which favored ignoring ARDE activities on Costa Rican soil. (Robert J. McCartney, "Costa Rica, Entangled in Nicaraguan Fighting, Vows to Seek Aid," *Washington Post*, 8 October 1983.)

invited by the minister of public security, a hard-liner, against the wishes of President Monge. The fact that no such reaction ever greeted Israeli advisors can be attributed to their perceived neutrality in regional disputes and their reputation for strict non-interference in internal affairs, an image which Israel has always cultivated in its dealings in the area.

Guatemala: A Special Case

Guatemala is a case unto itself. It is the only country of the region where the United States military involvement has not been paramount. It is no coincidence, then, that the Israeli presence has been strongest there. Indeed, Israel was Guatemala's principal military supplier for a number of years.[110] But the importance of Israel's assistance has not been so much in terms of arms sales, but in what can loosely be called "services," i.e., various forms of cooperation and use of advisors.

Other than Panama, Guatemala is the least involved of the Central American countries in anti-Sandinista activities largely because it is the farthest away from Nicaragua and has no Contras operating from its soil. This distance from the area of conflict, combined with its steadfast refusal to make even a gesture toward compliance with U.S. human rights requirements, resulted in a singular lack of U.S. aid, apart from humanitarian aid, to the country from 1977 to 1984, when President Reagan approved a relatively modest $300,000 for military training.[111]

During the relative absence of the United States from the Guatemalan scene, the military government subdued its guerrilla challenge and is proud to have done so without U.S. assistance. Indeed, the government attributes the success of its efforts in this regard to the lack of U.S. oversight and advice, enabling it to find its "own solutions." Such solutions—widely agreed to have been unparalleled in violence—included scorched earth campaigns, the bombing, burning and bulldozing of entire villages, massacres in the countryside, and death squad killings in the city. Although the United States remained in the background,

Guatemala obtained assistance to implement these solutions from South Africa, Argentina, Taiwan, and, especially, Israel.[112]

Israeli military sales to Guatemala (discussed earlier in this chapter), aside from Aravas, helicopters, and a handful of Dabur patrol boats, have not involved large items. Hard hit economically by disruptions in the countryside caused by the counterinsurgency campaign as well as by price drops in its major exports, Guatemala was not in a position to spend on state-of-the-art weaponry. Nor were such weapons needed in the war against the insurgents, where the Arava troop transports proved quite adequate. Israeli sales to Guatemala, therefore, have included such items as antiquated German-made bolt-action Mauser rifles from 1948 purchases from Czechoslovakia.

Far more significant has been Israel's advisory role to the Guatemalan government. In addition to police and military troop training, this has involved primarily assistance in electronic surveillance systems, intelligence gathering, and military-agricultural resettlement projects in former rebel areas.[113] It is impossible to estimate accurately the number of Israeli military advisors in Guatemala. At the time of the Rios Montt coup d'etat in March 1982, the Israeli press—which referred to the Montt coup as "the Israeli connection" because that group was "trained and equipped by Israel"—put the figure at 300.[114] The PLO ambassador to Nicaragua, Marwan Tahbub, was more conservative, estimating the number of advisors to be 150 to 200,[115] although his figure excluded agricultural and other advisors whose work is in fact of a military nature.[116] Nevertheless, the presence of a large body of Israeli advisors is undisputed. Rios Montt himself told ABC News reporters that his coup had been successful because "many of our soldiers were trained by the Israelis."[117]

Israeli technicians and advisors arrived with the first shipments of Arava planes in the mid-1970s,[118] and their role in the Guatemalan air force has gone beyond the upkeep of planes and instruction of pilots.[119] According to the CBS Evening News, they were involved in building an entire air base,[120] and Israeli pilots were reported to have carried out combat missions.[121]

An Israeli role in the police force has also been considerable, particularly following the February 1979 visit of Guatemala's interior minister to Israel for the purpose of obtaining equipment and know-how pertaining to internal security from the Israeli police and border guards.[122] In the course of his visit, which the Israeli press called "confidential and secret,"[123] the interior minister reportedly met with the representatives of Israeli companies that produce sophisticated police equipment.[124] Moreover, Israeli military advisors are said to work closely with Guatemala's secret police, and have offered instruction on interrogation tactics[125] as well as courses in urban counterinsurgency.[126]

With Israeli help, Guatemala also built a munitions plant to manufacture bullets for M–16 and Galil assault rifles. The munitions plant was inaugurated in May 1983 in Coban in the northern region of Alta Verapaz.* The 1984 yearbook of the Stockholm International Peace Research Institute (SIPRI) mentions the ammunition factory as well as Guatemalan plans to build a facility to produce rifles under Israeli license.[127] Other sources claim the plant is already in operation and manufactures armored vehicles.[128] The munitions plant, according to Guatemalan army spokesman Colonel Edgard Dominguez, is in keeping with the goal of Guatemala, El Salvador, and Honduras to standardize their military equipment.[129] Rebel sources, however, speak of a planned joint project to assemble helicopters.[130]

Israeli assistance for the installation of electronic equipment used in counterinsurgency has had greater impact. The most visible project is the Guatemalan Army School of Transmission and Electronics, unique in Latin America, which offers courses in ciphering, monitoring, and jamming radio transmissions. The school was inaugurated in November 1981 by Guatemala's chief of staff, General Benedicto Lucas Garcia (the brother of the president), who thanked Israel—represented at the ceremony by its ambassador—for the "gigantic job" it had done on behalf of

---

* According to David Gardner writing in the *Financial Times*, 12 July 1984, this plant, set up in the hometown of then-president General Romeo Lucas Garcia, is inefficient and has incurred high operating costs due to the humidity of the area.

Guatemala's armed forces in upgrading and improving their technical capabilities "thanks to the advice and transfer of electronic technology" from Israel.[131] The ambassador replied that more technical and scientific assistance agreements would follow, Guatemala being "one of our best friends."[132]

In addition to the school, which was funded, designed, and staffed by the Israelis,[133] the general's thanks were thought to refer to a computerized system installed by Tadiran that stores, coordinates, and communicates intelligence information about guerrilla and opposition group activities.* Another system monitors electricity and water consumption in various locations of Guatemala City. Sudden, large increases in consumption are investigated to detect safe houses, underground printing presses, bomb and mine factories, and other guerrilla activities.[134] These systems were particularly useful in dealing a severe setback to the ORPA (Organization of People in Arms) in the summer of 1981.[135] Israel has also installed a radar system composed of five receivers which have been used to detect arms smuggling by guerrillas.[136] Furthermore, in February 1983 CBS Evening News reported that Israel was organizing Guatemala's entire telecommunications system.[137]

But the most important aspect of Israeli assistance in Guatemala is billed as "agricultural." Aimed especially at the conflict areas such as the Frente Transversal del Norte (FTN) where the guerrilla movement is strong, this rural development is viewed by the Guatemalan government as "one of the most important political methods in the struggle against the revolutionary guerrilla movement."[138] Within the Guatemalan context, this rural development means, among other things, land clearing and road building in previously impenetrable areas, the destruction of hamlets thought to be guerrilla strongholds, and the forcible concentration of the native Indian populations† tradi-

---

* Other sources have confirmed this information. However, according to these sources, the computer center is located in the National Palace (*El Dia*, 8 May 1982).

† Indians constitute over half of Guatemala's population of 7 million (U.S. State Department Publication no. 7798, Background Note Series, July 1981).

tionally scattered over large areas in villages into easily guarded and controlled communities.[139] This has been achieved through the creation of cooperative model villages* in which peasants whose houses have been destroyed by the army are relocated and regrouped under army "protection."[140] Seventy-four such villages have been built to date by the army's Civilian Affairs Section, which is charged with the pacification of civilian populations in former rebel areas. The project has been notably successful in ending the local population's assistance to the rebels.[141]

Central to the program's success are the civil defense patrols into which 900,000 peasants between the ages of eighteen and fifty-five have been forcibly conscripted. Armed with sticks, machetes, and old Mauser rifles in a ratio of one gun per 100 men and operating under the close supervision of the army, they are used primarily for control of popular resistance, as informants, and as manpower reserves for building roads and other projects.[142] Their chief function, in fact, is to provide the army with a ready means of keeping tabs on virtually all men of fighting age.[143] The pacification program also involves reeducation and literacy campaigns, and, theoretically at least, the distribution of small parcels of land.

Israel has been in the forefront of these rural development efforts. The government-sponsored cooperatives are in part based on the kibbutz model, and the civic action programs are also patterned after those in Israel. Indeed, in March 1983 Colonel Eduardo Wohlers, head of the Plan of Assistance to Conflict Areas (PAAC), stated that Israel was the principal source of inspiration: "Many of our technicians are Israeli-trained. The model of the kibbutz and the moshav is planted firmly in our minds."[144] Other Guatemalan military men speak of the "Palestinization" of the native Indian populations.[145] Among the parallels cited are the Guatemalan Civil Defense Patrols and the Israeli-organized

---

* The U.S. Agency for International Development has allotted $1 million of its current $52.5 million program in Guatemala for facilities in these model villages (Loren Jenkins, "Guatemala Builds Strategic Hamlets," *Washington Post,* 21 December 1984).

armed village committees (even though the scale is not comparable, with some 900,000 Guatemalan peasants forcibly conscripted into the defense patrols),[146] as well as the government designation of compliant local mayors from the indigenous populations.[147]

But Israel has provided more than a model. Israeli advisors have been working since the late 1970s with the Guatemalan National Institute for Agrarian Transformation (INTA), the General Bureau of Agricultural Services (DIGESA), and the National Institute of Cooperatives (INACOP), which are the three major agricultural institutions in Guatemala.[148] In cooperation with the army, these organizations have helped direct rural development in conflict areas. Within the framework of these institutions, Israel has offered courses to government and army personnel on various facets of rural and regional development planning geared to the projects underway in the Northern Transversal region. Israeli advisors work with DIGESA in the region of Ixcan Quiche (the stronghold of the Guerrilla Army of the Poor—EGP), where they are particularly involved with civic action programs.[149] Guatemalans are also trained in Israel. Leonel Giron, head of the colonization programs in the Frente Transversal del Norte, spent time training in Israel in 1977.[150] The head of INTA, career army officer Colonel Fernando Castillos, spent two training periods in Israel, the first in the use of the Arava plane and the second in the establishment of agricultural cooperatives.[151] Technicians of his organization received grants to attend courses at Israel's Rehovot Center for Land Settlement Studies in February 1979,[152] following the initiation in 1978 of a two-year program of grants for Guatemalan officials to study cooperativization and rural development under the auspices of the Israeli Foreign Ministry's International Cooperation Division.[153]

Agricultural development programs, then, can be considered as synonymous with the struggle against the insurgents. The fine line between agricultural development and military needs can be seen even in the sale of the first Arava planes to Guatemala in 1976. The Guatemalan government affirmed that the plane was needed to transport agricultural products from remote areas to the markets because of lack of roads,[154] but it was soon used for military purposes ranging from the transport of troops and scouting to the bombing of villages.

With the crushing of the guerrilla movement, the government of General Oscar Mejia Victores, who seized power in a coup on August 8, 1983, held elections for a constituent assembly in July 1984. The general elections, which were to introduce the first civilian government in thirty years, were held in December 1985. Although the number of political killings and disappearances linked to the government security forces reached 950 in 1984,* this figure is a vast improvement over the 500 per month recorded in 1981:[155] President Reagan has finally been able to certify Guatemala's improvement on human rights to Congress and $10.3 million in "non-lethal" U.S. military aid was scheduled for 1985.[156] With the resumption of U.S. activity, the nature of Israel's role in Guatemala can be expected to change somewhat, especially since the ending of the insurgency and the installation of the civilian government.

Israel and the United States

Generally, Israel's role in Central America, at least in terms of actual sales of military hardware, has seemed to decline as the United States has reclaimed its preeminence. In a number of instances, the United States has actually impeded Israeli interests, for example by blocking the sale of Kfirs to Honduras (a very important sale from Israel's standpoint) and Guatemala. Nor can it be denied that the two arms manufacturers are competitors. When Israel's proposed sale of Kfirs to Mexico fell through, the United States stepped in with F–5s,† and Israel has on occasion

---

* A Roman Catholic Church report of July 1985 noted that over 60 peasants (11 of them members of the civil guard) around the single village of Patzun had been killed by security forces for suspected sympathy with the leftists since the beginning of 1985, most of them since March. At the same time, killings in the capital, mainly of university students, labor unionists, and political activists, had increased (James LeMoyne, "New Army Slayings in Guatemala Reported by Villages and Church," *New York Times*, 28 July 1985, p. 1).

† This can work both ways. Ecuador and Honduras both contracted for Kfirs only after having been refused F–5s.

openly accused the United States of thwarting its arms contracts for American commercial interests. Nevertheless, this competition is only one aspect of a very complex relationship, and it is helpful to remember that the United States and Israel often work in tandem.

On November 30, 1981, the United States and Israel signed the Memorandum of Understanding Concerning Strategic Cooperation, which laid the groundwork for joint military ventures "outside the east Mediterranean zone" and called for closer collaboration between the two countries in arms sales to third countries. Even before the memorandum—which was reaffirmed and upgraded in a November 1983 security agreement that created a U.S.-Israeli political-military planning group to organize joint military maneuvers and coordinate strategy—formalized cooperation between the two countries in the third world,[157] such cooperation existed, whether explicit or otherwise. Thus, although the United States publicly expressed displeasure at Israel's persistent sales to the Somoza regime after it had discontinued its own American support, an administration official indirectly approved the supplies that propped up the regime by saying: "If Somoza goes, we would prefer to see him go peacefully, we would not like to see him toppled in an armed revolt."[158] While the United States refused aid to Guatemala because of the latter's brutality in dealing with dissent, Secretary of State Alexander Haig reportedly asked Israel to do more there.[159] A State Department official, when asked if the United States viewed Israeli activities in the region favorably, replied: "Absolutely. We've indicated we're not unhappy they're helping out" but added, perhaps a bit disingenuously, "but I wouldn't say we and the Israelis have figured out together what to do."[160]

However, the U.S.-Israeli relationship has often been very explicit. Caught between perceived strategic national interests and congressional restraints that have limited maneuverability in Central America, the U.S. administration was obliged to circumvent these restraints by going through surrogates. Because the Israeli public was largely supportive of its arms export policies and it already possessed an extensive network in the region, Israel was perfect for the job. The use of Israel by the United

States as a means of "supplementing American security assistance to friendly governments"[161] has been on occasion strictly financial. In 1981 when President Reagan decided to send aid to El Salvador but found that the foreign aid funds had run out, he asked Israel to give El Salvador $21 million in military credits originally voted by Congress for Israel's own use, to be "repaid" the following fiscal year.[162]

But nowhere has this mutual assistance been more significant than to the anti-Sandinista forces in Honduras and Costa Rica, which Israel has supplied with captured PLO machine guns, artillery pieces, mortar rounds, and ammunition at the direct request of the U.S. government.[163] One-fourth of the Somocista FDN forces in Honduras were reported to have been armed by Israel with Kalashnikovs seized from the PLO in Lebanon.[164] Before U.S. funds for the Contras ran out, the shipments of PLO weapons to the FDN in Honduras and to Eden Pastora's ARDE in Costa Rica were paid for on a cash-and-carry basis out of CIA funds.[165] Subsequently, other means of financing became necessary. In April 1984 when Reagan's request for further funding for covert operations against Nicaragua was stagnating in Congress, the CIA reportedly "unofficially" asked Israel secretly to support the Contras. "U.S. sources" cited in the *Washington Post*[166] noted that Israel could be repaid for several million dollars worth of unofficial assistance to the Contras through Washington's annual military and economic aid package. On January 13, 1985, the *New York Times* reported that some U.S. military aid to Israel was being routed to the Contras and that Israeli arms shipments of "rifles, grenades and ammunition to the rebels had picked up since the summer when U.S. aid began to run out." A March 6, 1985, *New York Times* article entitled "U.S. Is Considering Having Asians Aid Nicaraguan Rebels" mentioned that Israel had increased its aid to the Contras.[167] This reportedly involved, in addition to the presence of Israeli military advisors, the provision of Israeli-manufactured equipment and uniforms (as differentiated from previous Israeli supplies which had been limited to captured PLO stocks).[168] Mention has also been made of direct Israeli monetary contributions of several million dollars.[169]

Israel has shown itself more than willing to assume a proxy role, although seldom with the overtly enthusiastic zeal displayed by Ya'acov Meridor, chief economic coordinator in Prime Minister Begin's government. In August 1981, Meridor proclaimed that Israel was negotiating an agreement with the United States to sell arms "by proxy" to countries Washington felt uncomfortable dealing with directly. "We are going to say to the Americans, 'Don't compete with us in Taiwan, don't compete with us in South Africa, don't compete with us in the Caribbean or in other countries where you couldn't directly do it. Let us do it!'"[170] Far more discreet was Yehuda Ben Meir, deputy foreign minister in the Shamir government, who noted: "It is no secret that there are agreements for U.S.-Israeli cooperation, in Asian countries, Africa, Latin America and Central America. The United States, as a world power, has interests throughout the world. Israel has its own interests in the countries of the world. In some of the places these interests overlap and the two countries cooperate."[171]

There are unquestionably advantages in this cooperation. According to Edy Kaufman, the costs Israel incurs in helping the Contras could, from an Israeli perspective, "be generously compensated for by receiving larger amounts of U.S. military aid as well as displaying good will towards an administration which has not enough room to maneuver south of its border."[172] But while appearing to have no qualms about being a "silent partner" with the United States, especially insofar as it provides better markets for Israeli weaponry in Central America and earns dividends from Washington at the bilateral level,[173] Israel has been reluctant to assume a high visibility role. This was particularly evident in 1984 when there was a considerable amount of foot-dragging on the part of the Likud government in carrying out the U.S. administration's wishes in the region. In April 1984 following talks in Washington between David Kimche, director of the Israeli Foreign Ministry, and State Department officials on U.S.-Israeli cooperation in Central America, the *Jerusalem Post* reported that the U.S. administration wanted Israel to "encourage its own supporters in the Congress, the Jewish community and elsewhere to become more assertive in backing the Contras" and that it was "more anxious to see a higher Israeli political profile in support of U.S. policy in Central America."[174] The revival of attempts by the United States to squeeze Central America into the mold of the Arab-Israeli conflict and to present Israel's role there as part of its drive against the PLO and international terrorism can be seen as part of this campaign. Thus, references to the Marxist-Arab coalition in Central America and President Reagan's statement that "it is no secret that the same forces which are destabilizing the Middle East—the Soviet Union, Libya, the PLO—are also working hand-in-glove with Cuba to destabilize Central America,"[175] followed a month later by the statement that greater involvement in Central America would give Israel the opportunity to fight the PLO there,[176] seem designed to prod Israel and to forestall criticism from pro-Israeli congressmen critical of U.S. policies in Central America.*

This approach appears to have borne some fruit, and the National Unity government under Shimon Peres has been less reticient than its predecessor to become openly involved in cooperation with Washington. Given the importance of the Contra issue for the U.S. administration and Israel's dependence on Washington's good will, it is likely that the Israeli role will remain significant in Central America for some time to come.

NOTES

1. *New York Times*, 17 December 1982.
2. *Israeli Foreign Affairs*, January 1985, p. 2; *Jerusalem Post*, 11 January 1986, p. 5.
3. Cynthia Arnson, "Arms Race and Central America," *New Outlook* 27 (March-April 1984): 19–22.
4. George Black, "Israeli Connection: Not Just Guns for Guatemala," *NACLA Report*, May-June 1983, pp. 43–45.
5. Esther Howard, "Sorcerer's Apprentice," *MERIP Reports*, February 1983; *Ma'ariv*, 22 November 1981, cited in *Le Monde Diplomatique*, October 1984.
6. Yoav Karni, *Yediot Ahronot*, 28 March 1982.

---

* For a detailed account of U.S. pressure on Israel in 1983 and 1984 to increase its involvement with the anti-Nicaraguan forces, see "Reagan's Unseen Ally in Central America," *Israeli Foreign Affairs*, December 1984.

7. ACAN–EFE, 23 April 1984, cited in *Israeli Foreign Affairs*, January 1985, p. 2.
8. Aaron Klieman, *Israel's Global Reach: Arms Sales as Diplomacy* (McLean, Va.: Pergamon-Brassey's, 1985), p. 14.
9. Stockholm International Peace Research Institute (SIPRI), *World Armament and Disarmament Yearbook 1982* (London: Taylor and Francis, 1982), p. 401.
10. *Ibid.*
11. Edy Kaufman, Yoram Shapiro, and Joel Barromi, *Israel-Latin American Relations* (New Brunswick, N.J.: Transaction Books, 1979), p. 106.
12. *Ibid.; El Dia*, 15 April 1977.
13. Ronald Slaughter, "Israel Arms Trade Cozying Up to Latin Armies," *NACLA Report* 16 (January-February 1982): 42–50.
14. Stockholm International Peace Research Institute (SIPRI), *World Armament and Disarmament Yearbook 1977* (London: Taylor and Francis, 1977) p. 317.
15. *New York Times*, 15 January 1977.
16. *Ibid.*
17. Black, "Israeli Connection," pp. 43–45.
18. *El Dia*, 12 August 1977.
19. Eric Hooglund, *Israel's Arms Exports* (Washington, D.C.: American-Arab Anti-Discrimination Committee Research Institute, 1982), p. 11; "Armas Israelies Contra America Latina," *OLP Informa* (Mexico City), February 1982, p. 8.
20. Mauricio Goldstein, *Punto Final Internacional*, August 1981, p. 14.
21. Emilcar, nom de guerre, interview with author and high-ranking official in the political wing of the Guatemalan EGP, Managua, Nicaragua. 18 August 1982; *News from Guatemala* (U.S.) 3 (October 1981):1.
22. Stockholm International Peace Research Institute (SIPRI), *World Armament and Disarmament Yearbook 1978* (London: Taylor and Francis, 1978), p. 262.; Stockholm International Peace Research Institute (SIPRI), *World Armament and Disarmament Yearbook 1979* (London: Taylor and Francis, 1978), p. 214–15.
23. *Christian Science Monitor*, 28 October 1981.
24. *Yediot Ahronot*, 11 March 1980.
25. *Excelsior*, 18 July 1977, p. 2A.
26. *Uno Mas Uno* (Mexico City), 4 December 1977.
27. *Uno Mas Uno*, 9 December 1977; *Agencia Latino Americana de Informacion* (ALAI), 15 December 1977.
28. Aaron Klieman, *Israeli Arms Sales: Perspectives and Prospects* (Tel Aviv: Jaffee Center for Strategic Studies, 1984) paper no. 24, p. 43.
29. SIPRI, *Yearbook 1982*, p. 188; Black, "Israeli Connection," p. 44.
30. Goldstein, *Punto Final Internacional*, August 1981, p. 14.
31. *Ha'aretz*, 25 December 1983, cited in Klieman, *Global Reach*, p. 174.
32. Steve Strasser, "Iran at the Brink?" *Newsweek*, 13 November 1978, p. 68.
33. *Jerusalem Post*, 15 November 1978.
34. *Ibid.*
35. *Excelsior*, quoted in the *Observer News Service*, 13 October 1978.
36. *Newsweek*, 20 November 1978, p. 68.
37. *Uno Mas Uno*, 26 April 1979; *Newsweek*, 20 November 1978, p. 68.

38. *Le Monde*, 4 July 1979.
39. Interview with Marwan Tahbub, PLO ambassador, Managua, Nicaragua, 9 and 15 August 1982.
40. *Jerusalem Post*, 30 January 1980.
41. Stockholm International Peace Research Institute (SIPRI), *World Armament and Disarmament Yearbook 1984* (London: Taylor and Francis) p. 519.
42. *Le Monde*, 21 July 1983.
43. Tommie Sue Montgomery, "El Salvador: The Descent into Violence," *International Policy Report*, March 1982, p. 9.
44. Sami Esmail, "Dictators Shop at Israeli Arms Bazaar," *Guardian* (U.S.), Special Issue, Winter 1982.
45. "El Salvador's Move to Jerusalem," *Israeli Foreign Affairs*, January 1985; Jacques Lemieux, "Le Rôle d'Israel en Amérique Centrale," *Le Monde Diplomatique*, October 1984, citing *Associated Press*, 20 April 1984.
46. "Keeping Track: Israeli Computers in Guatemala and El Salvador," *Israeli Foreign Affairs*, March 1985, p. 3.
47. *Ibid*.
48. *New York Times*, 15 February 1985.
49. Interview with George Salameh, PLO representative in Bolivia, in Managua, Nicaragua, 17 August 1982; *Latin America Weekly Report*, 13 November 1981, p. 3.
50. *Latin America Weekly Report*, 13 November 1981, p. 3; *Al-Fajr Palestinian Weekly*, 4–10 December 1981, p. 4.
51. Interviews with Miguel, nom de guerre, International Relations Department of the Salvadoran FMLN, Managua, Nicaragua, and with Santiago, nom de guerre, FMLN, Managua, Nicaragua, 17 August 1982.
52. Salameh interview.
53. Hooglund, *Israel's Arms Exports*, p. 8.
54. "El Salvador's Move to Jerusalem," *Israeli Foreign Affairs*, January 1985, p. 8.
55. *Ibid.*, p. 6.
56. Israeli Foreign Affairs, May 1985.
57. Sigifredo Ochoa, "Israel's Salvadoran Protégé," *Israeli Foreign Affairs*, April 1985, p. 6.
58. *Washington Post*, 7 December 1982.
59. Susan Morgan, "Israel Selling Fighter Jets, Tanks to Honduras?" *Christian Science Monitor*, 14 December 1982.
60. Kent Norsworthy, "Israeli Arms-Givers Active in Central America," *Guardian* (U.S.), 26 January 1983, p. 12; *Israeli Foreign Affairs*, October 1985.
61. *Ibid*.
62. Morgan, "Israel Selling Fighter Jets."
63. Jacques Lemieux, "Le Rôle d'Israel en Amérique Centrale," *Le Monde Diplomatique*, October 1984.
64. *Ibid.*; Norsworthy, "Israeli Arms-Givers."
65. *Washington Post*, 15 February 1982.
66. *Washington Post*, 24 March 1985.
67. Barbara Crossette, "Tensions Rise in Honduras as Bastion of Washington," *New York Times*, 10 July 1983.
68. SIPRI, *Yearbook 1984*, p. 526.

69. Philip Taubman, "Israel Said to Aid Latin Aims of US," *New York Times*, 21 July 1983.
70. NBC News, 23 April 1984.
71. SIPRI, *Yearbook 1982*, p. 397.
72. Joel Brinkley, "Nicaraguan Army: 'War Machine' or Defender of Besieged Nation?" *New York Times*, 30 March 1985; Joel Brinkley, "U.S. Military Advisors to Train Costa Rican Police," *New York Times*, 7 May 1985.
73. *Le Monde Diplomatique*, July 1983.
74. "Costa Rican Crisis Deepens," *Barricada* (Managua), 9 August 1982, p. 11.
75. U.S. Department of State, Publication No. 7768, November 1982.
76. Interview with Leonel Urbano, international editor of *Barricada*, Managua, Nicaragua, 13 August 1982.
77. Jacques Lemieux, "Le Rôle d'Israel en Amérique Centrale," pp. 16–17.
78. *Le Monde Diplomatique*, March 1983, citing *International Herald Tribune* (Paris), 25 June 1982.
79. "Strengthening Links with the Israelis," *Latin America Weekly Report*, 21 January 1983, p. 4.
80. Klich, "Israel et L'Amérique Latine."
81. *EFE*, 1 October 1982, quoting Ambassador to Israel Mme. Karen Olsen Beck, cited in *Le Monde Diplomatique*, February 1983.
82. Klich, "Israel et L'Amérique Latine."
83. *Financial Times*, 22 October 1982.
84. *Ibid.*; *Latin America Weekly Report*, 17 December 1982, p. 6.
85. *Financial Times*, 22 October 1982; Marwan Tahbub interview.
86. *La Nacion*, San José, 24 October 1982, cited in *Le Monde Diplomatique*, October 1984.
87. *Ha'aretz*, 1 November 1982.
88. "Strengthening Links with the Israelis," *Latin America Weekly Report*, 21 January 1983, p. 4.
89. *Jerusalem Post*, 7 January 1983.
90. *Le Monde Diplomatique*, 21 July 1983.
91. *Barricada* (Managua), 13 January 1983, cited in *Le Monde Diplomatique*, October 1984; *Latin America Weekly Report*, 21 January 1983; *Le Monde*, 21 July 1983.
92. *Financial Times*, 21 February 1984.
93. Leslie Gelb, "Israel Said to Step up Latin Role, Offering Arms Seized in Lebanon," *New York Times*, 17 December 1982.
94. *Ha'aretz*, July 1983, cited in *Le Monde Diplomatique*, October 1983.
95. Leslie Gelb, "Israel Said to Step up Latin Role."
96. Taubman, "Israel Said to Aid."
97. *Washington Post*, 14 February 1983.
98. *Ibid.*
99. *Ibid.*
100. *Ibid.*
101. Marlise Simons, "US Offers a Road Plan to Costa Rica," *New York Times*, 25 September 1983.
102. Jacques Lemieux, "Le Rôle d'Israel."
103. Edy Kaufman "The View from Jerusalem," *Washington Quarterly* 7, no. 4 (Fall 1984), p. 47.

104. Tim Coone, "Costa Rican Charge Counts Against Contras," *Financial Times*, 21 February 1984.
105. *Washington Post*, 20 December 1983.
106. Tim Coone, "Costa Rican Charge Counts Against Contras," *Financial Times*, 21 February 1984; *Washington Post*, 2 December 1983.
107. Simons, "US Offers a Road Plan."
108. Tim Coone, "Costa Rican Charge."
109. Joel Brinkley, "Costa Ricans at Odds over US Army Advisors."
110. Interview with Emilcar, Managua, Nicaragua, 17 August 1982; George Black, "Israeli Connection: Not Just Guns for Guatemala," *NACLA Report on the Americas*, May-June 1983; Israeli Television System Evening News, 25 January 1982.
111. *New York Times*, 2 March 1985; *Washington Post*, 14 December 1984.
112. David Gardner, *Financial Times*, 12 July 1984.
113. *Yediot Ahronot*, 28 March 1982.
114. *Haolam Haze*, 12 April 1982; "Guatemala on the World Stage," *NACLA Report on the Americas*, March-April 1983, p. 30.
115. Tahbub interview.
116. Salameh interview.
117. Lemieux, "Le Rôle d'Israel."
118. Black, "Israeli Connection," p. 44.
119. *El Dia*, 8 May 1982.
120. Dan Rather, *CBS Evening News*, 16 February 1983.
121. "Guatemala!" *Green Revolution* 37 (Winter 1981): 55; Goldstein, *Punto Final Internacional*, p. 51.
122. *Yediot Ahronot*, 7 February 1979.
123. *Ibid*.
124. *Ibid*.
125. Goldstein, *Punto Final Internacional*, August 1981, p. 15.
126. Slaughter, "Israel Arms Trade," p. 52.
127. SIPRI, *Yearbook 1984*, p. 521.
128. Salameh interview.
129. *Barricada* (Managua), 8 October 1983, cited in *Le Monde Diplomatique*, October 1984.
130. Interview with Miguel and Santiago, FMLN, Managua, Nicaragua, 17 August 1982.
131. John Rettie, *Manchester Guardian*, 10 January 1982.
132. *NACLA Report on the Americas*, May-June 1983, p. 44.
133. *Ibid*.
134. *Guardian*, 29 November 1981; *Ma'ariv*, 10 December 1982.
135. Rettie, *Manchester Guardian Weekly*, 10 January 1982.
136. *News from Guatemala* 3 (October 1981): 1; Emilcar interview.
137. Rather, *CBS Evening News*.
138. *News from Guatemala* 3 (October 1981): 2.
139. Loren Jenkins, "Guatemala Builds Strategic Hamlets," *Washington Post*, 20 December 1984.
140. *Ibid*.; Emilcar interview.
141. James Le Moyne, "Guatemala Crushes Rebels Its Own Way: Ruthlessly." *New York Times*, 13 January 1985.

142. Loren Jenkins, "Guatemala Enlists Indians to Patrol Against Guerrillas," *Washington Post*, 20 December 1984.
143. *Ibid.*
144. *NACLA Report*, May-June 1983, p. 45.
145. *Ibid.*
146. Le Moyne, "Guatemala Crushes Rebels."
147. *NACLA Report*, May-June 1983, p. 45.
148. Emilcar interview.
149. Rettie, *Manchester Guardian Weekly; NACLA Report*, May-June 1983, p. 45.
150. *NACLA Report*, May-June 1983, p. 45.
151. Emilcar interview.
152. "Israeli Involvement in Guatemala," *News from Guatemala* (U.S.) 3 (October 1981): 2.
153. *NACLA Report*, May-June 1983, p. 45.
154. Emilcar interview.
155. *New York Times*, 2 March 1985.
156. *Financial Times*, 12 July 1984.
157. Bernard Gwertzman, "U.S. and Israel Sign Strategic Accord To Counter Soviets," *New York Times*, 1 December 1981; *Latin America Weekly Report*, 18 December 1981, p. 9.
158. Arnson, "Arms Race."
159. Gelb, "Israel Said to Step Up Latin Role."
160. *Ibid.*
161. Taubman, "Israel Said to Aid."
162. *Davar*, 3 January 1983.
163. Taubman, "Israel Said to Aid;" *NBC Evening News*, 23 April 1984.
164. *NBC Evening News*, 23 April 1984.
165. Cody, *Washington Post*, 12 November 1984.
166. Bob Woodward, "CIA Sought Third Country Contra Aid," *Washington Post*, 19 May 1984.
167. "U.S. Is Considering Having Asians Aid Nicaraguan Rebels," *New York Times*, 6 March 1985.
168. *Israeli Foreign Affairs*, May 1985, p. 1.
169. *Ibid.*
170. Michael Brecher, "Israel and Arms Exports," *Boston Globe*, 18 August 1981.
171. *Al Hamishmar*, 18 November 1983, cited in *Israeli Foreign Affairs*, June 1985, p. 2.
172. Kaufman, "View from Jerusalem," p. 49.
173. *Ibid.*, p. 46.
174. *Jerusalem Post*, 22 April 1984.
175. Kaufman, "View from Jerusalem," p. 49.
176. *New York Times*, 21 July 1983, cited in *Israeli Foreign Affairs*, May 1985, p. 2.

CHAPTER SIX

Israel's Arms Export Policy: An Assessment

I srael's achievement in establishing an arms industry of impressive dimensions that produces a diversity of technologically sophisticated weapons is beyond dispute. The stunning growth of its exports over the past decade and a half from $100 million in 1970 to between $1 to $2 billion in the early 1980s is a reflection not merely of the growth of the industry and the high performance of its products, but also of Israel's ability to seize the opportunities offered by the vagaries of international politics, undeterred by the nature of the regime it is supplying.

Nevertheless, a number of factors militate against the continued expansion of the industry, and several authors believe that Israeli arms exports have reached their maximum growth.[1] Indeed, its undeniable success should not mask the fact that Israel is, and is likely to remain, a second tier supplier whose vulnerability to changing circumstances makes its current reliance on arms sales seem particularly unwise. With a limited domestic base and virtually no resources other than its human resource, Israel lacks both the staying power and financing capabilities of the larger suppliers. When Peru, for example, angered at the United States for refusal to sell F–5s, decided to seek another supplier, it turned not to Israel but to the Soviet Union in order to buy 36 SU–20s, lured by financing arrangements Israel could not possibly offer.[2] Given the increasing importance of loans and financing packages as an adjunct to sales, Israel's ability to compete on the international arms market will be seriously hampered. One way around this constraint would be for the United States to allow third countries to purchase Israeli arms using their U.S. military aid credits, but Israel's repeated requests for this have thus far fallen on deaf ears.

As we have seen, Israel's natural outlet for arms sales is the third world, the Soviet bloc being off limits and the Western countries either manufacturing their own weapons or purchasing them from each other. But it is precisely in the third world that Israeli arms purchases are the most politically sensitive. The question of Palestine, Israel's continued occupation of territories seized by force, and its frequent disregard for international law in the pursuit of its own objectives continue to cast long shadows, especially given Arab financial clout and the debt crises that have led many states to hope for Arab assistance. Thus, while many countries are content to buy Israeli products such as light arms and ammunition, these same countries often prefer to avoid the political risks entailed in purchasing items of high visibility.[3] Even the government of Taiwan, which is well known for its ability to stifle dissent, was obliged in the face of publicity to renounce its intention to buy Israeli Kfir jet fighters.[4] Hence the salience among Israeli arms clients of right-wing dictatorships and notorious human rights abusers unable to obtain weapons elsewhere. The concentration of this type of client tends to be self-reinforcing: the more Israel is identified with such regimes, the greater the potential political liabilities of overt military relations with it.

The temptation to avoid politically risky purchases from Israel is all the greater given the ready availability of alternate arms sources. Israel has to face stiff competition not only from the major suppliers, such as the United States, France, and the USSR, but increasingly from the third world itself. Thus, while it was the largest third world arms exporter prior to 1979,[5] Israel was surpassed that year by Brazil,[6] which manufactures armored vehicles, missiles, jet trainers, counterinsurgency and transport aircraft, frigates, and light arms.[7] Argentina, too, has registered impressive growth in its arms industry, manufacturing (mainly under license) light aircraft, helicopters, armored vehicles, and naval vessels.[8] Other Latin American states with growing arms industries include Chile, Colombia, Ecuador, Mexico, Peru, and Venezuela, all of which are now capable of producing some major weapons.[9] These countries all have the advantage of cheap labor; Mexico, Venezuela, and Brazil have important natural resources as well; and all have access to the lucrative markets closed off to Israel. Brazil, for example, has been selling arms to a number of Arab states, including Egypt, Iraq, Libya, the United Arab Emirates, Tunisia, and the Sudan.[10] Moreover, Latin American countries are increasingly turning to each other for arms purchases, which makes far more political sense than buying from an outsider. Thus, Brazil has sold large numbers of aircraft to Argentina, Colombia, Ecuador, Honduras, Bolivia, and Chile; and Argentina has sold weapons to Venezuela, Chile, El Salvador, and Uruguay.[11]

As a secondary supplier in a market dominated by big timers, Israel is particularly dependent on the vicissitudes of international politics for its arms sales. This situation unquestionably serves Israeli interests. Israel was able to capitalize on the international reluctance to supply human rights violators, or to contribute to arms escalations by supplying conflicting parties such as Honduras and El Salvador following the "soccer war," Chile and Argentina during the Beagle Channel dispute, and Ecuador and Peru at the time of the Amazon triangle flare-up. Israel also benefited from the international boycott on arms sales to Argentina during and following the Falklands/Malvinas War. Just as frequently, however, the ups and downs of regional and international politics have detrimental effects. The overthrow of Somoza; Ecuador's rising debt crisis, affecting its ability to purchase weapons, and its sensitivity to international political factors; and Argentina's return to civilian rule, all adversely affected Israeli exports. In the case of Somoza's fall in Nicaragua, Israel's arms sales ended abruptly. With the end of the junta in Argentina, Israeli arms sales showed a decline. Indeed, the reported $300 million decrease in Israeli arms revenues in 1983 was in large measure due to the Argentina setback.[12] The settlement of disputes, too, can mean a reduced role. According to Aaron Klieman, "The Central American market conceivably could dry up as quickly as it surfaced, especially if efforts at peace mediation such as those by the Contadora group were to succeed in putting a freeze on arms shipments and in negotiating the withdrawal of all foreign troops and military advisers from the region."*[13]

---

* Since its formation in 1983, the Contadora group, composed of Colombia, Mexico, Panama and Venezuela, has been attempting to end the Central American conflict. Its efforts have been supported by virtually all Latin American countries.

But more than anything else, Israel's arms sales are dependent on the United States. Time and again, Israeli sales of major weapons systems were either concluded or blocked as a direct result of U.S. actions: Venezuela, Ecuador, and Honduras all contracted to purchase Kfirs following the refusal of the United States to sell them F–5s, only to have the sales vetoed by the United States under the 1976 Arms Export Control Act. The law, which gives the United States the right to review all third country transfers of weapons containing U.S. components, affects major Israeli weapons systems such as the Kfir and Merkava as well as many refurbished, obsolete aircraft outfitted with U.S. engines or other elements. Between 1977 and 1980 the Carter administration rejected 30 petitions from Israel to present Kfirs to a number of Latin American countries,[14] resulting in important losses of revenue for Israel. When President Reagan finally authorized the Kfir sale to Ecuador on the grounds that Israel as a strategic ally should be helped to defray its own defense costs by facilitating its arms sales,[15] Ecuador ordered only half the number originally contracted. Venezuela and Colombia, too, probably bought fewer than they would have if they had been able to buy when they wanted.[16] Although President Reagan's policy toward individual sales has been more lenient, notwithstanding his veto of the Kfir sale to Honduras, the prerogative to approve or block sales remains, and such decisions are fraught with the kinds of political considerations that Israel sought to avoid by expanding its arms industry in the first place. Thus, while President Reagan lifted the veto on the Kfir deal with Ecuador partly to "offset Israeli displeasure at the approval of additional equipment for F–15 fighters being purchased by Saudi Arabia,"[17] the administration could just as easily block an important sale as an expression of displeasure over an Israeli action or to exert political pressure.

Despite President Carter's greater scrutiny of individual arms deals, in general Israel's exports of combat equipment flourished under his administration. Indeed, it was Carter's policies of limiting the proliferation of sophisticated weapons and then of banning arms sales to systematic human rights violators that allowed Israel to enter the Latin American market in a significant way. When the United States voluntarily withdrew to a large extent from such markets as Argentina, Chile, Nicaragua, Guatemala and El Salvador, Israel was able to move in. With President Reagan, the opposite situation occurred. Although more liberal concerning individual sales, his reversal of Carter's policy of restraint in American arms sales signaled the return of the United States to the region as the preeminent supplier, against which Israel was relatively powerless to compete. Thus, with an increased U.S. presence in Central America in the wake of the Sandinista victory in Nicaragua, Israel's role was reduced progressively from that of major supplier to what amounts to a back-up for the United States.

Politically, Israel has not obtained benefits from its arms transfers to Latin America. On the contrary, its position there has declined, as evidenced by eroded support at the United Nations and outspoken criticisms of Israeli policies in the occupied territories and in Lebanon. More important, its role as military advisor, supplier, and supporter of brutal and repressive regimes, and its growing reputation as a surrogate for the United States, have cost Israel the sympathy of large segments not only of progressive Latin American opinion, but of the local populations at large, thus canceling the goodwill generated in earlier years by its cooperative projects. Representative of the kinds of attitudes resulting from Israel's Central American activities is the following statement in the Costa Rican-based publication, *Human Rights in Central America:*

> Israel continues denouncing the Nazi genocides from World War II committed against the Jewish populations in Germany, Austria and Poland; thirty-five years later, it still pursues Nazis all over the world, but it has no reservations nor shame in cooperating with genocides of peasants in Central America, [or] the Indians of Guatemala and Nicaragua.[18]

Although Israel maintains that its concern for the safety of local Jewish communities is at the heart of its arms diplomacy, there is little evidence of this in Latin America, as was seen in the case of Argentina. Indeed, Israel's military activities can even adversely affect its position. In Ecuador, the Israeli embassy in Quito and the honorary consul's residence in Guayaquil were stoned simultaneously and their windows were smashed on 22 September 1982. A day earlier a bomb exploded in front of the Asociacion Israelita's community center in Quito.*[19] In November an Israeli-Ecuadoran goodwill association was slightly damaged by a bomb, and a more serious attack occurred toward the end of the month when two policemen and a bystander were killed as a youth tried to bomb the Israeli embassy.[20] Israeli embassies were also bombed in Guatemala,[21] Paraguay, and El Salvador.[22] The last two were closed down, and subsequently the mission in El Salvador was also closed after the kidnapping and murder of Honorary Consul Ernesto Liebes by the Salvadoran rebel group FARN (Armed Forces of the National Resistance).[23]

Anger over Israel's role has increased sympathy for the Palestine Liberation Organization (PLO), although, contrary to Israeli and U.S. claims, there has been little evidence of any PLO involvement in Central America beyond the provision of moral support. After the overthrow of the Somoza government, the Sandinista government froze relations with Israel, and then severed them entirely during the Lebanon invasion as a gesture of solidarity with the PLO. Furthermore, the PLO representative in Managua was elevated to the rank of ambassador. In El Salvador the leftist People's Revolutionary Army (ERP) stated that Israeli interests in Latin America were being attacked in "solidarity with the Palestinian people and their struggle for freedom" as well as to "expell the foreigners" that had been propping up repressive regimes.[24] When guerrillas of the FPL in Guatemala kidnapped the South African ambassador in November 1979, they demanded as conditions for his release the severance of Guatemala's ties with South Africa and Israel and the recognition of the PLO.[25] While Israel and the United States have often attempted *ex post facto* to attribute this sympathy for the PLO to local anti-Semitism, these allegations have not been borne out. Heszel Klepfisz, the Rabbi of Panama and an important Jewish figure in Central

---

* As early as May 1979 the Israeli consulate in Guayaquil was bombed. An organization called the Organization for the Liberation Forces of America claimed responsibility (*Nida' al-Watan* [Beirut, Arabic] 19 May 1979).

America, declared that Israeli arms supplies to Somoza had "pushed the Sandinistas into the arms of the PLO."[26] Edgar Bronfman, executive director of the World Jewish Congress, called the issue of anti-Semitism in Nicaragua a red herring,[27] while in July of 1983 U.S. Ambassador to Nicaragua Anthony Quainton sent a wire to Washington which read in part, "the evidence fails to demonstrate that the Sandinistas have followed a policy of anti-Semitism or have persecuted Jews because of their religion."[28] At another time, the ambassador called Sandinista anti-Semitism a "nonissue" and remarked that one of the "persecuted" Jewish emigres was reported to have been the middleman for Israeli arms sales to Somoza.[29]

Yoram Peri and Amnon Neubach restore the proper cause-and-effect sequence when they write that Israel's support of Somoza "not only led the Sandinista regime that succeeded Somoza to adopt an anti-Israeli posture, it also generated a wave of anti-Semitism in Nicaragua."[30] Similarly, the communique issued by Salvadoran FARN leader German Cienfuegos following the kidnapping and killing of Ernesto Liebes stated that he had been executed "as a war criminal due to the role he played in the sale of Israeli aircraft to the Salvadoran armed forces."[31] Although Liebes's murder accelerated the exodus of Salvadoran Jews, according to an official of the American Jewish Committee this was "not the result of anti-Semitism."[32] As the Israeli daily *Davar* pointed out on the eve of Somoza's overthrow:

> The people of Nicaragua did not become anti-Semitic by the influence of a new kind of bananas they have begun to grow. The Sandinista movement does not need such questionable justifications in order to achieve popularity—the fact that Somoza's regime is so corrupt and dirty is sufficient grounds for any reasonable man to support, either openly or covertly, those fighting Somoza. If more and more Nicaraguans are hating Israel more and more, it is not because they have become anti-Semitic suddenly. The reason is different: Because more and more of their children are being killed or wounded by weapons "made in Israel."[33]

The same could be said of other Israeli allies. Thus, Israel's political well-being in the region hinges on the survival of right-

wing military dictatorships. By associating so closely with hated
regimes, Israel alienates local populations and effectively rules
out the possibility of continued relations in the event of a change
in regime. Indeed, most liberation movements in Central America have explicitly expressed the intention of severing ties with
Israel immediately upon coming to power.[34]

In sum, Israel's goals in embarking upon a major arms industry almost two decades ago have not been met. Military self-
sufficiency has turned out to be a chimera, and Israel still obtains
two-thirds of its sophisticated weapons from the United States.
Far from assuring greater political independence from its suppliers, the arms industry has led to yet greater dependence.[35]
Not only do its ambitious projects such as the Lavi necessitate
ever larger injections of U.S. funds and technology, but the
export of these weapons systems, once developed, depends entirely upon the approval of the United States. Finally, despite the
preponderant role played by arms exports in the Israeli economy
and the contribution made by these transfers in alleviating the
balance of payments deficit, the Israeli economy has never been
as dependent on U.S. aid as it is today. Yoram Peri has likened
this dependence to "an addict's need for a fix: the larger the dose,
the greater the need becomes."[36]

The attitude of the Israeli public toward arms sales is, according to Klieman, "overwhelmingly supportive."[37] It is true
that certain members of the Labor Party have voiced concern
over sales to Central America,* but when it came to sponsoring
an individual motion by Labor M.P. Yossi Sarid that called for a
cessation of such sales, no one went along with it.[38] Furthermore,
while only 27.5 percent of the respondents to a January 1983
opinion poll conducted by the *Jerusalem Post* favored arms sales

---

* While the Likud party was in power, former Labor Prime Minister Yitzhak
Rabin criticized the government for supplying right-wing dictatorships in the
Israeli daily *Yediot Ahronot:* "Israel's military interference in Central America
only complicates and damages her position, image, and her interests with the few
friends she still has. That's all we need." (*Salt Lake Tribune*, 15 December 1982, p.
8A.) However, as already noted, the advent of the National Unity government led
by Labor has resulted in, if anything, even greater involvement in the region.

"to any country irrespective of the regime" (as opposed to 35.2 percent opposing exports to "racist and dictatorial regimes" and 27.9 percent condoning sales only to democracies), a clear majority of those polled approved of sales to Argentina[39] and this after the full scope of the junta's atrocities was known. For a variety of reasons, then—including limited access to information and a sense that whatever Israel does will earn it criticism—the Israeli public by and large continues to support the arms exports policy. As Benjamin Beit-Hallahmi of the University of Haifa wrote in a *New York Times* editorial:

> There is virtually no Israeli opposition to this global adventurism. There is no "human rights lobby" to oppose military involvement in Guatemala, Haiti or South Africa. There are no angry editorials or demonstrations when officials from repressive third world countries visit Jerusalem. . . . When Israeli military advisers train Angola Unita forces in Namibia, there are no angry congressional reactions and no oversight committees. The Knesset has nothing to say about such matters, which are defined as classified military business. The Peace Now movement would not dream of protesting Israeli involvement in Guatemala, Haiti or the Philippines. As far as the Israeli public is concerned, this is a non-issue.[40]

Nonetheless, the failure of the arms export program to realize its initial objectives coupled with uncertainties as to its viability in the long run have led a growing number of Israelis to call for a reassessment of current arms policy.[41] Among the arguments advanced is that Israel's long-term interests would be better served by deflecting productive capacity from the military industries toward civilian production, or at least by abandoning the excessively costly and ambitious programs in favor of a more limited number of economically viable product lines. Indeed, Israeli industry has already shown itself capable of making such a shift. Soltam, for example, which suffered a devastating setback with the loss of Iran as its major client, quickly diversified into kitchen equipment.

But given the depth of the government's commitment to its arms export policy and the particular structure of the Israeli political-military establishment, a change is not likely in the near future. Until such time as a reassessment occurs, Israel's arms clients are increasingly apt to be international pariah states or right-wing dictatorships waging war against their own people and in need of Israel's particular military expertise. And this will ultimately be to Israel's detriment politically, and certainly to the detriment of the populations of the countries it supplies.

NOTES

1. Aaron Klieman, *Israeli Arms Sales: Perspectives and Prospects* (Tel Aviv: Jaffee Center for Strategic Studies, 1984) paper no. 24, p. 1.
2. *Aviation Week and Space Technology*, 14 February 1977.
3. Yoram Peri and Amnon Neubach, *The Military Industrial Complex in Israel: A Pilot Study*. (Tel Aviv: International Center for Peace in the Middle East, 1985) p. 74.
4. Klieman, *Israeli Arms Sales*, p. 46.
5. Stockholm International Peace Research Institute (SIPRI), *World Armament and Disarmament Yearbook 1981* (London: Taylor and Francis, 1981) p. 116.
6. Stockholm International Peace Research Institute (SIPRI), *World Armament and Disarmament Yearbook 1982* (London: Taylor and Francis, 1982) p. 188.
7. *Ibid*. p. 405–406.
8. *Ibid*. p. 406–408.
9. *Ibid*. p. 395.
10. Stockholm International Peace Research Institute (SIPRI), *Trade in Major Conventional Weapons: Country by Country Listings* (London: Taylor and Francis: 1981–1984); SIPRI, *Yearbook 1982*, p. 406.
11. SIPRI, "Trade in Major Conventional Weapons."
12. Peri and Neubach, *Military Industrial Complex*, p. 81.
13. Aaron Klieman, *Israel's Global Reach: Arms Sales as Diplomacy* (McLean, Va.: Pergamon-Brassey's, 1985) p. 136.
14. *El Nuevo Diario* (Managua), March 1981.
15. *8 Days*, 11 July 1981.
16. Klieman, *Israeli Arms Sales*, p. 185.
17. Edward Cody, "U.S. Lifts Veto on Israeli Jet Sales to Ecuador," *Washington Post*, 21 March 1981.
18. *Human Rights in Central America*, last issue of 1978, quoted from an open letter to the Israeli government published by Hands Off Nicaragua Coalition. San Francisco, Calif., undated.
19. *Jewish Telegraphic Agency*, 8 November 1982.
20. *Washington Post*, 27 November 1982; *Jewish Telegraphic Agency*, 29 November 1982.
21. *Jerusalem Post*, 14 January 1982.
22. Ignacio Klich, Guatemala's Back-Door Arms Sales," *8 Days*, 13 March 1982, p. 33.

23. *Le Monde Diplomatique,* October 1982.
24. I.K.E. (Reuter), 13 December 1979.
25. *Le Monde Diplomatique,* October 1982.
26. Interview with Rabbi Heszel Klepfisz in the Jewish weekly *Nueva Presencia* (Buenos Aires), 8 November 1980, cited in Edy Kaufman, "The View from Jerusalem," *Washington Quarterly,* Fall 1984, p. 51.
27. *Israeli Foreign Affairs,* February 1985, p. 2.
28. Rabbi Balfour Brickner, "The Walls Are Not Smeared with Anti-Semitic Graffiti," *Washington Post,* 21 September 1985.
29. *Genesis 2,* July–August 1984, cited in *Israeli Foreign Affairs,* February 1985, p. 2.
30. Peri and Neubach, *Military Industrial Complex,* p. 82.
31. *International Herald Tribune,* cited in *Israeli Foreign Affairs,* February 1985, p. 2.
32. *Jewish Chronicle* (London), 30 May 1980, cited in *Le Monde Diplomatique,* October 1982.
33. *Davar,* 21 January 1979.
34. Interview with Marwan Tahbub, PLO ambassador, Managua, Nicaragua, 9 August 1982.
35. Peri and Neubach, *Military Industrial Complex,* p. 81.
36. *Ibid.,* p. 46.
37. Klieman, *Israel's Global Reach,* p. 112.
38. Kaufman, "The View from Jerusalem," *Washington Quarterly,* Fall 1984, p. 43.
39. *Jerusalem Post,* 2 February 1983.
40. Benjamin Beit-Hallahmi, "Israel's Global Ambitions," *New York Times,* 6 January 1983, p. 27a.
41. Peri and Neubach, *Military Industrial Complex,* pp. 43–47, 81.

Selected Bibliography

Magazines and Journals

Armed Forces Journal, August 1977; December 1977; October 1981.

Arnson, Cynthia. "Arms Race and Central America." *New Outlook* 27 (March–April 1984).

Aviation Week and Space Technology, 16, 23 February 1976; 17, 26 July 1976; 16 August 1976; 13 December 1976; 14 February 1977; 13, 14 March 1977; 4 July 1977; 8 October 1979; 21 May 1981; 10 January 1983; 25 July 1983; 5, 27 November 1983; 3 December 1984.

Bernier, Linda. "Israel Focuses on High Technology." *Journal of Commerce,* 7 December 1982.

Black, George. "Israel Connection: Not Just Guns for Guatemala." *NACLA Report* 17 (May–June 1983).

Dunn, Michael. "Israel's Elbit Is a Surprising Leader in Defense Computing." *Defense and Foreign Affairs,* February 1984.

The Economist, 3 March 1979; 12 June 1982; 20 October 1984.

Fortune Magazine, 13 March 1978.

Freedman, Lawrence. "The War of the Falkland Islands." *Foreign Affairs* 61 (Fall 1982).

Goldstein, Mauricio. *Punto Final Internacional,* August 1981.

"Guatemala!" *Green Revolution* 37 (Winter 1981).

Howard, Esther. "Israel: The Sorcerer's Apprentice." *MERIP Reports* 13 (February 1983).

Israel Business and Investor's Report, June 1979; August 1981.

Israel Economist, August 1971; February–March 1972.

Israel Export and Trade Journal, September 1973; May 1977, June–July 1977.

Israeli Foreign Affairs, December 1984; January 1985; March 1985; April 1985; May 1985.

Kidma (Tel Aviv), no. 25, 1982.

Klich, Ignacio. "Guatemala's Back-Door Arms Deals." *8 Days*, 11 July 1981.

———. "Israeli Arms." *South*, April 1982.

Kokalis, Peter. "Weapons Wizard—Israel Galili." *Soldier of Fortune*, March 1982.

"Latin America and the Middle East." *Middle East Economic Digest, Special Report*, September 1981.

Latin American Regional Reports—Andean Group, 22 January 1982.

Latin America Weekly Report, 16 May 1980; 5 September 1980; 10 April 1981; 25 September 1981; 9 October 1981; 13 November 1981; 18 December 1981; 1, 29 January 1982; 30 July 1982; 17, 24 December 1982; 21 January 1983; 17 February 1984; 9 March 1984; 7 September 1984.

Lernoux, Penny. "Israeli Arms Aimed at 'Terrorists.' " *National Catholic Reporter*, 25 December 1981.

———. "Israeli Arms Sales 'Imperil Vital Latin Friendships.' " *National Catholic Reporter*, 18 December 1981.

The Middle East Magazine, September 1980.

Mintz, Alex. "The Military-Industrial Complex: The Israeli Case." *The Journal of Strategic Studies* 6 (September 1983).

Montgomery, Tommie Sue. "El Salvador: The Descent into Violence." *International Policy Report*, March 1982.

Monthly Review, January 1973.

News from Guatemala 3 (October 1981).

Newsweek, 20 November 1978; 8 October 1984.

OLP Informa (Mexico City, Spanish), February 1982; April 1982.

Orfalea, Gregory. "Arms Buildup in the Middle East," *The Link* 14 (September–October 1981).

Perera, Victor. "Uzi Diplomacy." *Mother Jones*, July 1985.

Petroleum Intelligence Weekly, 28 May 1979.

Riding, Alan. "The Central American Quagmire." *Foreign Affairs* 61 (America and the World 1982).

Robinson, Clarence Jr. "Israeli Arms Exports Spur Concern."
    Aviation Week and Space Technology, 13 December 1976.
Slaughter, Ronald. "Israel Arms Trade Cozying to Latin Armies."
    NACLA Report 16 (January/February 1982).
Time, 18 May 1981; 28 March 1983.
Washington Report on the Hemisphere, 21 December 1984.
World Business, 6 October 1980.
Wright, Claudia. "South Atlantic: Hunting Season." *New States-
    man*, 16–23 December 1983.
Wright, Clifford. "The Israeli War Machine in Lebanon." *The·
    Journal of Palestine Studies* 53 (Winter 1983).

Books

Arendt, Hannah, *Eichmann in Jerusalem: A Report on the Ba-
    York: Theodora Herzl Foundation, 1958.
Glick, Edward. *Latin America and the Palestine Problem*. New
    York: Theodor Herzl Foundation, 1958.
Goldman, Richard, and Murray Rubenstein. *Shield of David: An
    Illustrated History of the Israeli Air Force*. Englewood
    Cliffs, N.J.: Prentice-Hall, Inc., 1978.
Garcia-Granados, Jorge. *The Birth of Israel: The Drama as I Saw
    It*. New York: Alfred A. Knopf, 1948.
Hammerman, Gay, ed. *The Almanac of World Military Power*,
    5th ed. San Rafael, Calif.: Presidio Press, 1980.
Hooglund, Eric. *Israel's Arms Exports*. Washington, D.C.:
    American-Arab Anti-Discrimination Committee Research
    Institute, 1982.
Israel Ministry of Defense. *Gadna, Youth Battalions*. Tel Aviv:
    Ministry of Defense, 1963.
———. *Nahal, Pioneering Fighting Youth*. Tel Aviv: Ministry of
    Defense, 1965.

Kaufman, Edy, Yoram Shapiro, and Joel Barromi. *Israel-Latin American Relations*. New Brunswick, N.J.: Transaction Books, 1979.

Khalidi, Walid. *From Haven to Conquest*. Beirut: Institute for Palestine Studies, 1971.

Klieman, Aaron. *Israel's Global Reach*. McLean, Va.: Pergamon-Brassey's, 1985.

Peri, Yoram, and Amnon Neubach. *The Military Industrial Complex in Israel: A Pilot Study*. Tel Aviv: International Center for Peace in the Middle East, January 1985.

Pierre, Andrew. *The Global Politics of Arms Sales*. Princeton, N.J.: Princeton University Press, 1982.

Safran, Nadav. *Israel the Embattled Ally*. 2nd ed. Cambridge: Harvard University Press, 1979.

Segre, D. V. "The Philosophy and Practice of Israel's International Cooperation." In *Israel in the Third World*. Edited by Michael Curtis and Susan Aurelia Gitelson. New Brunswick, N.J.: Transaction Inc., 1976.

Shahak, Israel. *Israel's Global Role: Weapons for Repression*. Belmont, Mass.: Association of Arab-American University Graduates Inc., 1982.

Slater, L. *The Pledge*. New York: Simon and Schuster, 1970.

Stauffer, Thomas. "US Aid to Israel." *Middle East Paper*, no. 24. Washington, D.C.: The Middle East Institute, 1983.

Interviews

Borja, Raoul. Journalist, Quito, Ecuador. Interview with author, 26 August 1982.

Chazan, Naomi. Coordinator, Africa Research Unit, the Truman Institute, Hebrew University, in Cambridge, Massachusetts, Interview with author, April 1983.

Emilcar (nom de guerre). High-ranking official in the political wing of the Guatemalan EGP, Managua, Nicaragua. Interview with author, 18 August 1982.

High-level official (who asked not to be identified). Central Bank of Ecuador, Quito, Ecuador. Interview with author, 24 August 1982.

Jijon, Samson. Former financial vice president of Ecuatoriana, Quito, Ecuador. Interview with author, 28 August 1982.

Lara, Antonio. Deputy Chairman, Foreign Relations Committee in Parliament, Quito, Ecuador. Interview with author, 27 August 1982.

Lasso, Xavier. Former vice president of CEPE's Foreign Marketing Department, Quito, Ecuador. Interview with author, 31 August 1982.

Miguel (nom de guerre). International Relations Department of the Salvadoran FMLN, Managua, Nicaragua. Interview with author, 17 August 1982.

Prominent TV journalist (who asked not to be identified). Quito, Ecuador. Interview with author, 30 August 1982.

Rodriguez, Carlos. President of the *Comite del Pueblo*, Quito, Ecuador. Interview with author, 27 August 1982.

Salameh, George. PLO representative in Bolivia, interviewed in Managua, Nicaragua. Interview with author, 17 August 1982.

Sandoval, Silvia. Member of the central committee responsible for the international relations of the Mexican Workers' Socialist Party (PST), Mexico City, Mexico. Interview with author, 3 August 1982.

Santiago (nom de guerre) FMLN, Managua, Nicaragua. Interview with author, 17 August 1982.

Tahbub, Marwan. PLO Ambassador, Managua, Nicaragua. Interview with author, 9 and 15 August 1982.

Veintimilla, Hernan. Undersecretary of State for Political Affairs, Ministry of Foreign Relations, Quito, Ecuador. Interview with author, 24 August 1982.

Yanez, Pablo. Director of the Department of Bilateral Economic Relations, Ministry of Foreign Affairs, Quito, Ecuador. Interview with author, 24 August 1982.

Zabaneh, Nabil. Political activist, Quito, Ecuador. Interview with author, 24 August 1982.

Zavala, Jaime Galarza. Noted author and political activist, Quito, Ecuador. Interview with author, 27 August 1982.

Newspapers

Aurora (Tel Aviv, Spanish), 2 January 1975.

Barricada (Managua, Spanish), 22 January 1981; 9 August 1982; 13 January 1983; 8 October 1983.

Boston Globe, 18 August 1981; 23 August 1981; 30 May 1982; 6 March 1983; 18 April 1983.

Buenos Aires Herald, 18 December 1983.

Chicago Tribune, 17 April 1977.

Christian Science Moniter, 6 January 1977; 28 October 1981; 14, 27 December 1982.

Davar, 13 September 1967; 13–14 November 1979; 3 January 1982; 27 August 1982; 13 May 1984.

El Dia (Mexico City), 15 April 1977; 12 August 1977; 14, 16 November 1978; 8 May 1982.

Excelsior (Mexico City, Spanish), 29 December 1976; 25 February 1977; 11, 27 April 1977; 29 December 1977; 13 September 1978; 13 October 1978; 10 October 1979; 14 March 1982; 11 August 1982; 4 August 1983.

Al-Fajr Palestinian Weekly (Jerusalem, English), 13–19 April 1981; 4–10 December 1981; 19–25 February 1982; 4–10 June 1982; 28 September 1984.

Financial Times (London), 14 June 1977; 24 October 1980; 10 August 1981; 25, 26 May 1982; 22 October 1982; 5 December 1982; 21 February 1984; 12 July 1984; 5 March 1985.

The Guardian, 30 July 1982; 10 December 1982.

Guardian (U.S.), 29 November 1981; 26 January 1983.

Ha'aretz (Tel Aviv, Hebrew), 5 September 1974; 7, 22, 23, 28 March 1977; 10 May 1978; 10 August 1978; 1 November 1982.

Hadashot (Tel Aviv, Hebrew) 2, 15 October 1984.

Al-Hamishmar (Tel Aviv, Hebrew), 9 April 1980.

Hoalam Haze (Tel Aviv, Hebrew), 4 October 1978; 12 April 1984.

International Herald Tribune (Paris), 25 June 1985.

Al-Ittahad (Haifa, Arabic), 24 June 1968.

Jerusalem Post, 22 June 1968; 15 November 1978; 30 January 1980; 12, 16, 26 January 1981; 29 May 1981; 14 January 1982; 5, 19, 22 February 1982; 24 March 1982; 2, 7, 12, 29 April 1982; 6, 13, 30 May 1982; 4, 6–12 June 1982; 18, 30 July 1982; 14, 15, 16, 21 December 1982; 7 January 1983; 2 February 1983; 13 June 1983; 25 March 1984; 22 April 1984; 20 September 1984; 4, 15, 17, 19, 23 October 1984; 12 March 1985.

Jewish Telegraphic Agency, 29 December 1980; 13 January 1981; 23, 29 December 1981; 7 January 1982; 5, 11 February 1982; 19 April 1982; 27 May 1982; 26 August 1982; 8, 29 November 1985.

Jewish Week, 13 August 1982.

Koteret Rashit (Hebrew), 4 April 1984.

Kuwait Times, 8 November 1981.

Los Angeles Times, 29 July 1981; 18 August 1981; 28 July 1982; 13 January 1983; 16 April 1984.

Ma'ariv (Tel Aviv, Hebrew), 17 September 1978; 4 April 1981; 20 October 1982; 10 December 1982.

Manchester Guardian Weekly, 10 January 1982.

Miami Herald, 13, 15 December 1982.

Le Monde, 15 March 1977; 25 January 1979; 4 July 1979; 19 February 1983; 21 July 1983.

Le Monde Diplomatique, October 1982; March 1983; October 1984.

El Nacional (Mexico City), 4 July 1977; 14 November 1978.

New York Times, 14 January 1972; 15 January 1977; 8 February 1977; 15 June 1977; 19 November 1978; 15 March 1981; 24 August 1981; 10 January 1982; 7 February 1982; 9, 27 May 1982; 6 June 1982; 1 October 1982; 15, 17 December 1982;

6, 14 January 1983; 14 April 1983; 10, 21 July 1983; 25 September 1983; 30 September 1984; 13 January 1985; 15 February 1985; 2, 6 March 1985; 19 May 1985.

Nuevo Diario (Managua), 28 September 1981; 21 July 1982; 31 August 1982.

The Observer, 12 December 1982.

Oilgram, 18 January 1980.

La Opinion (Spanish), 27 March 1974.

Philadelphia Inquirer, 14 December 1982.

Al-Quds (Arabic), 18 March 1983; 15 May 1983; 13 June 1983.

Salt Lake Tribune, 15, 16 December 1982; 21 November 1984.

El Sol (Mexico City), 10 February 1977; 7, 23 March 1977; 26 April 1977; 18 November 1978.

The Times (London), 17 November 1982; 10 December 1982.

Uno Mas Uno (Mexico City), 9 December 1977; 14 November 1978; 26 April 1979.

USA Today, 31 July 1985.

Wall Street Journal, 17 September 1981; 22 June 1984.

Washington Post, 21 March 1981; 15 February 1982; 21 July 1982; 27 November 1982; 7, 16 December 1982; 14 February 1983; 13 August 1983; 8 October 1983; 2, 20 December 1983; 8 May 1984; 14 November 1984; 14 December 1984; 28 January 1985; 24 February 1985; 22, 24 March 1985; 3 May 1985.

Ya (Madrid, Spanish), 14 December 1984.

Yediot Ahronot (Hebrew), 25 May 1976; 1 April 1977; 10 September 1978; 25 January 1979; 7 February 1979; 3 November 1980; 28 March 1982; 9 April 1984.

Yearbooks and Official Documents

Israeli Central Bureau of Statistics. *Montly Bulletin of Statistics* 32 (June 1981).

———. *Statistical Abstract of Israel, 1982.* Jerusalem: Hed Press Ltd., 1982.

———. *Statistical Abstract of Israel, 1983, 1984.* Jerusalem: Hed/Zonar Press.

———. *Israel Foreign Trade Statistics,* December 1973; December 1975; December 1976; December 1978; December 1979.

Israel Government Yearbook, 1968–69, 1969–70, 1970–71, 1971. Jerusalem: Central Office of Information.

The Israel Yearbook, 1978. Tel Aviv: Israel Publications Ltd.

Al-Kitab al-Sanawi lil-Qadiya al-Filastiniya [The Palestine Question Yearbook (Arabic)], 1969, 1970, 1972, 1975. Beirut: Institute for Palestine Studies.

Stockholm International Peace Research Institute (SIPRI). *Arms Trade Register,* 1975.

———. *World Armament and Disarmament Yearbook,* 1972, 1973, 1975, 1976, 1977, 1979, 1981, 1982, 1984.

U.S. Congress. House. Committee on Foreign Affairs. *Economic and Military Aid Programs in Europe and the Middle East. Hearings and Markup before the Subcommittee on Europe and the Middle East.* 96th Cong., 1st sess., 1979.

U.S. State Department Publication No. 7798. Background Series, July 1981.

Other Sources

Agencia Latino Americana de Informacion (ALAI), 1977–78.

CEPE, Unpublished Document, Quito, Ecuador, August 1982.

Klieman, Aaron. *Israeli Arms Sales: Perspectives and Prospects.* Tel Aviv: Jaffee Center for Strategic Studies, February 1984.

NBC News, 23 April 1984.

Partido Socialistica de los Trabajadores (PST). *Press Release,* 9 September 1978.

Rather, Dan. *CBS Evening News*, 16 February 1983.

Reuters, 13 December 1979.

U.S. General Accounting Office. "U.S. Assistance to the State of Israel." Uncensored draft report. Washington, D.C.: General Accounting Office, 1983.

Index

Book design by Diana Regenthal
Jacket design by Ernest Regenthal
Typography by
Mid Atlantic Photo Composition, Baltimore, Maryland
Text is set in Caledonia

ABOUT THE AUTHOR

Bishara A. Bahbah was born and raised in Jerusalem. He holds a B.A. in international relations from Brigham Young University and a doctorate in political science from Harvard University.

He has published articles in numerous journals and magazines including the *Journal of Communication*, *American-Arab Affairs Journal*, the *Journal of Palestine Studies*, and *Arab Perspectives*. His articles have appeared in a number of newspapers including the *Chicago Tribune*, the *Salt Lake City Tribune*, and *al-Fajr*, where he was editor-in-chief. He has been a visiting professor of political science at Brigham Young University. Bishara Bahbah currently serves on the Advisory Board of the *International Encyclopedia of Communication* and is an adjunct professor of political science at Brigham Young University.

Linda Butler was born in Wisconsin and holds a B.A. in French from Vassar College. She did graduate work at Columbia University in French literature and Middle Eastern studies. Ms. Butler lived and worked in the Middle East for seven years.

She is a writer and editor, most recently at the Aspen Institute for Humanistic Studies in New York, and has translated a number of books and articles, including *My Home, My Land, A Narrative of the Palestinian Struggle*, by Abu Iyad [with Eric Rouleau], (1981).

DATE DUE